Racial Discrimination

Racial Discrimination

Anjana Banerjee

GLOBAL VISION PUBLISHING HOUSE
20, Ansari Road, Daryaganj, New Delhi-110002 (INDIA)

GLOBAL VISION PUBLISHING HOUSE
F-4, 1st Floor, 'Hari Sadan' 20, Ansari Road,
Daryaganj, New Delhi-110002 (INDIA)
Tel.: 23261581, 23276291, 43037885 Mob: 9810644769
Email: nsingh_2004@vsnl.net, info@globalvisionpub.com
Website: www.globalvisionpub.com

Racial Discrimination

First Edition 2011

ISBN: 987-81-8220-378-5

PRINTED IN INDIA

Published by Dr. N.K. Singh for Global Vision Publishing House. New Delhi-2 and *Printed at* Balaji Offset, Naveen Shahdara, Delhi-32.

Preface

This book 'Racial Discrimination' looks at the theme of 'race,' 'racism' and 'racial discrimination' from socio-economic and political perspectives. Racial discrimination is treating people differently through a process of social division into categories not necessarily related to races. It differentiates between individuals on the basis of real and perceived racial differences, and has been identified by the government policy in several countries of the world. Scientific racism of Europe divided mankind into three 'great races', Caucasoid (white), Mongoloid and Negroid (black) in accordance with their own world-view. The populations of the Indian subcontinent, however, were problematic to classify under this scheme. They were assumed to be a mixture of an Indigenous and Dravidian race, tentatively with an Australoid grouping of the Caucasoid race, but some authors also assumed Mongolic admixture. Therefore, Indian racism presents a complicated mixture of all major types.

The book is critically examined in six chapters. First chapter deals with basic concept of race, racial classification, racism, different races in South Asian, African and American continents. Second chapter discusses conceptual and legal aspects of racial discrimination. In addition, it also examines various initiatives taken to address its problem. Third chapter covers scientific theory of racism and racial discrimination in physical anthropology, popular racist ideology, ideological applications, and racial legacy of orientalism and islamo-phobia. Fourth chapter examines statistical analysis of the issue covering causal, statistical, and experimental methods of assessment, study design, statistical analysis, and possible solutions to problems in using statistical models to infer discrimination. Fifth chapter covers attitudinal and behavioral indicators of discrimination in which it deals with perceptions of discrimination, challenge of direct measurement of discrimination, sources of observational data, scale measures used in surveys. Last chapter focuses on caste discrimination in the South Asian Diaspora, which looks at the various implications of the caste system in different spheres and also the initiatives that have been taken to tackle the problem.

The author has tried to discuss the theme in a lucid manner. The work is an invaluable source of information for the readers seeking to explore the burning issue.

Contents

1
Introduction

Racial discrimination is treating people differently through a process of social division into categories not necessarily related to races. Racial segregation policies may officialize it, but it is also often exerted without being legalized. Researchers, including Dean Karlan and Marianne Bertrand, at the MIT and the University of Chicago, found in their study that there was widespread discrimination in the workplace against job applicants whose names were merely perceived as 'sounding black'. These applicants were 50% less likely than candidates perceived as having 'white-sounding names' to receive callbacks for interviews. In contrast, institutions and courts have upheld discrimination against whites when it is done to promote a diverse work or educational environment, even when it was shown to be to the detriment of qualified applicants. The researchers view these results as strong evidence of unconscious biases rooted in the United States' long history of discrimination.

Racial discrimination differentiates between individuals on the basis of real and perceived racial differences and has been official government policy in several countries, such as South Africa in the apartheid era and the USA. In the United States, racial profiling of minorities by law enforcement officials has been called racial discrimination. As early as 1865, the Civil Rights Act provided a remedy for intentional race discrimination in employment by private employers and state and local public employers. The Civil Rights Act of 1871 applies to public employment or employment involving state action prohibiting deprivation of rights secured by the federal constitution or federal laws through action under color of law.

There is substantial evidence of differential outcomes for different racial and ethnic groups in many social and economic arenas in world today, ranging from hiring and promotion in the labour market, to loan approvals in mortgage lending, to rates of arrest and incarceration in the criminal justice system. These disparities—and others—describe social conditions that most Americans believe deserve some measure of attention. To understand such conditions and fashion appropriate responses, it is important to assess whether and how racial discrimination, along with other factors, may contribute to observed disparities among racial and ethnic groups.

Research in social psychology suggests that categorizing individuals on the basis of salient, observable characteristics such as race, gender, age and even patterns of dress and speech is inevitable, occurs automatically and activates biases associated with these characteristics (Allport, 1954; Brewer and Brown, 1998; Devine, 1989, 2001; Fiske, 1998). Some researchers posit that automatic categorization will fail to elicit biased responses among those motivated not to be prejudiced (Devine, 1989, 2001), yet people regularly use such categories to make distinctions and sometimes to perpetuate social inequalities among different groups. Although people categorize others in various ways, the focus on racial and ethnic distinctions and identifying methods that may make it possible to measure the presence and extent of racial and ethnic discrimination in a social or economic domain.

Before reviewing measurement methods, it is necessary first to define 'race' and 'racial discrimination' and to outline theories or models of how different types and mechanisms of discrimination may operate in various arenas. A clear conceptual framework is needed to guide appropriate data collection and analysis for measurement and to identify key assumptions of the underlying model.

Definition of Race

A race is a distinct population of humans distinguished in some way from other humans. The most widely observed races are those based on skin color, facial features, ancestry, genetics and national origin. Conceptions of race, as well as specific racial groupings, are often controversial due to their political and sociological uses and implications. Since the 1940s, evolutionary scientists have rejected the view of race according to which a number of finite lists of essential characteristics could be used to determine a like number of races. By the 1960s, data and models from population genetics called into question taxonomic understandings of race and many have turned from conceptualizing and analyzing human variation in terms of race to doing so in terms of populations and clines instead. That being said, many scientists still believe that race is a valid and useful concept.

Moreover, since the 1990s, data and models from genomics and cladistics have resulted in a revolution in our understanding of human evolution, which has led some to propose a new 'lineage' definition of race. These scientists have made related arguments that races are valid when understood as fuzzy sets, clusters, or extended families. Currently, opinions differ substantially within and among academic disciplines. Many social scientists, drawing on such biological research, believe common race definitions pertaining to humans have little taxonomic validity. They argue that race definitions are imprecise, arbitrary, derived from custom and that the races observed vary according to the culture examined. They further maintain that race is best understood as a social construct. Some scientists have argued that this shift is motivated more by political than scientific reasons.

Term once commonly used in physical anthropology to denote a division of humankind possessing traits that are transmissible by descent and sufficient to characterize it as a distinct human type (*e.g.*, Caucasoid, Mongoloid, Negroid). Today the term has little scientific standing, as older methods of differentiation, including hair form and body measurement, have given way to the comparative analysis of DNA and gene frequencies relating to such factors as blood typing, the excretion of amino acids and inherited enzyme deficiencies. Because all human populations today are extremely similar genetically, most researchers have abandoned the concept of race for the concept of the cline, a graded series of differences occurring along a line of environmental or geographical transition.

This reflects the recognition that human populations have always been in a state of flux, with genes constantly flowing from one gene pool to another, impeded only by physical or ecological boundaries. While relative isolation does preserve genetic differences and allow populations to maximally adapt to climatic and disease factors over long periods of time, all groups currently existing are thoroughly 'mixed' genetically and such differences as still exist do not lend themselves to simple typologizing. 'Race' is today primarily a sociological designation, identifying a class sharing some outward physical characteristics and some commonalities of culture and history.

The origin of the term 'race' is obscure. It may have derived from the Arabic *râs*, meaning 'chief', 'head' and 'origin'. The word entered Europe between the fifteenth and sixteenth centuries. Initially 'race' was understood to signify descent of an aristocratic breed. In particular, it referred to the lineages of the Frankish kings. Later, Europeans used 'race' as one of the possible translations of the Latin *natio* or *gens*; until the eighteenth century, it was interchangeable with terms such as 'stock' or 'tribe'. All ethnicities, whether they were called 'peoples' or 'races' or 'tribes', were classified according to their political traditions, their geographical habitat and climatic conditions. The European reference system of thought, being shaped by classical authors, was dominated by political paradigms and categories that paralleled natural and political phenomena. Only in the first decades of the nineteenth century did the term acquire its modern meaning. Implying that original difference is biologically founded, the concept presupposes the genealogical continuity of 'racial' traits that supposedly remain the same irrespective of environmental influences and it includes the idea that there are correlations between outward physiognomy and mental capacity.

The Greeks' emphasis on citizenship went hand in hand with the assumption that citizens were made, not born. From the Greeks onward, the state of government and civilization were seen to be the decisive characteristics of a people; some climates favoured the development of vigour of spirit and courage, instilling a war-like disposition, while others induced a phlegmatic attitude, laziness and the tendency to succumb to tyranny. The roots of this view were laid down in Hippocrates' *Airs, Waters, Places*. It was only in respect to this sort of theorizing — dubbed 'environmentalism' at the end of the nineteenth century — that the notion of descent played any role. 'Blood', by contrast, had been invested since antiquity with mythical meaning, transcending the common sphere of everyday life. In heathen Greek theory, notably in the writings of Aristotle, notions of 'species', 'genus' and physiognomy were closely linked to the concept of the 'essences', the basic elements of all matter. Therefore, Greek accounts of differing human physiognomies cannot be compared to modern-style theories of race or racism. The same applies *mutatis mutandis* to Roman theory.

The focus on measuring racial discrimination in this raises an initial question of "What is race?" Defining race is a task far more complex than can be accomplished in this chapter. In fact, there is little consensus on what race actually means (Alba, 1992; Anderson and Fienberg, 2000; Appiah, 1992; Fredrickson, 2002; Jones, 1997; Loury, 2002; Omi, 2001; Winant, 2001). Therefore, we only briefly describe ways in which race (and ethnicity) may be defined, rather than attempting an in-depth analysis. We first summarize biological and social concepts of race.

Biological Definition

Biological classifications of race were first developed from the work of eighteenth-century naturalists who studied population groups in what had been relatively isolated geographic areas (for further discussion, see Montagu, 1972; Zuberi, 2001). The term 'race' was used to distinguish populations in different areas on the basis of differing physical characteristics that had developed over time, such as skin color, facial features and other characteristics (van den Berghe, 1967; Zuckerman, 1990).

Recently, genetics researchers have found evidence of genetic clusters that correspond to geographically similar populations and yield the kinds of phenotypic variations that have been used to construct concepts of race. Rosenberg *et al.* (2002) report on a study of 1,056 individuals from 52 different populations. The researchers found that a 'soft' classification method using no a priori information on population groups identified six genetic clusters, five of which correspond directly to major geographic regions, as well as subclusters corresponding to specific populations. However, they concluded that within-population, differences accounted for 93–95 percent of genetic variation in these individuals, supporting the argument that there are only small genetic differences among geographically different groups.

Although not all scientists agree (see Crow, 2002; Mayr, 2002; van den Berghe, 1967; Zuckerman, 1990), many critics deny that meaningful distinctions among contemporary human groups can be derived from a biological notion of race. At this point, science has not identified a set of genes that correspond with social conceptions of race. The panel offers no further discussion of any such biological components and focuses on race as a socially constructed concept.

Social Concept of Race

In virtually all human societies, people take note of and assign significance to the physical characteristics of others, such as skin color, hair texture and distinctive features. Race becomes socially significant when members of a society routinely divide people into groups based on the possession of these characteristics. These characteristics become socially significant when members of a society routinely use them to establish racial categories into which people are classified on the basis of their own or their ancestors' physical characteristics and when, in turn, these categorizations elicit differing social perceptions, attitudes and behaviours toward each group (Hollinger, 2000; Loury, 2002; Smelser *et al.*, 2001).

The notion that race is about embodied social signification may be referred to as the social–cognitive approach to thinking about race (Fiske and Taylor, 1991; Loury, 2002). It is important to understand that this approach is conceptually distinct from biological–taxonomic notions of racial classification. No objective racial taxonomy need be valid to warrant the subjective use of racial classifications. In the social–cognitive sense, 'races' may be identified in a society, acknowledged over generations and believed to be biologically determined even though such groups may not exist in the biological–taxonomic sense.

Recent behavioural and social science evidence supports the social–cognitive notion that race is a construct based on observable physical characteristics (*e.g.*, skin color) that have acquired socially significant meaning (see Banton, 1983; Loury, 2002; Omi and Winant, 1986). In addition to physical features, ascribed and other characteristics such as given name, dress and diet may also contribute to racial categorizations (Nagel, 1994). Cultural factors, such as language, religion and nationality, have more often been used to refer to ethnicity—that is, groups of people who share a common cultural heritage, such as various European immigrant groups in the United States (Bobo, 2001).

The social meaning given to racial classifications activates beliefs and assumptions about individuals in a particular racial category. Consequently, if someone is perceived or identifies himself or herself as belonging to the African American or another racial group — regardless of the person's precise physical or other characteristics — that classification creates a social reality that can have real and enduring consequences. For instance, racial classification can affect access to resources (*e.g.*, education, health care and jobs), the distribution of income and wealth, political power, residential living patterns and interpersonal relationships. Moreover, the consequences of racial classification over time can create boundaries among racially defined groups that affect people today.

Races in India

Various attempts have been made, under the British Raj and since, to classify the population of India according to a racial typology. After the independence, in pursuance of the Government's policy to discourage community distinctions based on race, the 1951 Census of India did away with racial classifications. The national Census of independent India does not recognize any racial groups in India. Some scholars of the colonial epoch attempted to find a method to classify the various groups of India according to the predominant racial theories popular at that time in Europe. This scheme of racial classification was used by the British census of India. It was often mixed with considerations about the caste system.

Social Stratification

The majority (about 80%) of Indian society is broken up into about 2000 castes which can be further broken down into endogamous units which are called subcastes, the total number of these units in India is estimated to have been 75000 at its peak and still about 43000. Any genetic study needs to take these into account, as well as the 'gotra's (roughly speaking, exogamous lineages) within these. A preliminary study showed that about 87% of the subcastes were strictly endogamous and about 5% allowed 'anuloma' (hypergamous: woman marrying socially above herself) marriages. In almost all cases, the society is patrilocal (and patriarchal) and caste follows the father.

In addition to the Hindus who belong to the caste system, Moslems and other established religious groups, the rest of the mainland Indian population, about 7%, is tribal in nature; 427 separate tribes are officially recognized. These are usually divided into the tribes of the Himalayan, Middle, Western and Southern India; Bengal has tribes belonging to the first two groups (1941 census: population of tribal and aborigines defined linguistically as bhotiya, chakama, damai, gurun, hadi, kami, khasa, kuki, lepacha, limubu, mamgara, meca, mru, munda, neoyara, oraõ saotala, saraki, sunuoyara and Tipura: totalling in west bengal 1368780, in east bengal 287217, in

Coochbehar 2435, in hilly Chattagram 233392, in Sikkim 63206 and in Tripura 33633.

Knowledge of the exact affinities of the tribal with Australian or African Negrito populations would be interesting, but investigations have not been able to uncover direct genetic affinities except for known or suspected cases of recent contact. The tribes in Bengal have sometimes been divided into a australasiatic like saotala, õrao, munda, etc., Chinese-mongoloid like garo, kachadi, hadi, etc., the Tibetan-mongoloid like bhotiya, gurung, lepca, neoyar and the Arakan-burmese like chakama and kuki.

The castes can roughly be broken down into the upper castes, the middle castes and the lower castes based on their social status. The division, especially between the upper and middle castes, varies according to region. Genetic evidence points to the different social groups and geographical regions having different set of Y chromosomes, pointing to the social identity staying unchanged along male lines; similar data from mtDNA studies show only slightly higher admixture in the female lines. However, the statistical signficance of all these results is weak except to support a tribal versus caste hindu divide.

Historical Migrations

A study of the skulls from ancient South Asia showed presence of three groups of people.

1. Most of the hunter-gatherer skulls from South Asia clustered with upper paleolithic skulls from Europe.
2. The skulls from Harappa were sharply distinct from these.
3. The foraging and farming populations of South and Central India are intermediate between the other two.

In India, from anthropometric studies, one used to find traces of seven races of humans who intermixed to create the Indian race. Modern studies within regional contexts are still rare; so one mostly has to look back to the global genetic studies. Northwest India shares with west Asia and eastern Europe (and pockets in Africa and South East Asia) the maximum heterozygosity known among world populations, with means between 0.35 and 0.37; and the rest of India (and Europe) is only slightly lower: 0.33 to 0.35. This shows the vast amount of admixture that has gone on in these regions: to be contrasted against Australia which has a homozygosity of less than 0.25. It is currently accepted that at least four strata are visible in the populations in different parts of India.

1. An Australoid-Veddoid substratum
2. A migration from the east of Austrasiatic and Sino-Tibetan language speaking groups.
3. Neolithic migrations from western Iran, probably proto-Dravidian.
4. The Aryan expansion from north of Caspian sea via Turkmenia and Northern Iran.

Thus, for example, some researchers have concluded that the most likely synsthesis of different lines of evidence is that

i. the Austric language speakers came to India c. 50–65 Ka BP from the northeast;

ii. the Dravidian speakers c. 8–4000 BC from the mideast with knowledge of wheat cultivation and cattle, sheep and goat domestication (all middle eastern developments around 8000 BC);

iii. the Indo-europeans in several waves since 4000–1500 BC with horses (domesticated c. 4000 BC around Ukraine; appears to move from northwest India in about 1900 BC to southeast India in 100 BC) and/or iron (used around 3000 BC in Anatolia; also appears to move from North West India in 900 BC to South East India in 400 BC; iron and horses were almost certainly distinct cultural traits which were not associated with one another), they had distinctive burial styles and may have performed cremation, the painted grey ware pottery associated with these people fits the iron users more than the horse riders; and

iv. and in this mix, the Sino-Tibetans joined in in several waves since 8–6 Ka years BP bringing in rice cultivation (if it is not of separate origin in the Indian region, it may have started in south-east Asia around 8 Ka BP).

DNA evidence

The differences between different groups is small overall. But the differences that exist can be used to trace the history of human migrations. One word of caution is, however, due: human groups are rarely defined strictly genealogically. More often, it is cultural transmission that defines the groups one is studying and this transmission has both vertical (concordant with genetics) and horizontal (possibly discordant with genetics) components. Thus a group like 'Indoeuropeans' is defined by cultural features (language spoken, pastural nature, milk and domestic meat based diet, importance of the domesticated horse, a certain polytheistic religion with light/dark or day/night contrast symbolism etc.) and may correlate with a certain genetic makeup. On the other hand, except for genes like lactose tolerance which probably were important for surviving with their dietary peculiarities, no other gene *need* correlate with this cultural pattern. It is completely possible that the Indoeuropeans in various parts of the world, or associated with migrations at different times and places, have different genetic make up. Whether that is the case for any group (like the Indoeuropeans) needs specific study.

Overall, though with those caveats, the DNA data prefers the hypothesis that the Austro-Asiatic speaking tribals predate the Dravidian and the Tibeto-Burmese tribals in India (see here for one timing study). The caste populations are of more recent origins. The North-Indian muslims and the Tibeto-Burmese tribes stand apart in most comparisons, though there is some support for a grouping of north Indian muslims and the Indo-european upper castes of the same region. The Dravidian speaking groups seem to be related by paternal lineage. A change of Dravidian tribals to Indoeuropean caste population by an 'elite dominance' phenomenon is consistent with the data. However, there *is* significant admixture of the Central Asian populations, more in the North than the South and even less in the Northeast and more among the upper castes than among the lower.

mtDNA

Early mitochondrial DNA (which is maternally inherited) studies indicated that a vast number of Indian mtDNA lineages cluster with the East Asians, probably reflecting the proto-Dravidian. They also seem to be closely related to African (*e.g.*, Ethiopian) populations, probably indicative of the Australoid-Veddoid substratum.

Modern studies indicate that the major mtDNA lineages in India belong to the typically asian M haplogroup (see here and here), whose Indian variety (T at np16223) probably originated around 48000 +/- 1500 years before present (*i.e.*, about 46000 BC) and more than 98% of the M individuals carry this variety. This haplogroup is most common in the tribal population (for example, 96.7% amongst the Kotas of the South) and decreases as we go up in caste (reaching 18.5% amongst the Brahmins of Uttar Pradesh). It is also rare in the north Indian muslim community. Among its lineages M2 is the most diverse and occurs in significantly higher frequency among the Austro-asiatic tribals. The M3 (frequent among Dravidian tribals), M4 and M5 are also found in significant numbers. See here for relations between these.

The U haplogroup shows a contrasting distribution: it is most common among the North Indian muslim community (more than 30%), present at 15–20% in the various castes and less than 10% among the tribals. The haplotype U2i separated from an West Eurasian lineage around 53000 +/- 4000 before present (*i.e.*, about 51000 BC). The relative frequency of this subhaplogroup compared to the haplogroup U in general is highest amongst the tribals. Conversely, the tribals almost entirely lack the the West Eurasian subhaplogroup U2e which is more common among the upper castes and shows a caste linked gradation. The other subgroups significantly represented in Indian population are U1 and U7.

A small fraction of the Indian population (about 5–10%) belongs to lineages (W,H,K in upper castes; J,T in other castes) also common in Europe and which have more recent divergence dates. They probably have caste linkages, but the data set is, as yet, too small to be definite. Also, the divergence times have not been estimated, so it is difficult to pinpoint which migration this refers to.

Previous research, which had not detected the caste linkage of the European haplotypes had concluded that, assuming they were largely of Western Eurasian origin (*e.g.*, in accord with the Dravidian-protoElamite or the Indo-european hypothesis), the divergence time is about 9300 +/- 3000 BP (*i.e.*, about 7300 BC), which is deduced as an average over various number of unknown founders (*i.e.*, gradual migration model, rather than concentrated invasion model). Some minor geographical gradients from the Punjab to the Andhra in distribution of European haplotypes also needs further study.

Y chromosome

The Y chromosome (which is paternally inherited) data is broadly similar, but shows higher diversity than the mtDNA data (see here). India groups clearly with the South/Southeast Asia cluster (lineage M9(xM45) or K*(xO,P)?), though North India has a large fraction of R1a(M17) as illustrated by the map (YAP = DE, M130 = O?, M89 = F, M9 = K, M45 = P, M173 = R1*(xR1a1), M17 = R1a1; F is inherently F*(xK), K is K*(xP) and P is P*(xR)) of prevalence of the markers around Eurasia.

The Central Asian P* is significantly rarer among the tribals. The European ancestral lineage BR* is more common among the tribals, especially the Dravidian tribals, than the caste populations: the lineage itself may, however, be a heterogeneous group. The Tibeto-Burmese and to a smaller extent Austro-asiatic, tribals have higher frequencies of K*. It has been suggested that haplogroup J shows clines showing diffusion of agriculture from the middle east: Indian data does not show any clear evidence of this. The 'Indoeuropean' R1a and the L haplogroup are also found in significant numbers. See herc for details and here for one estimate of their ages in India. See here for data from a study concentrating mostly on the brahmins and the tribals and here for associated age estimates.

The major European haplotype (M173 or R1b?) is pretty rare, but some European haplotypes are found amongst the upper castes and in Punjab and Pakistan. A North African/Middle Eastern variety (M89(xM9) or F) is found at low levels all over India, but many of the Indian haplotypes seem to be of Indian origin, possibly due to genetic drift in small endogamous units. The interesting aspect is the much stronger caste linkage in the genetic distance between the Indian and European populations found in these studies compared to those dealing with the maternally inherited mtDNA. The data also shows multiple bottleneck events showing that the ethnic subgroups of India may have formed by widespread 'fission' resulting from pressures on natural resources and because of social regulations.

A recent paper by Sengupta *et al.,* has done a far more detailed study and claims a revision of this standard scenario is in order. The much larger and varied sampling, especially of the tribals, predictably leads to much better resolution of the phylogeny and greater clarity of the haplotype distributions, sometimes correcting the details of previous analyses. Thus they find that the haplogroups H* and its subclades H1*, H1c, H1a and H2 form the most common (26.4%) haplogroup in their Indian sample followed by R1a1-M17 (15.8%), O2a-M95 (14.6%), R2-M124 (9.3%), J2-M172 (9.1%), O3e-M134 (8.0%), L1-M76 (6.3%), F*-M89 (5.2%) and others accounting for the rest 4.2%.

Geographically, India lies between Pakistan (where they found R1a1-M17 which is predominant (24.4%), followed by L*-M20 (13.1%), J2-M172 (11.9%), R2-M124 (7.4%), R1b-P25 (7.4%), G-M201 (6.3%), C3-M217 (6.8%), H*-M69 (6.3%), L1-M76 (5.1%) and others, each less than 5%, accounting for the rest 16.4%) and East Asia (where O3e-M134 (15.4%), C3-M217(13.1%), N3-TAT (12.0%), O2a-M95 (10.9%), O3-M122(xO3e) (11%), N-M231(xN3) (6.3%) and R1b2-M73 (6.3%) are more than 5% and account for 75.4%). It is, however, in the study of diversity and divergence times that there are hints of disagreement with the standard model. The prevalence and diversity of H1, R1a1 and the R2 haplogroups peak in different regions.

Overall, the Indoeuropean speaking groups are more similar to the Pakistani populations than to the East Asian populations and than the Dravidian, Tibeto-Burman and Austro-asiatic groups are to the Pakistani population. As to the origin of the haplotypes, they note that C5-M356, F*-M89, H*-M69 (including H1-M52 and H2-

APT), R2-M124 and L1-M76 probably arose in India and F*-M89 and H*-M69 may have shared demographic history. Similarly, J2a-M410 and J2b-M12 probably came through the Indus valley, whereas O2a-M95 and O3e-M134 came from SE Asia, the former probably through Orissa.

The same study also finds considerable diversity in R1a1-M17 (and R2), especially in the northwest, possibly exceeding 10-15 Ka in time depth and this has been confirmed in another study. This may be inconsistent with a single recent (*i.e.*, about 5 Ka) entry of the comparatively recent (about 7 Ka) linguistic group called Indoeuropeans into India, though complicated exogamy rules can confound such simple conclusions. In fact, since the maximal diversity is around the Hindukush mountains, one can even postulate that as the source region, but the strong association with the Indoeuropean languages (which are unlikely to have arisen in that region) and its higher frequency (and lower diversity!) among caste Indians compared to tribals, both features confirmed in both these studies as well, points to a more complicated demographic history than the paper describes as its results.

Similar remarks apply to the spread of the other haplogroups like the Dravidian and neolithic associated J. A similar conclusion is drawn by Sahoo *et al.*, who show that the prevalence maps vary significantly between caste and tribal populations. They also conclude that there is very little to show the direction of R1a migrations: into or out of India. The data in the Sengupta *et al.*, however, argues that no such simple scenario is likely to fit: R1a1 probably marks multiple separate population movement which still remains to be deciphered. The issue of R1a1 is, studied in much more detail in a newer paper whose conclusions I summarize in my genealogy.

The R1a1 fraction in different populations (Sengupta *et al.* and Qamar *et al.*,): West Bengal Brahmins: 72%, Konkanasth Brahmins: 63%, Muslims: 58%, Sindhi Pakistani: 52/49%, Kashmiri Pakistani: 51%, Pathan Pakistani: 49%, Balti Pakistani: 46%, Tanti: 41%, Pathan Pakistan: 40/49%, UP Brahmins: 36%, Rajput: 31%, Baluchi Pakistanis: 28%. J2a is more common in India amongst the Iyengar,

Iyer and Kurumba and in Pakistan among the coastal, Sindhis, Makranis and Baluchis. See also here for another study which broadly agrees with this.

One possible summary

The National Geographic site tries to assign times to these migrations as follows, the details may sometimes need to be reconciled with what would be considered habitable at the different time periods. There were two ancient migrations–haplogroup C (marker M130) that arose in Arabian region around 50000 years ago out of the M168 lineage of 'Nonafrican Adam' who may have lived 80000 yrs ago in the African rift valley region of Sudan or Ethiopia and spread through the coastal regions of Southern India, Sri Lanka and further on; and haplogroup D (marker M174) which probably branched off from M168 early in Africa and accompanied them along the same coastal route (not found in mainland India, but in the Andamans). About 30000 years ago, two Indian lineages arose and populated large tracts of India for the first time–haplogroup L (marker M20) from Eurasian/American ancestor haplogroup K (marker M9) which arose around 40000 years ago from the haplogroup F (marker 89) in Central Asia; and the slightly later haplogroup H (marker M52) which arose out of an M69 lineage (called the 'Indian' marker, though it arose possibly in south central Asia around 30000 years ago), ultimately from the same common nonAfrican haplogroup F (marker M89) which itself had arisen out of the M168 lineage 45000 years ago. The precise relation of the haplogroup G (marker M201) which arose around 20000 years ago in the Indus region is not clear. The haplogroup O (marker M175) which arose 35000 years ago from haplogroup K (marker M9) might also have moved through eastern India. North India also has a large fraction of R1a individuals, probably associated with the Indoeuropean speakers, though one should be careful about possible caveats in genetically characterizing any cultural group. I myself belong to this lineage and you can see its history as part of my genealogy. A different branch of the R* M207 lineage described there is the M124 R2 lineage which probably arose 25000 years ago in Central Asia and a branch of them reached India. Similarly from the M45 P lineage described there, the Q M242 lineage arose, probably in Siberia around 15 to 20 thousand years back. This is the lineage that populated the Americas, but a few clades, such as the Q6 (M346) and Q1 (M120, M265=N14), especially Q1a (M378), is found in small proportions in India and Pakistan; and in East Asia.

On the female side, the African haplogroup L3 originated in the same region about the same 80000 years ago and gave rise to the haplogroup M which then spread out into Southern Asia including India, after the daughters C, D and Z branched off. L3 also gave rise to N* in Africa. This gave rise to many of the lineages of Eurasia and Americas. In particular, the R arose somewhere in the middle east out of this group and a few of its descendants are typical Indian. About 55000 years ago the haplogroup U arose from this somewhere in central Asia and some of its lineages are prominent in India. Haplogroup K arose 16000 years ago, as a part of this and spread mainly in Europe. Haplogroups J and T arose 10000 years ago from the R and have been associated with the spread of farming. H and V arose in Europe around 10–20000 years ago out of the preHV that arose around 40000 years ago from the R. The haplogroups A, B, F and X are also possibly daughters of R. The haplogroups N1, I and W are daughters of the N*. It should be noted that the history of one or two blocks on our chromosome is *not* the history of the entire human populations. The difference between these is discussed briefly in my page on human evolution.

Autosomal DNA

A similar caste linkage is also found in the autosomal studies: overall upper caste Indians are significantly closer to Europeans than other Indians. The autosomal locii are, however, inherited biparentally, so population admixture needs to be treated differently. A new study of 25 Indian populations and a few outside ones tries to draw a picture of migrations and intermixing. Assuming a notional generation time of 25 years in this period (so the early dates are likely to be too early in this discussion), one model they find to be consistent with their data is an out of Africa scenario in which an effective population of about 9,000 individuals expanded into a 18,000 strong West African and a 5,000 individual Eurasian population some 100,000 years back. The Eurasian population then expanded into a 10,000 large Ancestral European and a 5,000 strong Ancestral East-Eurasian populations about 50,000 years back. Within about 7500 years, this East Eurasian lineage expanded to 10,000 who gave rise to modern East Asian populations, a 3800 group of Andamanese and about 10,000 of a group called Ancestral South Indians. The Onge among the Andamanese remained almost unmixed when the Ancestral South Indians were undergoing further mixings later, but the Great Andamanese seem to have received recent gene flow, dominantly paternal, from the mainland for a couple of generations today.

The European lineage may have gotten a gene-flow from the East Asian group as late as 15,000 years back, but, the by then 20,000 strong lineage split off into the 30,000 individual Caucasian and 25,000 big West European groups about 7,000 years ago. Around 5,000 years back, a group of the West Europeans called Ancestral North Indians (ANI) started mingling with the Ancestral South Indians (ASI) to form the various Indian populations: Pathans about 80% ANI, Sindhi 75%, Kashmiri Pandit 70%, Vaish 65%, Meghawal 60%, Srivastava and Velama 55%, Tharu, Naidu and Lodi 50%, Vysya, Kamsali, Kurumba and Bhil 45%, to Chechu, Madiga and Mala about 40%. They correctly caution, however, that this is only a sketch of the story: gene flows between sister groups after a split (*e.g.*, between African and Eurasians before 50,000 years back; or between the Andamanese and the ASI before 5000 years back) is not detectable in their models and is thus consistent with mtDNA evidence that Andamanese and the tribal East Indians share a common ancestry in the last 24,000 years. Moreover, there is nothing to suggest that the mixture event that led to the Indians happened at an instant 5000 years ago: in fact, many groups seem to have small founder sizes, some as recently as a few hundred years back, others as much as a thousands of years back. Overall, caste divisions seem to be deep, with limited gene flows across caster boundaries in the historical period.

Physical Anthropological evidence

Physical anthropological studies very clearly separates the Indian populations (except some Andamanese tribals) from most of the other Asian populations, with people from the persian gulf, Arabia, Burma, SW China, Vietnamese and Malayan forming the border along the first principle coordinate. This component seems to be highly correlated with stature and hence with temperature. The second principle coordinate, which mainly measures facial and nasal shape, serves to separate the various groups of Indians: (i) Maharashtra upper caste, (ii) Gujarat and Konkan, (iii) West tribal and lower caste, (iv) Central and Eastern tribal, (v) Bihar and Bengal, (vi) Vedda and South Deccan tribal, (vii) Orissa upper caste, (viii) UP upper caste, (ix) Pahari bhotia, (x) South India and Ceylon and (xi) Kashmiri, Punjabi and Pahari. The third component clarifies the separation of (i)-(iv), (v)-(vii) and (ix) out of the rest.

In a limited genetic tree, Indians form a number of distinct clusters: (i) Central Indian and Brahmins, together with South Indians cluster with Westen Asians (cluster formed by Iranians, Uzbeks, Caucasians, Lebanese and Turkish, Jordanian, Assyrian, Armenians), (ii) Sri Lankans and South Dravidians break off earlier and (iii) North and Central Dravidians along with the East Indians break off before the cluster formed by the previous two groups and the Arabians including Bedouins. The first two principle components do not separate the Indian population: they only separate the caucasoid group discussed so far, from the South East Asians with Gurkhas and from the North East and East Asians with the Bhutanese.

When only the Indian populations are analyzed, the branching order changes somewhat. Now, the third of the Indian clusters mentioned is an inner group and consists of a cluster of Munda and North Dravidians with Central Dravidians and a separate one of Marathan and Maharashtrian Brahmins with Bhils and then Rajbanshis, with a cluster consisting of Bengali Brhamins and Parsis splitting off its base. A cluster consisting of the second and most of the first of the previous groups is sister to it. (The first group, of course, is now resolved: Punjabi, Central Indian form a group with

Punjabi Brahmins and the Rajputs; Vania and Jats form a sister cluster with Bombay Brahmins. Koli and Kerala Brahmins along with Pakistanis form a cluster off the base of all this.) Kanet and UP Brahmins seem to form a cluster branching off earlier and Gurkha and Tharu a cluster even earlier. The Kerala Kadar seems to come from a completely different branch.

The detailed structure of the clusters probably needs more data to be established. As far as Bengal is concerned, the tribals cluster with North and Central Dravidians; and Bengalis as a whole cluster with these and Maharashtrians. However, the importance of caste shows up; except in Punjab and Maharashtra, the Brahmins do not cluster with the other castes. On the other hand, the Brahmins of different regions do not cluster together either; in a two principle component analysis, Brahmins from Bombay, Kerala, UP, Punjab, Maharashtra and West Bengal show a steady progression along the diagonal. This could be due to genetic drift in these highly endogamous units.

Great Races

Scientific racism of Europe divided mankind into three 'great races', Caucasoid (white), Mongoloid and Negroid (black) in accordance with their own world-view. The populations of the Indian subcontinent, however, were problematic to classify under this scheme. They were assumed to be a mixture of an indigenous 'Dravidian race', tentatively with an 'Australoid' grouping, with an intrusive Aryan race, identified as a sub-race to the Caucasoid race, but some authors also assumed Mongolic admixture, so that India, for the purposes of scientific racism, presented a complicated mixture of all major types. Edgar Thurston identified a 'Homo Dravida' who had more in common with the Australian aboriginals than their Indo-Aryan or high-caste neighbors. As evidence, he adduced the use of the boomerang by Kallan and Marawan warriors and the proficiency at tree-climbing among both the Kadirs of the Anamalai hills and the Dayaks of Borneo.

In 1865, anthropologist Thomas Huxley said, "The so-called Dravidian populations of Southern Hindostan lead us back, physically as well as geographically, towards the Australians while the diminutive Mincopies of the Andaman islands lie between the Negro and Negrito races and, as Mr. Busk has pointed out, occasionally present the rare combination of brachycephaly, or short-headedness, with wooly hair." "The Hindoos of the Valley of the Ganges and the Indus, who there is every reason to believe result from the intermixture of distinct stocks... Aryan invaders were white men. It is hardly doubted that they intermixed with the dark Dravidian aborginees and that the high-caste Hindoos are what they are in virtue of the Aryan blood they inherited... I do not know any good reason for the physical differences between a high-caste Hindoo and a Dravidian, except the Aryan blood in the veins of the former"

The 'Negroid' status of the Dravidians however remained disputed. In 1898, ethnographer Friedrich Ratzel remarked about the 'Mongolian features' of 'Dravidians', resulting in his "hypothesis of their [Dravidians] close connection with the population of Tibet" whom he adds "Tibetans may be decidedly reckoned in the Mongol race" In 1899, a journal called 'Science' summarized Ratzel's findings over India with, "India is for the author [of the History of Mankind, Ratzel], a region where races have been broken up pulverized, kneaded by conquerors. Doubtless a pre-Dravidian negroid type came first, of low stature and mean physique, though these same are, in India, the result of poor social and economic conditions. Dravidians succeeded negroids and there may have been Malay intrusions, but Australian affinities are denied. Then succeeded Aryan and Mongol, forming the present pot porri through conquest and blending."

In 1900, anthropologist Joseph Deniker said, "the Dravidian race is connected with both the Indonesian and Australian... the Dravidian race, which it would be better to call South Indian, is prevalent among the peoples of Southern India speaking the Dravidian tongues and also among the Kols and other people of India... The Veddhas... come much nearer to the Dravidian type, which moreover also penetrates among the populations of India, even into the middle valley of the Ganges." Deniker groups 'Dravidians' as a 'subrace under the group of "Curly or Wavy Hair Dark Skin" in which he also includes the 'Ethiopian' and 'Australian'. Also, Deniker mentions that the "Indian race has its typical representatives among the Afghans, the Rajputs, the Brahmins and most of North India but it has undergone numerous alterations as a consequence with crosses with Assyriod, Dravidian, Mongol, Turkish, Arab and other elements." His theories have been discarded by post-modern anthropologists.

During 1930-2010, there were several historians and scientists who proved that there are no separate races of so called Aryans or Dravadians as they belong to the same race. This has picked up strong footing, as on one hand, there are no evidences till date in support of Aryan invasion theory and increased number of historical and scientific evidences that prove that there is only one race, on the other. Evidences include a ground-breaking research in 2009 that has been conducted jointly by Centre for Cellular and Molecular Biology (CCMB) Hyderabad along with Harvard Medical School, Harvard School of Public health, Broad Institute of Harvard and MIT of USA. The research team has made this claim after observing that north and south Indians are genetically similar.

Martial Races Theory

The Martial races theory was a British ideology based on the assumption that certain peoples were more martially inclined as opposed to the general populace or other peoples. The British divided the entire spectrum of Indian ethnic groups into two categories: a 'martial race' and a 'non-martial race'. The martial race was thought of as typically brave and well built for fighting. The non-martial races were those whom the British believed to be unfit for battle because of their sedentary lifestyle.

The question of loyalty and disloyalty cannot be debated on the simple fact that many of the races mentioned as 'loyal' actually did participate in the rebellion. One of the more famous rebels, Bhagat Singh, was a Sikh. The Indian rebellion of 1857 may have played a role in British reinforcement of the martial races theory. During this rebellion, some Indian troops, particularly in Bengal, mutinied, but the 'loyal', Sikhs, Punjabis, Dogras, Gurkas, Garhwalis, Devars and Pakhtuns (Pathans) did not join the mutiny and fought on the side of the British Army. Modern scholars have suggested that this theory was propagated to accelerate recruitment from among these races, while discouraging enlistment of 'disloyal' Indians who had sided with the rebel army during the war.

Race in the United States

We begin our discussion of race in the United States with its founding in 1789. The founding document, the U.S. Constitution, accorded de facto recognition to white and nonwhite racial categories in order to assign political representation to the states (Anderson and Fienberg, 2000). During the 1787 Constitutional Convention, northern and southern states compromised on counting slaves as three-fifths of a person for purposes of congres- sional reapportionment. In addition, Indians 'not taxed' were to be excluded from the reapportionment counts. The compromise on the treatment of slaves was key to the establishment of the new government; it was implemented in the U.S. decennial census, first conducted in 1790, when enumerators were instructed to classify people as white, other free person, or slave and to exclude Indians not taxed. Because all slaves were treated as a single racial group (*i.e.*, black), the enumeration of people by their civil status effectively produced a racial classification of whites, American Indians and blacks (free and enslaved).

Although slavery was abolished in the mid-nineteenth century, for more than 100 years federal and state laws and court decisions (*e.g.*, Jim Crow restrictions put in place in southern states and the 1882 Chinese Exclusion Act) upheld racial classifications as the basis for unequal treatment of groups, serving to maintain dominant and subordinate racial groupings in U.S. society (Feagin and Feagin, 1996). During this period, the concepts of 'white' and 'nonwhite' were defined in laws and customs to exclude people from white status if they had even a small amount of nonwhite blood. Thus, progeny of black and white unions were invariably classified as 'black', regardless of their skin color or appearance. Originating in the South, the so-called one-drop rule was associated with rigid social segregation and economic exploitation.

This narrow concept of whiteness even excluded many immigrant groups that are now classified as white but were not so in the nineteenth and early twentieth centuries. Being white once signified Anglo-Saxon heritage; thus, aside from the British, Dutch, Germans, Scandinavians and Scotch-Irish, many newly arrived Southern and Eastern Europeans, among others, had to struggle to be defined as 'white' in America. Irish immigrants (Ignatiev, 1995), as well as Jews, Italians and Poles (Roediger, 1991), were often treated negatively because of their ethnic origin. Initially, ethnic and cultural traits set these groups apart from the mainstream as 'nonwhites', but over time they acquired many traits of the larger society and were assimilated into 'white' U.S. culture. Immutable physical characteristics, however, made it difficult for many non-European groups to follow suit. Thus, such groups as Chinese or Japanese immigrants were denied citizenship for many decades and Chinese immigration was totally prohibited from 1882 to World War II.

In contrast to U.S. notions of race, Latin American and Caribbean societies have generally lacked a dichotomous classification of people as white or nonwhite; they also take account of social class as well as appearance in determining degrees of 'whiteness' (Degler, 1971; Toplin, 1974). Although U.S. society has generally not recognized gradations of whiteness, it has often recognized gradations within broad nonwhite racial categories on the basis of skin color and ancestry. For example, censuses from 1850 through 1890 and again in 1910 and 1920 included one or more black racial subcategories, such as black, mulatto, quadroon and octoroon. Censuses since 1890 have also distinguished subgroups of Asians on the basis of national origin

There is social scientific research on skin color differentiation (and discrimination) whereby members of a racial group are further distinguished (and treated differently) on the basis of their skin tone (*e.g.*, light-skinned versus dark-skinned African Americans). Empirical accounts of this type of differentiation within racial categories include Blair *et al.* (2002), Keith and Herring (1991), Krieger (2000), Maddox and Gray (2002) and Thompson and Keith (2001). However, we focus on the broad classifications, which, in the United States, have carried social meaning and consequences for all their members.

Most recently in the United States, stigmas attached to some nonwhite groups have appeared to diminish and there has been increased interest by such groups as Native Americans and people of mixed race to identify themselves as such. In addition, increased immigration from Latino and Caribbean countries has highlighted ambiguities in the measurement of race for these populations. Results from recent censuses document that many Hispanic groups think of their ethnicity (as it is termed in the census) as a racial category. These people often check 'other race' rather than a specifically named category, or they do not answer the race question at all. We discuss these developments, which underscore the fluid and socially and politically influenced nature of racial classification, in the next section.

Racial Categories in Federal Statistics

The meaning of race in the United States has shaped and been shaped by the data collected and reported by federal agencies in the census, house- hold surveys and administrative records systems. These data are used for many purposes, including to describe and analyze social, economic and other differences among racial and ethnic groups and to monitor compliance with civil rights laws.

Decennial Census

The U.S. census, as noted above, has included questions on race in every census beginning in 1790. Reflecting evolving conceptions of race and the political power of different groups over time, the racial categories in the census have changed from one decade to the next. The census has also often included additional items related to racial categorization, such as questions on national origin, birthplace of parents, language spoken in the home and ancestry.

The identification of Hispanic origin in the census has varied substantially over time. In 1930 the census included 'Mexican' as a separate nonwhite racial category; but after protests from the Mexican government, the category was omitted in subsequent censuses. Prior to 1970, there was no nationwide standard for identifying people of Latin American origin. From 1940 to 1970, the census coded people in five southwestern states who reported Spanish language or surname as 'of Spanish origin', and in 1960 and 1970 the census tabulated people of Puerto Rican birth or heritage in three northeastern states.

The 1970 census included a Hispanic origin item that was asked of a 5 percent sample of the U.S. population. Respondents were to indicate whether their origin or descent was Mexican, Puerto Rican, Cuban, Central or South American, or some other Spanish origin. Subsequent censuses have asked everyone whether they are of Hispanic origin and to indicate a specific subgroup. The ethnic origin question is separate from the race question; thus, Hispanics can be of any race. We are in agreement that 'Hispanic' is an ethnicity and not a race in the way that Americans have conceptualized such racial groups as whites, blacks and Asians. However, disadvantaged Hispanics face many of the same barriers to full participation in U.S. society as disadvantaged racial groups. Moreover, from census reporting patterns, significant proportions of Hispanics consider their origin to be synonymous with their race. For these reasons, we include Hispanics when discussing discrimination against different racial groups in this.

Federal Classification Standards

Since 1977, the U.S. Office of Management and Budget (OMB) has provided federal statistical and program administration agencies with classification standards for collecting and reporting data on race and ethnicity (these standards were most recently revised in 1997). OMB currently defines five major racial categories for use in federal data collection: American Indian or Alaska Native; Asian; black or African American; Native Hawaiian and other Pacific Islander; and white. In addition, there are two ethnic categories:

Hispanic or Latino and Not Hispanic or Latino. The OMB standards state a preference for separate questions to ascertain race and ethnicity, but agencies may use a combined question in which Hispanic is treated as a race. The standards also state a preference for self-reporting of race and ethnicity as opposed to reporting by an observer.

Under the 1997 standards, respondents for the first time have the option of checking more than one racial category. This option reflects changes in the nation's diversity as a result of immigration and intermarriage among different racial groups. Although a 'multiracial' option was considered, many critics believed it would hamper the ability to identify the racial groups to which 'multiracial' respondents belonged (Harrison, 2002). Other critics argued that "mark one or more races" might complicate racial classification as well. OMB emphasizes that its classification standards are designed to monitor adherence to and enforce civil rights laws. "The categories in this classification are social-political constructs and should not be interpreted as being scientific or anthropological in nature" (Office of Information and Regulatory Affairs, 1997: 58,788).

Federal statistical and program evaluation and administrative agencies use the OMB standards to count and classify the U.S. population. Administrative data on race are collected by such agencies as the U.S. Department of Education and others to monitor equal access to opportunity in social and economic domains for groups that have experienced discrimination and that may continue to face unequal treatment because of their race or ethnic origin. Census and household survey data on race and ethnicity are collected by the Census Bureau and other statistical agencies and are widely used by federal, state and local government agencies, private firms, nonprofit organizations, academic researchers, the media and the general public. Uses of these data include redrawing congressional and state legislative district boundaries; calculating and analyzing vital demographic information (*e.g.,* birth rates, infant mortality rates); monitoring compliance by employers with equal opportunity employment laws; and many other applications for research and program planning, implementation and evaluation.

The federal classification system is not an attempt to categorize all the ethnic and racial groups in the United States. For instance, the classification system does not support separate identification of many subgroups within racial populations (*e.g.*, Caribbean-born blacks versus U.S.-born African Americans, or foreign-born versus native-born Asians) or of the large numbers of immigrant groups to the United States. Federal agencies such as the Census Bureau can use more detailed subcategories of race (*e.g.*, Vietnamese, Korean, or Filipino for Asian groups) as long as they collapse to the basic five categories cited above. The census is also allowed to use a category of 'other race'.

Measurement Issues

The Ambiguity of Race

As a social–cognitive construct, the meaning of race in the United States has changed and will likely continue to change over time with changing sociopolitical norms, economic patterns and waves of immigration (*e.g.*, the assimilation of some European immigrant groups from 'nonwhite' to 'white' status in the first half of the twentieth century and the growing acknowledgment of mixed-race origins in the twenty-first century). Moreover, race has and may continue to have different meanings for different groups, sometimes overlapping and sometimes not (Lieberman, 1993). For instance, some Hispanics, who can be of any race in the OMB classification system, identify themselves primarily by ethnic or national origin (*e.g.*, Mexican, Cuban, or Puerto Rican) (de la Garza *et al.*, 1992). In contrast, other Hispanics consider Hispanic or Latino to be a race on a par with black, white, Asian and American Indian (Denton and Massey, 1989; Harris, 2002; U.S. Office of Management and Budget, 1997). Furthermore, whereas historically Americans have most often viewed racial categories as mutually exclusive, Hispanics have tended to see race along a continuum (Nobles, 2000). Thus, there is research evidence that many Latin American and Latin Caribbean immigrants who come to the United States see themselves as being of mixed origin, most commonly European and American Indian or European and African.

Shifts in societal views on race, political pressures from different groups, increasing diversity in the country's population and consequent changes in data collection standards and practices add ambiguity to the way we understand race and interpret data on race. Two specific measurement problems are inconsistent reporting for individuals and groups, currently and over time and different data collection practices, such as self-reporting in surveys and, frequently, reporting by others in administrative records systems. Some researchers have suggested that multiple indicators are needed to fully understand racial categorization in American society today.

Inconsistent Reporting

Population groups and individuals vary in their consistency of reporting race when comparing surveys across time and with each other. In particular, there has always been considerable confusion regarding the responses of Latin American and Caribbean groups to the separate race question used in the census and surveys. Many Latin Americans and Caribbeans reject the racial categories on the census, select 'other race', and write in a word that to them best describes their racial identity. For instance, Latin Caribbeans might use 'Moreno', 'Trigeño', or 'Boricua' and Central and South Americans might use 'Mestizo', 'La Raza', 'Mexicano' or some other term denoting a mix of races (Denton and Massey, 1989). From 1940 through 1970, the Census Bureau assumed that such responses were incorrect because Hispanic respondents misunderstood the race question. Accordingly, all such responses were recoded as 'white.' In 1980, however, the Census Bureau for the first time accepted such responses, grouped them into one category and treated Hispanic data as 'racial' data (*i.e.*, responses were recoded as 'Spanish race')—a practice generally continued in 1990 and, with greater complexity, in 2000. This practice further adds to the confusion about how to classify Hispanics as a group.

Different question formats or wording can also affect responses and enumeration of Hispanics. For instance, according to various studies, when questions about race and Hispanic origin are reversed so that the race question follows the ethnic origin question (as was done in the 2000 census), response rates for Hispanic origin are higher and fewer respondents choose 'other race' (Anderson and Fienberg, 2000; Bates *et al.*, 1994; del Pinal, 2003; Martin *et al.*, 1990; Tucker and Kojetin, 1996; see also Harris, 2002). For another example, a 1995 supplement to the Current Population Survey found that a smaller proportion of respondents identified themselves as Hispanic when a combined race and Hispanic origin question was used, compared with having separate questions on race and ethnicity. Finally, studies that have compared responses for the same individuals with separate surveys show high rates of consistency for reporting of Hispanic origin but low rates of consistency for reporting of race by Hispanics (see del Pinal, 2003).

Inconsistent reporting of race on surveys is also problematic for other groups, although not to the same extent as for Hispanics. For American Indian and Native Hawaiian or other Pacific Islander groups—both small populations—rates of inconsistent reporting across surveys can be high. For instance, census counts of American Indians and Alaska Natives increased dramatically following the 1950 census—by 51 percent from 1950 to 1960, 50 percent from 1960 to 1970 and 71 percent from 1970 to 1980. Factors driving the increases included not only increased life expectancy but also the change from observer to self-reporting in the census, growing ethnic pride and reduction in stigma from being identified as anything other than white. There are no data on how many people changed their racial category between censuses, but such people likely accounted for a major part of the growth in the American Indian population after 1950 (Snipp, 2000).

High levels of inconsistent reporting also characterized people who chose more than one race in the 2000 census, which was the first census to allow multiracial identification. Overall, only 2.4 percent of the population marked more than one race, but 8 percent of children ages 0 to 4 had two or more races marked, indicating that the multiracial population is likely to grow in number. However, nearly one-third of multiracial respondents were of Hispanic origin, many of whom checked 'white' and 'some other race'. Also, results from the National Health Interview Survey suggest that, if prompted, a majority of people choosing more than one race will select one primary racial category.

Overall, these results illustrate how respondents have different concepts for race and ethnicity, leading to subjective responses (Anderson and Fienberg, 2000). Subjectivity and ambiguity of responses make it difficult to collect complete and reliably reported information on race and ethnicity. Furthermore, with changes to questions or to category labels for some groups over time (*e.g.*, the Asian or Pacific Islander category was split into two separate categories), differences in who reports the race of an individual (the individual, another household member, or an observer) and changing political reasons for identifying with a particular race (*e.g.*, civil rights enforcement, collective identity), responses can be inconsistent and difficult to interpret. Despite these problems, it is important to note that 98 percent of the U.S. population identified with one race in the 2000 census. Moreover, studies conducted in conjunction with the census find high levels of consistent reporting for people reporting African American, Asian, or white race, even when the data are collected by different methods (*e.g.*, computer-assisted personal interviewing versus mail response) and use different question formats.

Self-Identification of Race

According to OMB's 1997 revised standards, self-identification or self-reporting is the preferred method of collecting data on race and ethnicity (U.S. Office of Management and Budget, 1997). Self-identification is used in most surveys (and has been used in the census for most of the population since 1960), but many administrative racial identification forms are filled out by someone other than the person being surveyed (*e.g.*, by a parent, survey administrator, health care worker, or police officer).

Some people believe self-identification is the only reasonable method because it allows people to express their own racial identity (see Harris, 2002). Others argue against self-identification because they believe federal racial data, if used to monitor and enforce civil rights, should capture the observer's report of an individual's race—

after all, people are most often discriminated against on the basis of observers' beliefs. The revised OMB standards state that, although the data are used for civil rights enforcement, the government should not tell individuals how to classify their race (Harris, 2002; U.S. Office of Management and Budget, 1997).

Using different approaches to identify and report race and ethnicity can make it difficult to compare racial categorizations across time and among data sets. Moreover, reporting procedures are not often the same even within a single data set. For example, 78 percent of occupied households mailed back a questionnaire in the 2000 census, but the remaining forms were obtained by enumerators in follow-up, sometimes from neighbors or landlords (Stackhouse and Brady, 2003). In addition, one person typically fills out a census questionnaire for an entire household, which can result in different racial categorizations from those that each household member would have chosen individually.

Multiple Indicators of Racial Identification

Harris (2002) argues that classifying race is a social process that varies across contexts and observers. He uses a matrix to illustrate the multidimensional, socially constructed nature of racial classification (see Figure 1-1).

	Genotype/Ancestry	Phenotype	Culture
Internet	1 "Iknow that my background is X"	2 "I know that I look X"	3 "I know that I feel/act X"
Expressed	4 "My background is X"	5 "I look X"	6 "I feel/act X"
External	7 "He/she has X ancestry"	8 "He/she looks X"	9 "He/she acts X" "He/she thinks he/she is X"

Figure 1-1 A matrix of race.
Source: Harris (2002).

To determine an individual's race, people may use one or more ancestry or biological bases, phenotypic or physical characteristics and cultural bases, such as ideology and language. Furthermore, racial classifications for an individual may differ according to the perspective of the person making the classification: internal (self-classification based on an individual's beliefs about his or her own race); expressed (self-classification based on how an individual presents his or her race to others—*e.g.*, choosing not to identify as a member of a nonwhite group to avoid stigmatization); and external (classification by observers based on their views of an individual's race). These dimensions are not mutually exclusive; they all interact within a social context. Thus, a mixed-race individual may identify herself as multiracial in private settings but express her dominant race in public and be classified in different categories by different observers.

Obtaining multiple indicators of racial identification would likely provide helpful data to inform racial classification and analysis. As Harris notes, however, indicators for race along these lines are not available in most current data sets. To collect these data, it would be necessary to add specific additional categories and observations, still further complicating the measurement and analysis of race data.

Racial Classification and Racism

Attempts have been made to classify humans since the 17th cent., when scholars first began to separate types of flora and fauna. Johann Friedrich Blumenbach was the first to divide humanity according to skin color. In the 19th and early 20th cent., people such as Joseph Arthur Gobineau and Houston Stewart Chamberlain, mainly interested in pressing forward the supposed superiority of their own kind of culture or nationality, began to attribute cultural and psychological values to race. This approach, called racism, culminated in the vicious racial doctrines and anti-Semitism of Nazi Germany and was used to justify slavery and segregation (see integration) in the United States, apartheid in the Republic of South Africa and European imperialism and colonialism generally.

Summary

There is no single concept of race. Rather, race is a complex concept, best viewed for social science purposes as a subjective social construct based on observed or ascribed characteristics that have acquired socially signifi- cant meaning. Indeed, for the purpose of measuring racial discrimination, a social–cognitive concept of race is integral to meaningful analysis. The reason is that racial discrimination historically has been and continues today to be a phenomenon of social attitudes and behaviours, stemming from people's perceptions. There is no scientifically objective information that people use or can use as a basis for creating unambiguous, consistent racial classifications that have social meaning and effects.

In the United States, ways in which different populations think about their own and others' racial status have been affected over time by changing patterns of immigration, social and economic change and changes in societal norms and government policies. The subjectivity of race and the heterogeneity within population groups add further ambiguity to classifying different populations by race. Overall, federal racial categories provide only a partial picture of the heterogeneity and growing diversity of the U.S. population and of the complexity of racial classification. Moreover, factors related to survey and administrative records design and implementation—such as changes in racial categories, methods of reporting data (self-reports or observer reports) and allocation rules for single races and multiple-race combinations—have implications for the collection, use and interpretation of data on race (especially when attempting to compare data for racial categories in different data sets). Yet most people continue to identify with a single race and consistency of reporting is high for some major racial groups.

2

Racial Discrimination: Conceptual and Legal Analysis

In the previous chapter, we discussed race as a social–cognitive construct that evolves over time and in which racial categories reflect one's own or one's ancestors' physical features and associated characteristics that have acquired socially significant meaning. In this chapter, we turn to the concept of racial discrimination, defining it from a social science perspective, which includes not only legal definitions of discrimination but also aspects that go beyond legal concepts. We provide examples of the large and persistent differential outcomes by race in various social and economic domains that make racial discrimination an important topic for social science analysis and motivate our examination of methods for measuring the role that race-based discrimination may play in those differences. For completeness, we examine the legal definitions of discrimination. Although discrimination is often understood in legal terms because, once it has been identified, legal consequences ensue, our definition encompasses forms of discrimination that may not be explicitly unlawful or easily measured.

Racial Discrimination

Racial discrimination is the practice of letting a person's race or skin color unfairly become a factor when deciding who receives a job, promotion, or other employment benefit. It most often affects minority individuals who feel they have been unfairly discriminated against in favor of a Caucasian (or white) individual, but there have been recent cases where whites have claimed that reverse discrimination has occurred—that is, the minority received unfairly favorable treatment at the expense of the white individual. Court rulings handed down through the years have determined that a company's responsibility not to discriminate based on race begins even before an individual is hired. Companies can be held liable if pre-employment screening or testing is determined to be discriminatory, if applications ask unacceptable questions designed to screen for race, or if the overall selection process is deemed to be unfair. One of the main indicators that racial discrimination has occurred in the hiring process involves the qualifications of the job applicants. While a slight difference in qualifications between a minority and nonminority candidate do not automatically indicate racial bias (if the lesser qualified nonminority candidate is hired over the minority candidate), a drastic difference in qualifications has almost always been upheld by the courts as a sure sign of racial discrimination.

Racial discrimination is a high-profile issue in the business world and is a very real problem that still exists—and in some cases is getting worse. In a 1998 study by the nonprofit group Catalyst called "Women of Color in Corporate Management: A Statistical Picture," it was shown that minority women, while now accounting for almost a quarter of all women in the workplace, occupied only 15 percent of the management positions held by women. The study determined that a combination of racial discrimination and the glass ceiling (a term that describes the difficulty women in general have in reaching management positions) was responsible for the disparity in those numbers.

Theories of Discrimination

We developed a two-part definition of racial discrimination: differential treatment on the basis of race that disadvantages a racial group and treatment on the basis of inadequately justified factors other than race that disadvantages a racial group (differential effect). We focus our discussion on discrimination against disadvantaged racial minorities. Our definition encompasses both individual behaviours and institutional practices.

To be able to measure the existence and extent of racial discrimination of a particular kind in a particular social or economic domain, it is necessary to have a theory (or concept or model) of how such discrimination might occur and what its effects might be. The theory or model, in turn, specifies the data that are needed to test the theory, appropriate methods for analyzing the data and the assumptions that the data and analysis must satisfy in order to support a finding of discrimination. Without such a theory, analysts may conduct studies that do not have interpretable results and do not stand up to rigorous scrutiny.

The purpose of this chapter is to help researchers think through appropriate models of discrimination to guide their choice of data and analytic methods for measurement. We begin by discussing four types of discrimination and the various mechanisms that may lead to such discrimination. The first three types involve behaviours of individuals and organizations: intentional discrimination, subtle discrimination and statistical profiling. The fourth type involves discriminatory practices embedded in an organizational culture. Next, we compare these discriminatory behaviours and institutional practices with existing legal standards defining discrimination in the courts.

We then discuss how these discriminatory behaviours and practices might operate within the domains of education, employment, housing, criminal justice and health. Finally, we discuss concepts of how cumulative discrimination might operate across domains and over time to produce lasting consequences for disadvantaged racial groups. This chapter is not concerned with identifying the relative importance of the various types of discrimination; rather, it is designed to present a set of conceptual possibilities that can motivate and shape appropriate research study designs.

Legal Definition of Discrimination

Thus far we have presented a definition of discrimination and examined racial disparities across several domains. As a point of comparison, in this section we look at the legal definitions of discrimination and identify the circumstances under which a legal finding of discriminatory behaviour can be made. The law represents an important venue in which racial discrimination is often identified and measured. In a legal setting, once an act has been labeled as discriminatory, legal remedies, both monetary and injunctive, may be awarded.

An elaborate array of federal and state constitutional, statutory and administrative provisions broadly prohibit discrimination on the basis of race in a vast range of public and private behaviours. A large body of law has developed to give content to this broad prohibition by defining specifically what constitutes impermissible discrimination. Because the foundations of these laws emanate from different jurisdictions and legal authorities, there is no single definition of impermissible racial discrimination; standards depend on the particular jurisdiction or actor involved. Nonetheless, as noted above, two important doctrinal concepts—disparate treatment and disparate impact discrimination—are useful in defining the nature of the legal prohibition. Each is discussed in turn below.

Disparate Treatment Discrimination

The core concept of disparate treatment discrimination emanates from the constitutional requirement of equal protection under the law and is codified in the main federal statute prohibiting racial discrimination in employment—Title VII of the 1964 Civil Rights Act. This statute prohibits an employment practice that affects an individual's employment "because of such individual's race…." Thus, an employer who refuses to hire, fails to promote, or discharges a worker because of his or her race is guilty of disparate treatment discrimination. So, too, is an employer who decides to pay nonwhite workers less than white workers or to discipline the former more heavily for identical conduct.

The language 'because of' is interpreted as requiring proof that race was a motivating factor for the employment practice. In theory, the requirement that the discrimination be intentional before it runs afoul of the law may protect an employer who acts without conscious awareness of having discriminated, a phenomenon that the research literature in psychology indicates is common. For this reason, some legal scholars have suggested that the legal theory of intentional discrimination is flawed and should be expanded to prohibit unconscious or negligent acts of discrimination (Allen, 1995; Oppenheimer, 1993).

In practice, however, a defense that the discrimination is 'unconscious' is virtually never encountered in an employment discrimination litigation, which typically focuses on two issues: (1) the plaintiff's threshold demonstration of racial disparity in treatment and (2) the credibility of the nondiscriminatory reasons for this disparate treatment offered by the employer. Therefore, although in theory any nondiscriminatory reason will constitute a defense against a charge of disparate treatment discrimination, in practice an employer will be more likely to lose the case if the reason does not appear to be sufficiently linked to the plaintiff's lack of ability to perform the job or demonstrated misconduct. Nonetheless, the courts have held that the burden of persuading the court that the employment decision was discriminatory remains with the plaintiff. Even if the plaintiff establishes that the employer's proffered reason for the employment action is not truthful, the employer will prevail if the plaintiff cannot persuade the court that race was a motivating factor.

Once it has been established that an employer has intentionally discriminated on the basis of race, the reason for the differential treatment will ordinarily not be relevant (unless it is pursuant to the implementation of a valid affirmative action plan). Accordingly, intentional racial discrimination will be deemed unlawful whether the employer acted because he or she dislikes nonwhites (say, blacks), prefers a nonblack ethnic group that is consequently favored, or believes that blacks will be on average less productive. Similarly, an employer cannot engage in disparate treatment on the grounds that customers or other employees demand such racial exclusion or would otherwise prefer it.

On the other hand, a decision to locate a plant in a suburb or in a state with a low black (or other nonwhite) or Hispanic population may have serious adverse consequences for potential black (or other nonwhite) and Hispanic employees. But this locational decision, even if motivated by racial animus, will not be prohibited unless it is deemed an 'employment practice'. Cases focusing on infrequent institutional behaviours (as opposed to regularly implemented procedures) are essentially unknown for both doctrinal and practical reasons, a fact that underscores how potentially significant choices that may be affected by discriminatory motives can impair the employment prospects of minority groups without generating any legal response.

The task of measuring racial discrimination in a legal case often begins with the documentation of various racial disparities in such areas as income, wealth, educational attainment, incarceration or involvement in the criminal justice system and health. Of course, as noted above, the mere presence of large disparities in some of these measures does not necessarily mean that discrimination exists. For example, in the United States it is well documented that women live far longer than men, but it is rarely thought that discrimination against men explains their substantially higher rates of death. Similarly, men commit suicide and are incarcerated at vastly higher rates than women, yet again discrimination against men is unlikely to play a large explanatory role in these male–female disparities. Moreover, as discussed above, even when a racial or other group disparity is the product of discrimination, it is not necessarily the result of discrimination occurring at the point in time at which the disparity becomes manifest. For example, employers are generally not held liable under Title VII of the 1964 Civil Rights Act for disparities resulting from pre–labour market discrimination against blacks.

Disparate Impact Discrimination

Although disparate treatment was the original conception of unlawful discrimination, in 1971 the Supreme Court established a second, potentially broader notion of discrimination—the disparate impact standard. Under this doctrine, which, like disparate treatment, was judicially crafted in the arena of employment discrimination, the court first asks if an employment practice, even though facially neutral, has an adverse impact on members of a protected group. Once a finding of disparate impact has been made, the court will rule the challenged practice unlawful unless a sufficiently compelling business justification can be supplied for retaining it. The precise legal standard for this justification defense, first legislatively articulated in the Civil Rights Act of 1991, is that the defendant must prove "that the challenged practice is job related for the position in question and consistent with business necessity." Moreover, this justification will be dismissed if the employer's proffered legitimate business interest could be satisfied by another equally effective employment practice having a less racially adverse impact.

Everything from minimum educational requirements to rules against hiring those with arrest records to grooming standards that prohibit beards to certain types of seniority systems has been deemed under certain circumstances to constitute disparate impact discrimination against disadvantaged racial groups in employment. The goal of the doctrine has been to remove artificial barriers that prevent the economic progress of members of protected groups. At the same time, the rationalization of employment processes that has followed in the wake of the development of the disparate impact doctrine may have brought greater fairness to the process of selection of all employees.

Discrimination Law Regarding Governmental Actions

Government actions fall under a somewhat different set of legal rules. The constitutional prohibition against violations of equal protection (directly applied to the states under the Fourteenth Amendment and indirectly applied to the federal government under the due process clause of the Fifth Amendment) prohibits racial classifications unless justified by a 'compelling interest' and unless the policy is 'narrowly tailored' to serve that interest. However, the definition of racial discrimination for purposes of evaluating constitutional violations is narrower than the two-part legislative standard that governs employment discrimination law.

Specifically, although the equal protection clause prohibits disparate treatment discrimination that fails to have the most compelling societal justification, the Constitution prohibits only intentional discrimination; evidence of disparate impact alone will not establish a violation. Thus, the Constitution does not restrict a government from engaging in acts that harm disadvantaged racial groups unless the harm is caused intentionally. Moreover, knowing that a certain practice will cause harm is not enough to render it an intentional act of discrimination barred by the equal protection clause. As the court has emphasized, a government is not prohibited from acting in spite of harm to members of disadvantaged racial groups; it is banned only from causing harm because of race.

This constitutional interpretation reflects the fact that many neutral governmental actions have predictable effects that either benefit or harm certain racial groups and that allowing all these actions to be challenged on equal protection grounds would make the federal courts the arbiters of a vast array of legislative and executive conduct. For example, the mortgage interest deduction for residential housing disproportionately benefits whites because of their greater housing wealth and possibly dampens investments in other types of productive capital that might generate more jobs that could disproportionately advantage blacks. Similarly, the war on drugs is designed to identify and punish the tens or even hundreds of thousands of workers in the illegal drug trade, a disproportionate number of whom will inevitably be drawn from disadvantaged groups having less abundant opportunities in the legitimate economy. Yet no doctrine of law would permit either of these ostensibly neutral governmental programs to be challenged as racially discriminatory. Similarly, governmental social programs that disproportionately benefit a racial or ethnic group cannot be challenged on that basis alone on equal protection grounds.

Comparison of Legal Standards with the four Types of Discrimination

The legal definition of discrimination includes two standards: disparate treatment discrimination whereby an individual is treated less favorably because of race and disparate impact discrimination whereby treatment on the basis of nonracial factors that lack sufficiently compelling justification has an adverse impact on members of a disadvantaged racial group. The quintessential case of disparate treatment discrimination involves intentional behaviour motivated by explicit racial animus. However, disparate treatment applies in other types of discrimination as well. For instance, a black cab driver who refuses to pick up blacks may be acting without racial animus but may be engaging in statistical discrimination by making probabilistic predictions about the risk of being victimized by crime, of receiving a lower tip, or of ending up in a distant neighborhood from which the prospect of receiving a return fare is small. Employers and police officers who profile job candidates or security risks can be motivated by similar beliefs or concerns and their probabilistic assessments may be correct or completely inaccurate. In any event, as noted above, this type of statistical discrimination is considered intentional differentiation on the basis of race and falls squarely in the category of unlawful disparate treatment discrimination. In evaluating a job applicant, for example, it is unlawful to consider what the 'average' black worker would be like and then to treat individual blacks in conformity with this stereotypical prediction.

In short, although vexing issues of proof complicate real-world cases, the law has clearly identified the theoretically prohibited discriminatory actions that emanate from either racial animus or the rational calculation of risk using race as a proxy. More subtle types of discrimination, however, are more difficult to deal with legally. As discussed above, there may be no conscious bias or rational calculation that prompts someone to treat whites differently from nonwhites. Such precognitive patterns of conduct have been well documented and are in practice treated as cases of unlawful disparate treatment discrimination if they are found to generate differential treatment of blacks. Note, however, that issues of proof make it more difficult to establish these unconscious forms of discriminatory behaviour, although statistical approaches are commonly used to ferret out just such unconscious bias. Indeed, the legal requirement that unlawful disparate treatment discrimination must involve intentional discrimination may result in many indirect, subtle and ambiguous types of discrimination being overlooked. In some cases, nonetheless, an organization has been found guilty of intentional discrimination for failing to compensate for the unconscious, automatic discrimination of its employees.

Prohibition of Racial Discrimination by Federal Laws

Since the social unrest of the 1960s, the federal government has been actively involved in preventing racial discrimination in the workplace. The most important law covering racial discrimination on the job is the Civil Rights Act of 1964— specifically, Title VII of that act, which strictly prohibits all forms of discrimination on the basis of race, color, religion, sex, or national origin in all aspects of employment. Written during a tumultuous period in American history when many people expected the federal government to right social wrongs, the law was a monumental piece of legislation that changed the American employment landscape.

The law stated that it was unlawful for an employer to "fail or refuse to hire or to discharge any individual, or otherwise discriminate against any individual with respect to his compensation, terms, conditions, or privileges of employment, because of such individual's race, color, religion, sex, or national origin." The law covers hiring, dismissals, compensation and all other aspects of employment, while also covering actual employment opportunities that are available. Examples of racial discrimination that would fall under the scope of the act include:

(*i*) An employee who alleges that his or her manager only promotes nonminority employees and keeps minorities in entry-level positions.

(*ii*) An employee who alleges that a manager or other person in power tells jokes or makes statements that are demeaning, insulting, or offensive to members of a minority group.

(*iii*) A manager who makes it clear that he or she believes in racial stereotypes by admitting that he or she refuses to promote a certain minority group because "all [members of that group] are lazy."

The law covers businesses with 15 or more employees and applies to all private, federal, state and local employers. In many states, businesses with fewer than 15 employees face the same rules thanks to local or state statutes. In addition to the hiring provisions, the law dictates that employers cannot in any way limit or segregate employees based on race in any way that would adversely affect their chances at promotions. It does allow for two narrow exceptions to the law—businesses may use a 'bona fide' seniority or merit system and measure performance and earnings based on a quantity or quality measuring system and employers may use ability tests to determine the most qualified candidates for a job as long as the test does not discriminate racially in any way.

In 1991, the 1964 law was significantly amended for the first time by the passage of the Civil Rights Act of 1991. The law was passed to override several Supreme Court decisions that had made it much more difficult for employees to prove that racial discrimination had occurred. One of the many changes of the 1991 law is that it closed a loophole in the 1964 act that also involved a Civil War-era statute known as 42 U.S.C. Section 1981. The Supreme Court had held that Section 1981 applied to hiring and sometimes to promotions, but that it did not cover racial harassment that occurred in the workplace once a person was hired. The 1991 act said that all racial discrimination was covered by U.S. law, including post-hire harassment.

The other major enhancement under the 1991 act involved monetary damages. Before the law was passed, employees who sued an employer for discrimination and won could only recover lost wages or salary, lost benefits, attorney fees, other legal costs and the costs associated with reinstatement. The 1991 law said that employees could also recover punitive monetary damages for pain and emotional suffering, mental anguish, future lost wages and benefits and more. Those damages could only be collected if it was proven that the discrimination was intentional and there was clearly 'malice' or 'reckless indifference' exhibited, but this was a radical change from the previous legislation. To protect employers from overly large court settlements, the amount of punitive damages was capped at $300,000 for certain cases of discrimination, although no caps apply in cases of ethnic or racial discrimination.

Other changes in the 1991 law involve employment practices that have a 'disparate impact' on racial groups (that is, affect them more than nonminority groups), make it easier for a plaintiff to receive damages in cases where a discriminatory practice and a nondiscriminatory practice both played a part in a hiring or promotion decision and allow employees to challenge seniority systems that are put into place if the systems are later determined to be discriminatory (in the past, workers could only sue at the time the system was first put into place). Together, all of these changes made it easier for workers to prove discrimination claims, which has increased the number of lawsuits nationwide.

The Equal Employment Opportunity Commission

To oversee the federal civil rights legislation, a separate administrative body was created as part of the Civil Rights Act of 1964. The Equal Employment Opportunity Commission, or EEOC, was created to enforce laws that prevent discrimination based on race, sex, color, religion, national origin, disability, or age when hiring, firing, or promoting employees. Four groups—race, color, sex and creed—were given 'protected status' under the law, which was to be upheld by the EEOC. The commission is an independent regulatory body that has the power to launch investigations, file lawsuits and create programs to eliminate discrimination.

The EEOC has been a controversial organization throughout its nearly 40-year history. Liberal politicians believe that the agency was long overdue and that it is absolutely imperative that the agency be proactive in identifying and fighting discrimination in the courts, while conservatives believe that the organization is a perfect example of 'big government' that intrudes far too deeply into citizens' lives. The agency's strong enforcement of affirmative action policies (which actively seek to promote minorities over equally qualified nonminorities in order to address past discrimination) has been its most controversial action, as many Americans oppose affirmative action.

Even with political opposition, the EEOC continues to be effective in fighting racial discrimination. In 1997, for example, the agency collected $111 million in judgements for people who claimed to have been harmed by racial discrimination, including a $34 million settlement with Mitsubishi Motor Manufacturing. Each year, the EEOC handles nearly 50,000 claims.

Steps Taken by Employers to End Discrimination

Because racial discrimination can have disastrous results for a company—including lower morale, a divided workplace, expensive lawsuits and public embarrassment—most companies are taking highly visible steps to curtail discrimination in the workplace. Steps taken include in-house workshops and training sessions on racial sensitivity and diversity in the workplace, training on employment laws and adopting strict new rules against discrimination. Training magazine reported in 1998 that more than half of the approximately 137,000 companies in the United States, with more than 100 employees, had instituted some form of racial sensitivity training.

Unfortunately, many companies do not take action against racial discrimination until faced with an incident at their workplace or until they are named defendant in a large lawsuit. Instead of being proactive and instituting training programs before a problem arises, companies tend to be slow to act. In November of 2000, the Coca-Cola Company agreed to settle a racial discrimination suit by paying a penalty of $192.5 million. Sara Lee Corporation was forced to make a large cash settlement to a former employee who says that he was the butt of racist jokes, disparaging remarks and was even forced to view a noose hanging in his workplace. In addition to the cash settlement, which was confidential, Sara Lee also agreed to establish training programs to raise awareness of the company's anti-discrimination policies.

To make sure that it is on the cutting edge of preventing racial discrimination, IBM has established individual employee task forces for almost every group that is employed by the huge company, including men, women, blacks, Hispanics, Asians, Native Americans, gays and lesbians and disabled persons. The groups, which are established at many of the company's offices, meet regularly to discuss diversity and workplace concerns. This represents an extreme example of the steps companies are taking to prevent discrimination, but actions of this type are becoming more common.

Companies need to take steps to ensure that the training programs they adopt are appropriate and serve the purpose for which they are intended. For example, publishing giant R.R. Donnelly & Sons was sued in 1998 because elements of its training program were deemed discriminatory. Scenes from a training film that depicted the lynching of black slaves, as well as offensive questions from a questionnaire designed to make white workers confront racism, were challenged by a group of 3,500 black Donnelly employees that filed suit against the company. The training program had been instituted after the company was hit with a discrimination lawsuit in 1993. There are so many examples of diversity training gone bad that a new group of consultants has come into existence—their sole job is to visit companies to correct the damage caused by faulty diversity training programs.

Affirmative Action

Affirmative action is a controversial policy that is intended to counteract racial discrimination. West's Encyclopedia of American Law defines affirmative action as referring "to both mandatory and voluntary programs intended to affirm the civil rights of designated classes of individuals by taking positive actions to protect them." In other words, affirmative action actively promotes the interest of minorities over nonminorities in order to correct past discrimination. For example, in a situation where a test is required before starting a particular job or to earn a promotion, minorities may be given preference over nonminorities for that job or promotion even though they score lower on the test than the nonminority worker. While this may seem wrong to some people, those who support affirmative action argue that past acts of discrimination have been so blatant that extraordinary steps are required to overcome those acts. At the start of the twenty-first century, however, affirmative action programs are under fire across the United States, with numerous court challenges occurring across the country.

One effect of affirmative action has been an increase in 'reverse discrimination' lawsuits, in which nonminority workers allege that they have been discriminated against. In situations where companies have used affirmative action to help undo decades of blatant discrimination, white workers have become upset over being passed over for jobs and promotions. They claim that, if it is unfair to not hire a qualified worker just because he or she is a minority, then it should be equally unfair to not hire a qualified worker just because he or she is white. White employees have argued that, even though they have higher qualifications, experience and skill, they are being passed over for jobs in favor of less-qualified candidates who are minorities.

In response to reverse discrimination lawsuits involving affirmative action programs, courts have recognized the need to overcome past racial bias, but have also sided with the nonminority workers in many cases. For example, in an attempt to redress past problems, a public university ruled that women and minorities would no longer have to take a test to qualify for a special employment program. As a result, for nine years, every job opening in the program went to a woman or a minority, even though white males represented half of the applicant pool. When the university's program was challenged in a lawsuit brought by white males, the courts ruled that the test exemption ensured that "the sole purpose of the affirmative action plan was to circumvent a lawful ... preference program" and that the exemption violated Title VII because it caused white men to be excluded from the job in question. The school was forced to pay $113,000 to settle the case and correct the reverse discrimination.

Reverse discrimination does not always have to involve affirmative action, however. In 1999, five white instructors at traditionally black Livingstone College sued the college and charged it with racial discrimination. The five faculty members argued that documents proved that college administrators were attempting to fill all faculty positions with black teachers, going so far as to remove whites from department chairs and other positions. One of the plaintiffs in the case even filed a separate lawsuit, arguing that he had suffered "emotional pain and suffering" when he was passed over in favor of less-qualified black teachers.

Racial Discrimination Still on the Rise

While great strides have been made to improve race relations in some areas, there is statistical evidence to show that racial discrimination in the workplace is still disturbingly commonplace. In 2000, the EEOC reported the results of a study of workplaces in North Carolina that showed that accusations of racial harassment on the job nearly quadrupled between 1996 and 2000, jumping from 16 reported incidents in 1996 to 62 in 2000 in just one region of the state. Mindy Weinstein, attorney at the EEOC office in Charlotte, North Carolina, was uncertain of what caused the increase, but she had some ideas. "There's a new generation of workers today who were not raised in the civil rights movement, who may not have been aware of the laws that came about because of that time," she said in the Raleigh News & Observer. "We think it's largely a reflection of what's going on in society as a whole." Another potential cause of the increase is the fact that, thanks to earlier efforts to wipe out racial discrimination, there are more minorities than ever before in the workplace and also in high-level positions of power. Because minorities have been able to compete on a level playing field, they have been able to rise through the ranks more quickly, often taking jobs that were traditionally held by white workers. This can lead to resentment among the formerly dominant workers who are now lower on the employment ladder.

Another example of how racial discrimination is on the rise despite efforts to combat it involves wages. Traditionally, there has been a 'wage gap' between minority and nonminority employees. That means that, when a minority worker and a nonminority worker held the exact same job, the minority worker was paid less money for his or her efforts. From the 1940s to the 1970s, that gap between minority and nonminority workers actually narrowed as civil rights legislation was enacted and prevailing attitudes changed. However, in the 1980s and 1990s, the gap has actually reversed directions and begun to widen once again, according to Nation's Cities Weekly. The gap is increasing for both men and women and for all educational levels. In addition, the unemployment level for black workers has risen at the same time. A study by the Catalyst nonprofit group reported in HR Focus showed that men of color in management earned 75 cents for every dollar earned by white males in the same job in 1998, while women of color earned 57 cents.

Limiting the Discussion

The experience of discrimination and its consequences may vary with several factors, including the domain in which it occurs (*e.g.*, the labour market, the health care system, the criminal justice system, the housing market); the actors involved (*e.g.*, employers, insurance companies, police officers, mortgage lenders, neighbors); and the targets (*e.g.*, African Americans, whites, Hispanics, American Indians, Asians). Within the scope of our broad definition of discrimination, we focus our analysis on specific aspects of racial discrimination in the United States. We are concerned primarily with discrimination that has adverse social and economic consequences for disadvantaged racial groups. We use the term disadvantaged racial groups interchangeably with minority groups and nonwhite groups and refer to non-Hispanic whites as the majority group. These terms describe the social stratification (rather than the numerical proportions) of different racial groups in the United States. We recognize that racial groups in different communities, institutions and even countries (*e.g.*, South Africa) can be in the numerical majority but still experience discrimination.

Various forms of Discrimination

There are following various forms of discrimination, they are Age discrimination, Sex and Gender discrimination, Caste discrimination, Employment discrimination, Sexual Orientation

Discrimination, Language discrimination, Disability discrimination and Religious discrimination.

Age Discrimination

Age discrimination is discrimination on the grounds of age. Although theoretically the word can refer to the discrimination against any age group, age discrimination usually comes in one of three forms: discrimination against youth (also called adultism), discrimination against those 40 years old or older and discrimination against elderly people. In the United States, the Age Discrimination in Employment Act prohibits employment discrimination nationwide based on age with respect to employees 40 years of age or older. The Age Discrimination in Employment Act also addresses the difficulty older workers face in obtaining new employment after being displaced from their jobs, arbitrary age limits.

In many countries, companies more or less openly refuse to hire people above a certain age despite the increasing lifespans and average age of the population. The reasons for this range from vague feelings younger people are more 'dynamic' and create a positive image for the company, to more concrete concerns about regulations granting older employees higher salaries or other benefits without these expenses being fully justified by an older employees' greater experience. Unions cite age as the most common form of discrimination in the workplace. Workers ages 45 and over form a disproportionate share of the long-term unemployed – those who have been out of work for six months or longer, according to the U.S. Bureau of Labour Statistics.

Some people consider that teenagers and youth (around 15–25 years old) are victims of adultism, age discrimination framed as a paternalistic form of protection. In seeking social justice, they feel that it is necessary to remove the use of a false moral agenda in order to achieve agency and empowerment. This perspective is based on the grounds that youth should be treated more respectfully by adults and not as second-class citizens. Some suggest that social stratification in age groups causes outsiders to incorrectly stereotype and generalize the group, for instance that all adolescents are equally immature, violent or rebellious, listen to rock tunes and do drugs. Some have organized groups against age discrimination.

Ageism is the causal effect of a continuum of fears related to age. This continuum includes:

- Ephebiphobia: the fear of youth.
- Gerontophobia: the fear of elderly people.
- Pediaphobia: the fear of infants or small children.

Related terms include:

- Adultism: Also called adultarchy, adult privilege and adultcentrism/adultocentrism, this is the wielding of authority over young people and the preference of adults before children and youth.
- Jeunism: Also called 'youthism' is the holding of beliefs or actions taken that give preference to 'younger' people before adults.

Gender and sexual discrimination

Gender discrimination, also known as sexual discrimination, is the practice of letting a person's sex unfairly become a factor when deciding who receives a job, promotion, or other employment benefit. It most often affects women who feel they have been unfairly discriminated against in favor of a man. But there have also been cases where males have claimed that reverse discrimination has occurred—that is, the woman received unfairly favorable treatment at the expense of the man.

Court rulings handed down through the years have determined that a company's responsibility not to discriminate based on sex begins even before an individual is hired. Companies can be held liable if pre-employment screening or testing is determined to be discriminatory, if applications ask unacceptable questions designed to screen for sex, or if the overall selection process is deemed to be unfair. One of the main indicators that gender discrimination has occurred in the hiring process involves the qualifications of the job applicants. While a slight difference in qualifications between a female and a male candidate does not automatically indicate gender bias (if a lesser qualified male candidate is hired instead of a female candidate, that is), a drastic difference in qualifications has almost always been upheld by the courts as a sure sign of gender discrimination. For example, if a male who dropped out of high school without receiving a diploma is hired in an administrative position over a female who had obtained her master's degree, then it is likely bias was a factor.

In addition to gender discrimination in hiring and other circumstances, there is a particular form of sexual discrimination called sexual harassment. This form of discrimination involves inappropriate words or actions of a sexual nature directed at an employee by employees of the opposite sex. To meet the criteria for harassment, the behaviour in question must be both unwanted and sexual in nature. The U.S. legal system has determined that there are two main types of sexual harassment. 'Quid pro quo', or 'this for that', occurs when one employee offers another employee a job or benefit, or threatens to deny that job or benefit, unless sexual favors are granted. A 'hostile work environment' occurs when an employee, or a group of employees, repeatedly make lewd comments or suggestive noises, make unwanted sexual advances, or otherwise use sex to such a degree that the behaviour interferes with another employee's ability to perform her job, or she feels intimidated or threatened on the job.

Though gender discrimination and sexism refers to beliefs and attitudes in relation to the gender of a person, such beliefs and attitudes are of a social nature and do not, normally, carry any legal consequences. Sex discrimination, on the other hand, may have legal consequences. Though what constitutes sex discrimination varies between countries, the essence is that it is an adverse action taken by one person against another person that would not have occurred had the person been of another sex. Discrimination of that nature in certain enumerated circumstances is illegal in many countries.

Currently, discrimination based on sex is defined as adverse action against another person, that would not have occurred had the person been of another sex. This is considered a form of prejudice and is illegal in certain enumerated circumstances in most countries. Sexual discrimination can arise in different contexts. For instance, an employee may be discriminated against by being asked discriminatory questions during a job interview, or because an employer did not hire, promote or wrongfully terminated an employee based on his or her gender, or employers pay unequally based on gender.

In an educational setting, there could be claims that a student was excluded from an educational institution, program, opportunity, loan, student group, or scholarship due to his or her gender. In the housing setting there could be claims that a person was refused negotiations on seeking a house, contracting/leasing a house or getting a loan based on his or her gender. Another setting where there have been claims of gender discrimination is banking; for example, if one is refused credit or is offered unequal loan terms based on one's gender. Another setting where there is usually gender discrimination is when one is refused to extend his or her credit, refused approval of credit/loan process and if there is a burden of unequal loan terms based on one's gender.

Socially, sexual differences have been used to justify different roles for men and women, in some cases giving rise to claims of primary and secondary roles. While there are alleged non-physical differences between men and women, major reviews of the academic literature on gender difference find only a tiny minority of characteristics where there are consistent psychological differences between men and women and these relate directly to experiences grounded in biological difference. However, there are also some psychological differences in regard to how problems are dealt with and emotional perceptions and reactions which may relate to hormones and the successful characteristics of each gender during longstanding roles in past primitive lifestyles.

Unfair discrimination usually follows the gender stereotyping held by a society. The United Nations had concluded that women often experience a 'glass ceiling' and that there are no societies in which women enjoy the same opportunities as men. The term 'glass ceiling' is used to describe a perceived barrier to advancement in employment based on discrimination, especially sex discrimination. In the United States in 1995, the Glass Ceiling Commission, a government-funded group, stated: "Over half of all Master's degrees are now awarded to women, yet 95% of senior-level managers, of the top Fortune 1000 industrial and 500 service companies are men. Of them, 97% are white." In its report, it recommended affirmative action, which is the consideration of an employee's gender and race in hiring and promotion decisions, as a means to end this form of discrimination. In 2008, women accounted for 51% of all workers in the high-paying management, professional and related occupations. They outnumbered men in such occupations as public relations managers; financial managers; and human resource managers. The China's leading headhunter, Chinahr.com, reported in 2007 that the average salary for white-collar men was 44,000 yuan ($6,441), compared with 28,700 yuan ($4,201) for women. The PwC research found that among FTSE 350 companies in the United Kingdom in 2002 almost 40% of senior management posts were occupied by women. When that research was repeated in 2007, the number of senior management posts held by women had fallen to 22%.

Transgender individuals, both male to female and female to male, often experience problems which often lead to dismissals, underachievement, difficulty in finding a job, social isolation and, occasionally, violent attacks against them. Nevertheless, the problem of gender discrimination does not stop at trandgender individuals nor with women. Men are often the victim in certain areas of employment as men begin to seek work in office and childcare settings traditionally perceived as 'women's jobs'. One such situation seems to be evident in a recent case concerning alleged YMCA discrimination and a Federal Court Case in Texas. The case actually involves alleged discrimination against both men and blacks in childcare, even when they pass the same strict background tests and other standards of employment. It is currently being contended in federal court, as of fall 2009 and sheds light on how a workplace dominated by a majority (- women in this case) sometimes will seemingly 'justify' whatever they wish to do, regardless of the law. This may be done as an effort at self-protection, to uphold traditional societal roles, or some other faulty, unethical or illegal prejudicial reasoning. Affirmative action also leads to white men being discriminated against for entry level and blue collar positions. An employer cannot hire a white man with the same 'on paper' qualifications over a woman or minority worker or the employer will face prosecution.

Caste Discrimination

According to UNICEF and Human Rights Watch, caste discrimination affects an estimated 250 million people worldwide. Discrimination based on caste, as perceived by UNICEF, is prevalent mainly in parts of Asia (India, Sri Lanka, Bangladesh, Nepal, Japan) and Africa. Currently, there are an estimated 160 million Dalits or Scheduled Castes (formerly known as 'untouchables') in India.. Dalit people face severe problems, such as segregation and violence against them An estimated 40 million people in India, most of them Dalits, are bonded workers, many working to pay off debts that were incurred generations ago. There have been substantial improvements in the position of Dalits in post-independence India, consequent to the strict implementation of the rights and privileges enshrined in the Constitution of India, as implemented by the Protection of Civil rights Act, 1955. India has had a Dalit president, K.R. Narayanan and the practise had disappeared in urban public life, though persist very strongly in rural areas, where modern ideas have not penetrated and ancient ethnic divisions and hostilities against Dalits often dominate the discourse of inter-community relations, resulting in underrepresented Dalits facing discrimination and violence.

In modern times, Dalits, tribal people and members of the lowest castes in India benefit from broad affirmative action programmes and are enjoying greater political power. The Constitution of India places special emphasis on outlawing caste discrimination, especially the practice of untouchability. In addition, the Indian penal code inflicts severe punishments on those who discriminate on the basis of caste. Anti-Dalit prejudice and discrimination exists primarily in rural areas, where small societies can track the caste lineage of individuals and discriminate accordingly.

Employment discrimination

Employment discrimination (or workplace discrimination) is discrimination in hiring, promotion, job assignment, termination and compensation. It includes various types of harassment. Many jurisdictions prohibit some types of employment discrimination, often by forbidding discrimination based on certain traits (protected categories). In other cases, the law may require discrimination against certain groups. In places where it is illegal, discrimination often takes subtler forms, such as wage discrimination and requirements with disparate impact on certain groups. In addition, employees sometimes suffer retaliation for opposing workplace discrimination or for reporting violations to the authorities. Like most discrimination, employment discrimination may occur intentionally or unintentionally, because of prejudice or ignorance.

Discrimination in the workplace negatively affects businesses in that discriminatory policies can hurt a company's reputation. A business self-limits itself when it restricts advancement to certain groups or types of employees. Speaking negatively about a former employee can be damaging for a potential client. There is also a direct correlation between loyalty, retention and discrimination. Employees are more likely to be looking for new jobs when they feel they have been wronged. According to a report on discrimination at the workplace by the International Labour Organization, "workplace discrimination remains a persistent global problem, with new, more subtle forms emerging." Sending wrong signals to potential clients can also cause conflict because customers can sense when employees aren't enthusiastic or donot believe in their company. This is one reason that it is important for a job applicant to observe the attitudes of people they wish to work with. Sending positive signals to employees attracts future potential employees.

Inequalities suffered by discriminated groups spreads. Due to affirmative action policies, a new middle class has been created that consists of formerly discriminated people in some countries but in others, people who are from discriminated groups are frequently involved in the worst jobs, denied benefits, capital, land, social protection, training, or credit. Discrimination at a workplace can lead to poverty. "Discrimination creates a web of poverty, forced and child labour and social exclusion, (seeking to eliminate discrimination is indispensable to any strategy for poverty reduction and sustainable economic development)." In December 2005, a Gallup poll showed that job satisfaction was lowest when employees experienced discrimination.

Even though there are regulations that are used to promote equality within the workplace, discrimination is still rampant. Women still do not measure up to men when it comes to income, employment rates and occupational range. Women's average salary is 72 to 88 percent of men's, even when variables such as education, age, position level and job tenure are considered. In most countries, the glass ceiling is ever present for women and the wage differences are significant compared to men. Based on a report by Catalyst in 2005, only "one in eight woman were CEO's in the Fortune 500; an additional nine were CEO's in Fortune 501-1000 companies." Women are also more likely to be stuck in low-paid and insecure jobs. They face higher unemployment rates. "Discrimination can occur at every stage of employment, from recruitment to education and remuneration, occupational segregation and at time of layoffs."

Unintentional discrimination (often termed statistical discrimination) occurs when neutral selection practices produce a substantial disparity of outcomes between one group and another. Such practices include the use of standardized tests (which may disadvantage certain groups) or height (which may disadvantage women and some ethnic groups) in the hiring process. If the requirements are job-related and a 'business necessity', the disparity is irrelevant. Some laws prohibit unintentional as well as intentional discrimination, but may have different standards for deciding what is acceptable. Substantial disparities in outcome are not necessarily illegal, if the practices that produce them are necessary.

Sexual Orientation Discrimination

Whether you are heterosexual, homosexual, lesbian or bisexual, you have the same rights under the Equal Opportunity Act. That means it is against the law for someone to discriminate against you because of your sexual orientation. Sex between consenting adults is no-one's business but the people involved. Our laws protect us all from discrimination on the basis of lawful sexual activity. That means who you have sex with should have no bearing on whether you get a job, a promotion, accommodation, a loan or place on a sporting team. Though people may use other labels, or none at all, sexual orientation is usually discussed in terms of three categories, heterosexuality, homosexuality and bisexuality; and asexuality is increasingly recognized as a fourth. The first three exist along a continuum that ranges from exclusively heterosexual to exclusively homosexual, including various forms of bisexuality in between. This continuum does not suit everyone, however, as some people identify as asexual. This linear scale is a simplification of the much more nuanced nature of sexual orientation and sexual identity; many sexologists believe it to be oversimplified.

Classifying sexual desires or people on the basis of sexual orientation is a modern Western concept. Doubts have been raised about the validity of this concept in non-Western and indigenous societies, as well as in the pre-modern West.

While sexual orientation is reported in this article primarily within biology and psychology, including sexology, for reports within anthropology and history, including social constructionism.

In 2009, ILGA published a report based on research carried out by Daniel Ottosson at Södertörn University College, Stockholm, Sweden. This research found that an of the 80 countries around the world that continue to consider homosexuality illegal, five carry the death penalty for homosexual activity and two do in some regions of the country. In the report, this is described as 'State sponsored homophobia'. This happens in Islamic states, or in two cases regions under Islamic authority. South Africa has one of the world's most progressive constitutions, but same-sex unions are often decried as 'un-African'. Research shows 86% of black lesbians from the Western Cape live in fear of sexual assault

Language Discrimination

Diversity of language is protected and respected by most nations who value cultural diversity. However, people are sometimes subjected to different treatment because their preferred language is associated with a particular group, class or category. Commonly, the preferred language is just another attribute of separate ethnic groups. Discrimination exists if there is prejudicial treatment against a person or a group of people who speak a particular language or dialect. Language discrimination is suggested to be labeled linguicism or logocism. Anti-discriminatory and inclusive efforts to accommodate persons who speak different languages or cannot have fluency in the country's predominant or 'official' language, is bilingualism such as official documents in two languages and multiculturalism in more than two languages.

Language discrimination occurs when a person is treated differently because of that person's native language or other characteristics of that person's speech. In an employment situation, for example, an employee may be being subjected to language discrimination if the workplace has a 'speak-English-only' policy but the employee's primary language is something other than English. The employee may also be the victim of language discrimination if he or she is treated less favorably than other employees because he or she speaks English with an accent, or if the employee is told he or she does not qualify for a position because of a lack of English proficiency. Outside the employment context, language discrimination may also occur if a person is denied access to businesses or government services because he or she does not speak English. Although the law in this area is still developing, many courts and governmental agencies consider language discrimination to be a form of discrimination on the basis of race or national origin, which are prohibited by well established civil rights laws.

Discrimination because of accent also violates an employee's civil rights. In general, the standard applied in these cases is that the employee's accent must "materially interfere with job performance" in order to justify any adverse action. In other words, an employee's accent must have a significant negative effect upon the employee's ability to do the job. Moreover, the employer must fairly and objectively assess the accent. Often there are subtle prejudices against some accents more than others. An employer may not deny a person an employment opportunity because that person is not proficient or fluent in English, unless the job that person performs: 1) actually requires some English language skills and 2) the person does not possess the particular type and level of English language skill required. For example, if a person is told that he or she does not qualify for a position because he or she is unable to speak or read English well enough, but the position is one which requires little or no communication, the person may have a claim of language discrimination.

Language discrimination exists outside the workplace as well. For instance, if a person is denied services by a business because he or she lacks English skills, this may be a violation of civil rights law. Such laws may also be violated if a person is unable to communicate with a government agency because the agency does not offer materials in that person's language or have personnel who speak that person's language. This fact sheet is intended to provide accurate, general information regarding legal rights relating to employment in California. Yet because laws and legal procedures are subject to frequent change and differing interpretations, the LAS-ELC and the ACLU Foundation of Northern California cannot ensure the information in this fact sheet is current nor be responsible for any use to which it is put. Do not rely on this information without consulting an attorney, the Language Rights Information Line, or the appropriate agency about your rights in your particular situation.

Reverse Discrimination

Reverse discrimination, also known as positive discrimination, is a controversial specific form of discrimination against members of a dominant or majority group, or in favor of members of a minority or historically disadvantaged group. Groups may be defined in terms of race, gender, ethnicity, or other factors. This discrimination may seek to redress social inequalities where minority groups have been denied access to the same privileges of the majority group. In such cases it is intended to remove discrimination that minority groups may already face. 'Reverse discrimination' may also be used to highlight the discrimination inherent in affirmative action programs.

In the United States of America, the term 'reverse discrimination' has been used in past discussions of racial quotas or gender quotas for collegiate admission to government-run educational institutions. Such policies were held to be unconstitutional in the United States, while non-quota based methods, which may include race as a factor, including some affirmative action programs (race as a factor, ethnic minorities and physical, mental, or learning disabilities) can be legal. Nevertheless, some city governments still utilize racial quotas when awarding government contracts. The city of Chicago has mandated that all government construction contracts must award 25% of their value to minority owned businesses.

In 2009, a group of firefighters in New Haven, Connecticut filed suit against the city for reverse discrimination after promotion test results were thrown out because no African-American firefighters passed the test. Sixteen Caucasian and three Hispanic firefighters passed the test. The Roberts Court in Ricci v. DeStefano found that disregarding the test results was unconstitutional.

In India, the term is often used by citizens protesting against reservation and quotas. In November of 2007, David Rosin, a former vice-president of the Royal College of Surgeons wrote in the magazine Hospital Doctor: "It is time that someone spoke up concerning the reverse discrimination with respect to merit awards" and criticising the fact that "female and ethnic minority consultants are being given preferential treatment to meet artificial quotas."

Disability Discrimination

Disability discrimination occurs when an employer or other entity covered by the Americans with Disabilities Act, as amended, or the Rehabilitation Act, as amended, treats a qualified individual with a disability who is an employee or applicant unfavorably because she has a disability. Disability discrimination also occurs when a covered employer or other entity treats an applicant or employee less favorably because she has a history of a disability (such as cancer that is controlled or in remission) or because she is believed to have a physical or mental impairment that is not transitory (lasting or expected to last six months or less) and minor (even if she does not have such an impairment).

The law requires an employer to provide reasonable accommodation to an employee or job applicant with a disability, unless doing so would cause significant difficulty or expense for the employer (undue hardship). The law also protects people from discrimination based on their relationship with a person with a disability. For example, it is illegal to discriminate against an employee because her husband has a disability.

- **Disability Discrimination and Work Situations**: The law forbids discrimination when it comes to any aspect of employment, including hiring, firing, pay, job assignments, promotions, layoff, training, fringe benefits and any other term or condition of employment.
- **Disability Discrimination and Harassment**: It is illegal to harass an applicant or employee because he has a disability, had a disability in the past, or is believed to have a physical or mental impairment that is not transitory (lasting or expected to last six months or less) and minor (even if he does not have such an impairment).
- **Disability Discrimination & Reasonable Accommodation**: The law requires an employer to provide reasonable accommodation to an employee or job applicant with a disability, unless doing so would cause significant difficulty or expense for the employer. Reasonable accommodation might include, for example, making the workplace accessible for wheelchair users or providing a reader or interpreter for someone who is blind or hearing impaired.
- **Disability Discrimination & Reasonable Accommodation & Undue Hardship:** An employer doesnot have to provide an accommodation if doing so would cause undue hardship to the employer. Undue hardship means that the accommodation would be too difficult or too expensive to

provide, in light of the employer's size, financial resources and the needs of the business. An employer may not refuse to provide an accommodation just because it involves some cost. An employer does not have to provide the exact accommodation the employee or job applicant wants. If more than one accommodation works, the employer may choose which one to provide.

Religious Discrimination

Religious discrimination is valuing or treating a person or group differently because of what they do or do not believe. A concept like that of 'religious discrimination' is necessary to take into account ambiguities of the term religious persecution. The infamous cases in which people have been executed for beliefs perceived to be heretic are generally recognisable as persecution. Other cases in which adherents of different religions (or denominations) are treated unequally before the law are sometimes difficult to assess. If behind laws, regulations or acts of authority perceived to be discriminating against a certain religion, there is the intention 'encourage' people to abandon their beliefs, the laws are religious persuction. Laws which only carry light punishments are described as mild forms of religious persecution or as religious discrimination.

Furthermore, even in societies where Freedom of Religion is a constitutional right, sometimes adherents of religious minorities voice concerns about religious discrimination against them. Insofar as legal policies are concerned, cases that are perceived as religious discrimination might be the result of an interference of the religious sphere with other spheres of the public that are regulated by law (and not aimed specifically against a religious minority.) Generally, people are free to have these issues clarified through the juridical system.

In a 1979 consultation on the issue, the United States commission on civil rights defined religious discrimination in relation to the civil rights guaranteed by the Fourteenth Amendment to the United States Constitution. Whereas religious civil liberties, such as the right to hold or not to hold a religious belief, are essential for

Freedom of Religion (in the United States secured by the First Amendment), religious discrimination occurs when someone is denied the equal protection of the laws, equality of status under the law, equal treatment in the administration of justice and equality of opportunity and access to employment, education, housing, public services and facilities and public accommodation because of their exercise of their right to religious freedom.

However, cases of religious discrimination might also be the result of an interference of the religious sphere with other spheres of the public that are regulated by law. Although, for example, in the United States the Free Exercise Clause of the First Amendment states that "Congress shall make no law respecting an establishment of religion, or prohibiting the free exercise thereof", in Reynolds v. United States the U.S. supreme court decided that religious duty was not a suitable defense to a criminal indictment. In this specific case a law against bigamy was not considered to be discriminating against Mormons, who, at that time sometimes practiced Polygyny. Similar current issues in the United States are about the policy towards drugs or environmental policy. Practitioners of one branch of the native American religion perceive the regulations regarding the use of Peyote and the eagle feather law in the United States as discriminating. Similar cases can be found in many other western countries.

Caste Discrimination

Discriminatory and cruel, inhuman and degrading treatment of a vast global population has been justified on the basis of caste. In much of Asia and parts of Africa, caste is the basis for the definition and exclusion of distinct population groups by reason of their descent. Over 250 million people worldwide continue to suffer under what is often a hidden apartheid of segregation, modern-day slavery and other extreme forms of discrimination, exploitation and violence. Caste imposes enormous obstacles to their full attainment of civil, political, economic, social and cultural rights.

Caste is descent-based and hereditary in nature. It is a characteristic determined by one's birth into a particular caste, irrespective of the faith practiced by the individual. Caste denotes a system of rigid social stratification into ranked groups defined by descent and occupation. Under various caste systems throughout the world, caste divisions also dominate in housing, marriage and general social interaction-divisions that are reinforced through the practice and threat of social ostracism, economic boycotts and even physical violence.

Among the communities discussed in this report are the *Dalits* or so-called *untouchables* of *South Asia*-including Nepal, Bangladesh, India, Sri Lanka and Pakistan-the Buraku people of Japan, the Osu of Nigeria's Igbo people and certain groups in Senegal and Mauritania. The prominence of caste as a social and economic indicator for the widespread *South Asian diaspora* is also discussed. These communities share many features; features that have allowed even the most appalling practices to escape international scrutiny. In many cases, caste systems coexist with otherwise democratic structures. In countries such as India and Nigeria, governments have also enacted progressive legislation to combat abuses against lower-caste communities. Despite formal protections in law, however, discriminatory treatment remains endemic and discriminatory societal norms continue to be reinforced by government and private structures and practices, in some cases through violent means.

Lower-caste communities are almost invariably indistinguishable in physical appearance from higher-caste communities. This is not, as some would say, a black and white issue. For most outsiders then, the visual cues that otherwise accompany race or ethnicity are often completely lacking. Stark economic disparities between low and high-caste communities also get buried under a seemingly homogenous landscape of poverty. Poverty can be quite deceptive. It makes one conclude that all suffer from it equally. A closer look reveals the discrimination inherent in the allocation of jobs, land, basic resources and amenities and even physical security. A closer look at victims of violence, bonded labour and other severe abuses also reveals disproportionate membership in the lowest ranking in the caste order. A perpetual state of economic dependency also allows for abuses to go unpunished, while a biased state machinery looks the other way, or worse, becomes complicit in the abuse.

The language used to describe low and high-caste community characteristics in the examples that follow are striking in their similarity, despite the variation in geographic origin, with ideas of pollution and purity and filth and cleanliness prevalent. In turn, these designations are used to justify the physical and social segregation of low-caste communities from the rest of society, their exclusion from certain occupations and their involuntary monopoly over 'unclean' occupations and tasks.

The exploitation of low-caste laborers and the rigid assignment of demeaning occupations on the basis of caste keep lower-caste populations in a position of economic and physical vulnerability. The triple burden of caste, class and gender effectively ensures that lower-caste women are the farthest removed from legal protections. Only with the honest implementation of the International Convention on the Elimination of All Forms of Racial Discrimination (ICERD) and of domestic laws designed to abolish the vestiges of various caste systems and to protect the economic, social, cultural, civil and political rights of all, can the process of attaining economic and physical security and human dignity, begin.

In August 2000, the U.N. Subcommission on the Promotion and Protection of Human Rights passed resolution 2000/4 on Discrimination Based on Work and Descent. The resolution, aimed at addressing the issue of caste, reaffirmed that discrimination based on work and descent is prohibited under international human rights law. The Subcommission also decided to further identify affected communities, examine existing constitutional, legislative and administrative measures for the abolition of such discrimination and make concrete recommendations for the effective elimination of such practices.

In August 2001, subcommission expert R.K.W. Goonesekere presented his working paper on work and descent-based discrimination to the subcommission's fifty-third session. The paper was submitted pursuant to Subcommission resolution 2000/4. Because of time and other constraints, Mr. Goonesekere limited the paper's focus to the Asian countries of India, Nepal, Pakistan, Sri Lanka and Japan but stated that further study of African countries in particular was warranted. The presentation of the paper and the ensuing debate amongst subcommission experts that followed, marked the first time that caste discrimination was discussed as a major source of human rights violations worldwide by a U.N. human rights body. The subcommission also determined by consensus to extend the study to other regions of the world where work and descent-based discrimination continues to be experienced.

This important resolution underscores the notion that caste systems are inherently economic and social in their consequences and that the exclusion of lower-caste communities extends to the economic and social realms of wages, jobs, education and land. This report discusses the manifestations of caste and descent-based discrimination and abuse in over a dozen countries. It is not meant to be an exhaustive review but an introduction to the prevalence and global dimensions of this underreported problem. It is also an appeal to governments to give close and systematic attention to the problem of caste discrimination at the World Conference Against Racism, Racial Discrimination, Xenophobia and Related Intolerance and beyond. Despite the magnitude of the problem, as of this writing, caste-based discrimination had been systematically cut out of the WCAR's intergovernmental process through the actions of a handful of governments. This has occurred despite the Committee on the Elimination of Racial Discrimination's repeated affirmations that caste, as a form of descent-based discrimination, falls within the definition of racial discrimination under article 1 of the ICERD.

Differential Outcomes by Race

Evidence of large and persistent differentials in social, economic and political outcomes among racial and ethnic groups in the United States characterizes virtually every social domain. Indeed, were there not such marked differences, there would be little reason to convene a panel of social scientists to study methods for measuring race-based discrimination. Even though prejudices and stereotyping might be present and individual cases of discrimination might occur, an absence of observable differences in outcomes among racial groups would almost preclude social science measurement of the role of racial discrimination in American society.

We provide examples of differential outcomes among racial groups in five domains: education, the labour market, the criminal justice system, the housing market and mortgage lending and health care. In these examples, we draw no conclusions about whether or to what extent differential outcomes by race are caused by discrimination. The magnitude of the differentials in these—and other—domains, however, is a primary reason to be concerned about our ability to identify and measure racial discrimination. Also, the greater the extent to which differential outcomes are the result of discriminatory behaviours or processes, the greater is the likelihood that antidiscriminatory efforts would be needed to reduce these differences.

Education

Racial classification and many factors that are correlated with race (*e.g.*, family structure, parental education, poverty, access to computers and linguistic diversity) are associated with different educational experiences and levels of educational attainment (Choy, 2002; Lloyd *et al.*, 2002; Mare, 1995). Research shows that blacks, Hispanics, American Indians and Native Hawaiians and other Pacific Islanders—compared with whites and Asians—are more likely to attend lower-quality schools with fewer teachers and material resources and greater concentrations of poor, homeless, limited English-speaking and immigrant students (Kahlenberg, 2001; Lee *et al.*, 2001; Natriello *et al.*, 1990; Van Hook, 2002). They are also more likely to have lower test scores, drop out of high school, not graduate from college and attend lower-ranked programs in higher education. For example, the U.S. Department of Education (2001a) reports that African American and Hispanic students are less likely to have completed advanced levels of math and science coursework compared with Asian and Pacific Islander and white students. However, overall educational attainment may vary substantially among Asian groups—for example, Japanese, Koreans and Asian Indians versus Cambodians, Laotians and Hmongs (U.S. Census Bureau, 1993).

Hispanics continue to face obstacles to educational achievement. Between the late 1970s and 1998, they had significantly lower educational attainment and higher dropout rates than both blacks and whites (Hauser *et al.*, 2002). In 2000, 57 percent of Hispanics aged 25 and over had obtained at least a high school degree, compared with 79 percent of blacks and 85 percent of whites (U.S. Census Bureau, 2002). One factor influencing the education gap between whites and Hispanics is the increasing numbers of disadvantaged Hispanic immigrant groups entering the United States. Poor educational outcomes for many Hispanic groups may lead to subsequent disadvantages in social and economic opportunities.

Employment and Income

Black Americans are more likely to experience unemployment as teens and adults, to work at lower wages, to have lower wage growth over time and to accumulate less wealth relative to whites (Altonji and Blank, 1999). Indeed, unemployment rates for blacks are generally twice those for whites. In 2002, the average annual unemployment rate for black workers aged 16 and over (10.3 percent) was nearly twice the overall unemployment rate (5.8 percent) and just over twice the rate for whites (5.1 percent). The unemployment rate for Hispanics was 7.6 percent that year (Bureau of Labour Statistics, 2003).

The gap between Hispanics and Whites has grown at a particularly rapid rate, a fact that may be attributable to differences in educational achievement (Bureau of Labour Statistics, 2003). These earnings differentials are reinforced by substantial differences in the occupational categories in which various racial groups are clustered, with disadvantaged racial groups generally having lower-status as well as lower-wage occupations. Empirical research on labour market outcomes for Asians and American Indians is more limited, reflecting the lack of data on these groups (Altonji and Blank, 1999). Perhaps the largest racial differences are observed with respect to wealth, which reflects not just current earnings but cumulative lifetime (and even cross-generational) differences. The average net worth of blacks is just a fifth that of whites (Conley, 1999; Oliver and Shapiro, 1995).

Criminal Justice

Disadvantaged racial groups (particularly blacks) are disproportionately represented in the criminal justice system compared with non-Hispanic whites. Racial differences are largest in the corrections system, in which the incarceration rate for blacks is about eight times that for whites (Blumstein, 1982, 1993). In large part, this differential reflects more frequent arrests of blacks for serious crimes (*e.g.*, murder and robbery), for which the ratio of black to white arrest rates is about 7, relative to less serious crimes (*e.g.*, burglary and drugs), for which the ratio is closer to 3.

In some cases, the punishment for crimes committed by blacks is significantly different from that for similar crimes committed by whites. One reason is lower thresholds for mandatory minimum sanctions for crimes that are more likely to be committed by blacks. This difference is particularly striking in a provision of the federal Anti-Drug Abuse Act of 1986: A mandatory minimum sentence of 5 years is imposed for possession of as little as 5 grams of crack cocaine; in contrast, a possessor of powder cocaine must have at least 500 grams to receive a mandatory minimum sentence of 5 years. In 2000, 85 percent of sentenced crack cocaine offenders, who were sentenced for possessing very small amounts of cocaine, were black, but only 31 percent of sentenced powder cocaine offenders, who had to have large amounts of cocaine to be sentenced, were black (51 percent were Hispanic and 18 percent white). Although the disparate sentencing thresholds are associated with the crime rather than the race of the offender, they have a marked differential racial impact.

Blacks are disproportionately represented not only as offenders but also as victims of crime (Sampson and Lauritsen, 1997; Walker *et al.*, 1996; Weich and Angulo, 2002). Sampson and Lauritsen report that crime victimization rates vary systematically across racial and ethnic groups. Compared with whites, blacks were six times more likely to be murdered in 2000 In criminal justice research, there is a lack of consistent data on crime for Asian Americans and American Indians. However, Weich and Angulo (2002) point out that Asian American youths are far more likely than whites to be transferred to adult courts, convicted in adult courts and incarcerated in youth and adult prisons. Also, although African Americans are overrepresented in federal and state prisons relative to their proportion in the population (Walker *et al.*, 1996), American Indians actually have the highest incarceration rate for any race: In 1997, 1,083 of every 100,000 American Indians in the United States were incarcerated (Smelser and Baltes, 2001). Moreover, American Indian youths, who are subject to federal rather than state prosecution, often end up facing harsher sentences than if they were subject to state prosecution (Weich and Angulo, 2002). As a result, approximately 60 percent of youths in federal custody are American Indian.

Housing Markets and Mortgage Lending

Housing segregation among black Americans is far greater than among any other identifiable group. For example, blacks are much more likely to live in segregated neighborhoods, to rent rather than own a home and to have a lower-valued home when they are homeowners (Charles and Hurst, 2002; Massey, 2001). Although legal segregation and exclusion ended in 1968 with the Fair Housing Act, racial disparities in certain neighborhoods and housing markets continue. In addition, disparities in aggregate lending to black and white neighborhoods continue to exist in many communities (Ladd, 1998; Munnell *et al.*, 1992, 1996; Turner and Skidmore, 1999; Turner *et al.*, 2002a; Wyly and Holloway, 1999). For example, Wyly and Holloway found that applicants were more likely to have their loans approved in Atlanta neighborhoods in which their race was predominant (*i.e.*, blacks were approved more in black neighborhoods and whites in white neighborhoods). Other studies have shown significant differences in the probability of mortgage loan approval by race in Boston (Carr and Megbolugbe, 1993; Munnell *et al.*, 1992) and Milwaukee (Squires and O'Connor, 2001).

Health Care and Health Outcomes

African Americans, Hispanics, Asian Americans and American Indians and Alaska Natives face large barriers to health care services as compared with whites (for recent reviews, see Institute of

Medicine, 2003; Mayberry *et al.*, 2000). These groups tend to experience lower levels of access to care and to receive lower-quality health care (Institute of Medicine, 2003). For instance, African Americans and Hispanics compared with non-Hispanic whites are less likely to receive kidney dialysis or transplants (Epstein *et al.*, 2000), are less likely to receive appropriate cancer diagnostic tests or treat- ments (Imperato *et al.*, 1996; McMahon *et al.*, 1999) and are more likely to receive less-than-desirable procedures, such as limb amputation for diabetics (Chin *et al.*, 1998).

Disadvantaged racial groups are also more likely than whites to suffer from adverse health status and outcomes (Institute of Medicine, 2003; Keppel *et al.*, 2002; National Research Council, 2001a). Thus, substantial racial differentials exist for rates of infant mortality, certain cancers, cardiovascular disease and kidney disease (Keppel *et al.*, 2002). For example, American Indians are more likely than other racial groups to die from diabetes, liver disease and cirrhosis and unintentional injuries. There is also considerable evidence that African Americans have disproportionately high levels of hypertension compared with other racial groups.

Interpreting Differential Outcomes

Differences in outcomes by race do not themselves provide direct evidence for the magnitude or even the presence of racial discrimination in any particular domain. These outcome differences are the result of any number of factors that may or may not include racial discrimination in that domain. For instance, racial disparities in the labour market (*e.g.*, in hiring or wages) may reflect differences in school quality and achievement rather than any racial animus within the labour market per se.

Although racial disparities continue to exist in many domains, both social and legal changes have improved opportunities for many nonwhites in the United States. Recently, the Brookings Institution (2000) reported the federal government's 50 most important achievements in the past 50 years, including expanding the right to vote (ranked 2), promoting equal access to public accommodations (ranked 3), reducing workplace discrimination (ranked 5), increasing access to postsecondary education (ranked 19) and increasing low-income families' access to health care (ranked 34). Examples of legislative acts designed to promote equal opportunity and reduce discrimination include the Civil Rights Act of 1964 banning discrimination in employment and in public accommodations; the Voting Rights Act of 1965 (and its subsequent extensions and amendments), allowing full political participation of nonwhite groups once excluded from voting; Federal Executive Order 11246, requiring compliance by government contractors with federal antidiscrimination policies and the development of administrative systems to monitor compliance; and the Fair Housing Act of 1968, banning discrimination in housing.

Nonetheless, differential outcomes by race persist and motivate analysis to understand contributing factors, including the possible role of racial discrimination. Black–white gaps in income, employment, higher education, test scores, housing segregation, health care and treatment within the criminal justice system are large. Such sizable and persistent differences in outcomes, by themselves, are problematic and important to address. Even if differential outcomes do not in and of themselves prove that discrimination is occurring, they tell us where to look when seeking to assess whether discriminatory behaviour occurs in various social arenas. In the example cited above, for instance, racial disparities in the labour market may reflect not only discrimination in that domain at that time (*e.g.*, wage differentials) but also discrimination in earlier interactions (*e.g.*, labour market experience) and in other domains (*e.g.*, education).

Differential outcomes might be less informative if we believed that the groups involved were innately different. Yet, as noted, scientists have not determined a genetic basis for the socially based racial and ethnic categories in American society—categories whose meaning has changed over time (*e.g.*, the assimilation of previously 'nonwhite' European immigrant groups into the 'white' category). We can then infer that these differential outcomes reflect deep differences in the historical and current experiences and environment of disadvantaged racial groups versus non-Hispanic whites. For instance, surveys show that nonwhites perceive much greater discrimination toward nonwhite racial groups and experience much more discrimination themselves compared with whites (Bobo, 2001; Morin, 2001; Schuman *et al.*, 1997). Cumulative disadvantage across generations—in access to nutritious food, decent housing, remunerative employment and secure and stress-free environments—is a possible way to interpret the differences in current outcomes among nonwhite Americans.

Role of Cumulative Disadvantage

Much of the discussion of the presence of discrimination and the effects of antidiscrimination policies assumes discrimination is a phenomenon that occurs at a specific point in time within a particular domain. For instance, discrimination can occur in entry-level hiring in the labour market or in loan applications in mortgage lending. But this episodic view of discrimination occurring may be inadequate. Here we explore the idea, that discrimination should be seen as a dynamic process that functions over time in several different ways.

First, the effects of discrimination may cumulate across generations and through history. For instance, impoverishment in previous generations can prevent the accumulation of wealth in future generations. Similarly, learned behaviour and expectations about opportunities and life possibilities can shape the behaviours and preferences of future generations for members of different racial groups.

Second, effects of discrimination may cumulate over time through the course of an individual's life across different domains. Outcomes in labour markets, education, housing, criminal justice and health care all interact with each other; discrimination in any one domain can limit opportunities and cumulatively worsen life chances in another. For instance, children who are less healthy and more impoverished may do worse in school and in turn, poor education may affect labour market opportunities. The possibility that the effects of discrimination cumulate over an individual's lifetime is rarely discussed in the literature on the measurement of discrimination.

Yet even small initial disadvantages, experienced at key points in an individual's life, could well have long-term cumulative effects.

Third, effects of discrimination may cumulate over time through the course of an individual's life sequentially within any one domain. Again, small levels of discrimination at multiple points in a process may result in large cumulative disadvantage. For instance, children who do not learn basic educational skills in elementary school because of discrimination may face future discrimination in the way they are tracked or the way their test scores are interpreted in secondary school. Small effects of discrimination in job search (*e.g.*, application or interviewing stages), job retention, job promotion and wage setting may result in large differences in labour market outcomes when these effects cumulate over time, even if no further discrimination occurs.

There are many instances in which the application of neutral rules harms a member of a disadvantaged racial group because of discrimination at some other time or place in the social system. However, there is presently no case law that addresses these broad social effects; the law frequently will not deem the challenged conduct to be unlawful if it merely transmits, rather than expands, the extent of racial discrimination. Similarly, the law does not hold any agents or institutions responsible for problems outside their legitimate purview. Discrimination occurring in other domains or in society generally need not be remedied; hence, cumulative discrimination is not a legal issue. An employer who needs highly educated workers can hire them as he or she finds them, even if doing so means that only a small percentage of black or Hispanic workers will be hired because prior discrimination in educational opportunities limited the number of members of these groups with the requisite skills.

Whether cumulative discrimination is important across generations, across a lifetime in different domains and over time within a specific domain are empirical questions. However, these questions have not been addressed to any great extent by empirical social scientists. we return to the issue of the importance of developing methods focused not just on measuring discriminatory behaviour at a particular point in time in a specific process but also on understanding the cumulative and dynamic effects of discrimination over time and across processes.

Summary

We adopt a broad definition of racial discrimination for use in social science research, which includes individual behaviours and institutional processes but not attitudes or beliefs as such. Our definition includes two components that are related to (but broader than) a large body of case law: differential treatment on the basis of race that disadvantages a racial group and treatment on the basis of inadequately justified factors other than race that disadvantages a racial group (differential effect). In defining discrimination for this report, we focus primarily on discrimination that has harmful consequences for disadvantaged racial minorities.

The definition is not limited to those actions defined as discriminatory within a legal framework but also encompasses subtle behaviours and processes and cumulative discriminatory effects that may not be explicitly unlawful or easily measured. In the next chapter, we discuss in more detail the possible ways in which discrimination may manifest itself and return to a discussion of when these discriminatory behaviours may or may not be explicitly unlawful. There is a history of racial exclusion in the United States and a persistence of large disparate outcomes for racial groups across many societal domains. Although such disparities may not in themselves signal the presence of discrimination in any particular domain or event, they are problematic and motivate our work to assess social science analytical methods for measuring the role of racial discrimination in American society today

Discrimination manifests itself in multiple ways that range in form from overt and intentional to subtle and ambiguous, as well as from personal to institutional, whether through statistical discrimination and profiling or organizational processes. Discrimination also operates differently in different domains and may cumulate over time within and across domains. Regardless of which form it takes, discrimination can create barriers to equal treatment and opportunity and can have adverse effects on various outcomes. Clear theories about how discriminatory behaviour may occur are important in order to develop models that help identify and measure discrimination's effects.

Although discrimination is sometimes still practiced openly, it has become increasingly socially undesirable to do so. Consequently, such discrimination as exists today is more likely to take more subtle and complex forms. Subtler forms of discrimination can occur spontaneously and ambiguously and go undetected, particularly at the institutional level. Although legal standards address specific forms of unlawful intentional or statistical discrimination, subtler forms are more difficult to address within the law. Thus, shifts in kinds of discriminatory behaviour have implications for the measurement of discrimination. As we discuss in the next chapter, some types of discrimination may be more difficult to identify and may require collecting new and different data and the further development of new methods of analysis.

3

Scientific Racism and Racial Discrimination

Scientific racism is the use of scientific or ostensibly scientific findings and method to investigate differences among the human races, specifically in a historical context of ca. 1880 to 1930. As a term, scientific racism denotes the contemporary and historical scientific theories that employ anthropology (notably physical anthropology), anthropometry, craniometry and other disciplines, in fabricating anthropologic typologies supporting the classification of human populations into physically discrete human races.

Racial anthropology was most common during the New Imperialism period (ca. 1880s–1914), in the second half of the 19th century, wherein theory conflated with racial supremacism in justifying white European imperialism. Since the end of the Second World War (1939–45) and the occurrence of the Holocaust, scientific racism in theory and action was formally denounced, especially in The Race Question (18 July, 1950), the UNESCO moral condemnation of racism and official debunking of scientific racism: "The myth of 'race' has created an enormous amount of human and social damage. In recent years, it has taken a heavy toll in human lives and caused untold suffering."

Beginning in the later 20th century, scientific racism has been criticized as obsolete and as historically used to support or validate racist world-views, usually based upon belief in the existence and significance of racial categories— typically with a hierarchy of superior and inferior races. Today, 'scientific racism' refers to politically motivated research attempting to scientifically justify racist ideology. The accusation of scientific racism often is cast upon researchers claiming the existence of quantifiable differences in intelligence among the human races, especially if the differences are partly genetic in origin.

The critics of these authors, such as Stephen Jay Gould and Richard Lewontin, write that their works are motivated by racist presumptions unsupported by available evidence. The authors in turn reply that their work is objective and that criticisms are motivated by professional prejudice, political correctness and censorship. Publications, such as the *Mankind Quarterly*, an anthropology journal accused of scientific racism for publishing articles on controversial interpretations of human evolution, intelligence, ethnography, language, mythology, archaeology and race subjects.

The term 'scientific racism' is a pejorative adjective applied to contemporary theories, such as in *The Bell Curve* (1994), claiming that scientific evidence show significant evolutionary differences among the human races and ethnic groups. As such, 'scientific racism' criticizes human genetics studies claiming to establish a connection between race and intelligence, to so establish the existence of a 'natural racial hierarchy', hence, there exist discrete, 'superior' and 'inferior', human races.

Racial Theories in Physical Anthropology (1850-1918)

The scientific classification established by Carl Linnaeus is requisite to any human racial classification scheme. In the 19th century, unilineal evolution (aka classical social evolution) was a conflation of competing sociologic and anthropologic theories proposing that Western European culture was the acme of human socio-cultural evolution. The ideologic proposal that social status is unilinear — from primitive to civilized, from agronomic to industrial

— became popular among philosophers, including Friedrich Hegel, Immanuel Kant and Auguste Comte. In said context, the Christian Bible was interpreted to sanction slavery and, from the 1820s to the 1850s, was an oft-cited, pro-slavery legalism used in the antebellum Southern United States, by writers such as the Rev. Richard Furman and Thomas R. Cobb, for the de jure and de facto enforcement of the racialist idea that negroes had been created unequal and thus suited to slavery.

In *An Essay on the Inequality of the Human Races* (1853–55), Arthur de Gobineau proposed three human races and that miscegenation led to the collapse of civilization. Polygenist theory proposed different genetic origins of the species man, thus making it conceptually possible to conceive different, biologically discrete, human races and so classify people as animals are classified— without rights. In On the Origin of Species by Means of Natural Selection, or the Preservation of Favoured Races in the Struggle for Life (1859), by Charles Darwin, proved culturally influential in assessing the place of the species Man in Nature; and in The Descent of Man and Selection in Relation to Sex (1871) he reports no racial distinctions indicating that the human races are discrete species; to wit: "It may be doubted whether any character can be named, which is distinctive of a race and is constant... they graduate into each other and... it is hardly possible to discover clear, distinctive characters between them.... As it is improbable that the numerous and unimportant, points of resemblance, between the several races of man, in bodily structure and mental faculties (I do not here refer to similar customs) should all have been independently acquired, they must have been inherited from progenitors who had these same characters" (Darwin, 1871).

In establishing a sole human species, Darwin contrasted the 'civilized races' with the 'savage races'; like most of his contemporaries— except the naturalist Alfred Russel Wallace— he did not distinguish 'biological race' from 'cultural race'. Moreover, beyond the biology, he note that savage races risked extinction more from white European colonialism, than from evolutionary inadequacy; moreover, scientific racism was epitomised with in the phrase survival of the fittest, an 1864 coinage by Herbert Spencer. In the 1940s, the term Social Darwinism denoted ideologies, including pre-Darwinian racialism and racism, derived from facile interpretations of evolution by natural selection.

At the end of the 19th century's end, scientific racism conflated Græco–Roman eugenicism with Francis Galton's concept of voluntary eugenics in the form of coercive, anti-immigrant government programs influenced by other socio-political discourses and events. Such institutional racism was effected via Phrenology, telling character from physiognomy; craniometric skull and skeleton studies; thus skulls and skeletons of black people and other colored volk, were displayed between apes and white men. In 1906, Ota Benga, a Pygmy, was displayed as the 'Missing Link', in the Bronx Zoo, New York City, alongside apes and animals. The most influential theorists included the anthropologist Georges Vacher de Lapouge (1854–1936) who proposed 'anthroposociology'; and Johann Gottfried Herder (1744–1803), who applied 'race' to nationalist theory, thereby developing the first conception of ethnic nationalism. In 1882, Ernest Renan contradicted Herder with a nationalism based upon the "will to live together", not founded upon ethnic or racial prerequisites. Scientific racist discourse posited the historical existence of 'national races' such as the Deutsche Volk in Germany and the 'French race' being a branch of the basal 'Aryan race' extant for millennia, to advocate for geo-political borders parallel to the racial ones.

Craniometry and Physical Anthropology

The Dutch scholar Pieter Camper (1722–89), an early craniometric theoretician, used 'craniometry' (interior skull-volume measurement) to scientifically justify racial differences. In 1770, he conceived of the facial angle to measure intelligence among species of men. The facial angle was formed by drawing two lines: a horizontal line from nostril to ear; and a vertical line from the upper-jawbone prominence to the forehead prominence. Camper's craniometry reported that antique statues (the Græco–Roman ideal) had a 90-degree facial angle, Europeans an 80-degree angle, Blacks a 70-degree angle and the orangutan a 58-degree facial angle — thus he established a racist biological hierarchy for mankind, per the Decadent conception of history. Such scientific racist researches were continued by the naturalist Étienne Geoffroy Saint-Hilaire (1772–1844) and the anthropologist Paul Broca (1824–80).

In the 19th century, an early physical anthropologist, the American physician Samuel George Morton (1799–1851), collected human skulls from worldwide and attempted a logical, classification scheme. Influenced by contemporary racialist theory, Dr Morton said he could judge racial intellectual capacity by measuring the interior cranial capacity, ergo a large skull denoted a large brain, thus high intellectual capacity, conversely, a small skull denoted a small brain, thus low intellectual capacity; superior and inferior established.

The craniometric data yielded Morton the information with which to determine the evolutionary point at which Caucasians ceased being racial Caucasians and the evolutionary point where began racial Negro-ness. The craniometry of Ancient Egyptian skulls determined that the ancient Egyptians were white people, not black-skinned Africans. Dr Morton's major monographs, 'Crania Americana' (1839), 'An Inquiry into the Distinctive Characteristics of the Aboriginal Race of America' (1844) and 'Crania Aegyptiaca' (1844) synthesize his racialist presumptions. In 'Crania Americana', he reported that the mean cranial capacity of white skulls was 87 in.^{3} (1,425 cm^3); the mean cranial capacity of black skulls was 78 in.^{3} (1,278 cm^3); and the mean cranial capacity of red skulls was 82 in.^{3} (1,344 cm^3).

In '*The Mismeasure of Man*' (1981), the historian of science Stephen Jay Gould claimed that Samuel Morton had falsified the craniometric data with over-packed skulls, to so produce results that would legitimize the racist presumptions he was attempting to prove. A subsequent study by John Michael found Morton's original data to be more accurate than Gould describes, concluding that "contrary to Gould's interpretation... Morton's research was conducted with integrity." In 1873, Paul Broca, founder of the

Anthropological Society of Paris (1859), found the same pattern of measures — that Crania Americana reported — by weighing specimen brains at autopsy. Other historical studies, proposing a black race–white race, intelligence–brain size difference, include those by Bean (1906), Mall (1909), Pearl (1934) and Vint (1934).

Monogenism and Polygenism

Samuel Morton's followers, especially Dr Josiah C. Nott (1804–1873) and George Gliddon (1809–57) extended Dr Morton's ideas in Types of Mankind (1854), claiming that Morton's findings supported the notion of polygenism — mankind has discrete genetic ancestries; the races are evolutionarily unrelated and is predecessor of the modern human multiregional origin hypothesis. Moreover, Morton, himself, had been reluctant to espouse polygenism, because it theologically challenged the Christian creation myth espoused in the Bible. Later, in The Descent of Man (1871), Charles Darwin proposed the single-origin hypothesis, *i.e.*, monogenism— mankind has a common genetic ancestry, the races are related, opposing everything that Creationism and the polygenism of Nott and Gliddon proposed.

Typologies

One of the first typologies used to classify various human races was invented by Georges Vacher de Lapouge (1854–1936), a theoretician of eugenics, who published in 1899 L'Aryen *et son rôle social* (The Aryan and his social role). In this book, he classified humanity into various, hierarchized races, spanning from the "Aryan white race, dolichocephalic", to the 'brachycephalic' 'mediocre and inert' race, best represented by the 'Jew.' Between these, Vacher de Lapouge identified the "Homo europaeus (Teutonic, Protestant, etc.), the 'Homo alpinus' (Auvergnat, Turkish, etc.) and finally the 'Homo mediterraneus' (Neapolitan, Andalus, etc.) Vacher de Lapouge became one of the leading inspiration of Nazi anti-semitism and Nazi racist ideology.

Vacher de Lapouge's classification was mirrored in William Z. Ripley in The Races of Europe (1899), a book which had a large influence on American white supremacism. Ripley even made a map of Europe according to the alleged cephalic index of its inhabitants. He was an important influence of the American eugenist Madison Grant.

Furthermore, according to John Efron of Indiana University, the late 19th century also witnessed "the scientizing of anti-Jewish prejudice," stigmatizing Jews with male menstruation, pathological hysteria, and nymphomania. At the same time, several Jews, such as Joseph Jacobs or Samuel Weissenberg, also endorsed the same pseudo-scientific theories, convinced that the Jews formed a distinct race. Chaim Zhitlovsky also attempted to define Yiddishkayt (Ashkenazi Jewishness) by turning to contemporary racial theory.

Joseph Deniker (1852–1918) was one of William Z. Ripley's principal opponents; whereas Ripley maintained, as did Vacher de Lapouge, that the European populace comprised three races, Joseph Deniker proposed that the European populace comprised ten races (six primary and four sub-races). Furthermore, he proposed that the concept of 'race' was ambiguous, and in its stead proposed the compound word 'ethnic group', which later prominently featured in the works of Julian Huxley and Alfred C. Haddon. Moreover, Ripley argued that Deniker's 'race' idea should be denoted a type, because it was less biologically rigid than most racial classifications.

Popular Racist Ideology

Human zoos, sometimes called 'ethnographic exhibitions' or 'Negro villages', were objects of anthropology and anthropometry and also an important means of bolstering 'popular racism'. Human zoos were popular from the 1870s until World War II, and the concept survived into the 21st century. Ethnographic zoos were often predicated on unilinealism and a version of Social Darwinism. Many placed indigenous people (particularly Africans) in a continuum between Europeans and the non-human hominids. Fundamental to scientific racism, unilinealism claimed Western culture was the contemporary pinnacle of social evolution. It was upheld by famous thinkers such as Auguste Comte (1798–1857), Edward Burnett Tylor (1832–1917), Lewis Henry Morgan (1818–1881) and Herbert Spencer (1820–1903). Social evolutionism attempted to scientifically formalize social thinking, and was later influenced by the biological theory of evolution.

Displaying human beings in cages to demonstrate scientific racist theories was common in the second half of the 19th century. The 1889 World Fair in Paris had as major attraction a 'Negro village' where 400 indigenous people were displayed. Carl Hagenbeck, a German merchant in wild animals, exhibited in 1874 Samoans and Sami people described as 'purely natural' populations. Two years later, he sent an emissary to Sudan to capture wild beasts for his circus attractions, along with Nubians. Geoffroy de Saint-Hilaire, son of Edouard Geoffroy Saint-Hilaire and owner of the Parisian Jardin d'acclimatation, presented Nubians and Inuit in 1877.

In 1906, Madison Grant, head of the New York Zoological Society, had Congolese pygmy Ota Benga displayed at the Bronx Zoo in New York City alongside apes and other animals. At the behest of Grant, a prominent eugenicist, the zoo director placed Ota Benga in a cage with an orangutan and labeled him The Missing Link, illustrating that in evolutionary terms Africans like Ota Benga were closer to apes than were Europeans. Historians Pascal Blanchard *et al.* said:

Human zoos, the incredible symbols of the colonial period, and the transition from the nineteenth to the twentieth century, have been completely suppressed in our collective history and memory. Yet they were major social events. The French, Europeans, and Americans came in their tens of millions to discover the 'savage' for the first time in zoos or 'ethnographic' and colonial fairs. These exhibitions of the exotic (the future 'native') laid the foundations on which, over an almost sixty-year period, was spun the West's progressive transition from a 'scientific' racism to a colonial and 'mass' racism affecting millions of 'visitors', from Paris to Hamburg, London to New York, Moscow to Barcelona.

Ideological Applications

Ideological Applications discuss as Nordicism, slavery justified, South African Apartheid, Eugenic, an Popular racist ideology.

Nordicism

Joseph Deniker's historic contribution to racial theory was la race nordique (the Nordic race), a generic, racial-stock descriptor, which the American eugenicist Madison Grant (1865–1937) presented as the white racial engine of world civilization. Having adopted Ripley's three-race European populace model, but disliking the 'Teuton' race name, he transliterated la race nordique into 'The Nordic race', the acme of the concocted racial hierarchy, based upon his racial classification theory, popular in the 1910s and 1920s.

Slavery Justified

In the United States, scientific racism justified Black African slavery to assuage moral opposition to the Atlantic slave trade. Alexander Thomas and Samuell Sillen described black men as uniquely fitted for bondage, because of their "primitive psychological organization". In 1851, in antebellum Louisiana, the physician Samuel A. Cartwright (1793–1863), considered slave escape attempts as 'drapetomania', a treatable mental illness, that "with proper medical advice, strictly followed, this troublesome practice that many Negroes have of running away can be almost entirely prevented". The term drapetomania (mania of the runaway slave) derives from the Greek drapetes, (a runaway [slave]) and mania (madness, frenzy). Cartwright also described dysaethesia aethiopica, called 'rascality' by overseers. By 1840, the political challenges to American slavery increased; yet the 1840 census indicated that Northern, free blacks suffered mental illness at higher rates than did their Southern, enslaved counterparts. Moreover, Southern slavers concluded that escaping Negroes were only suffering from 'mental disorders' and the census mental health data became a political weapon against abolitionists.

At the time of the American Civil War (1861–65), the matter of miscegenation prompted studies of ostensible physiological differences between Caucasians and Negroes. Early anthropologists, such as Josiah Clark Nott, George Robins Gliddon, Robert Knox, and Samuel George Morton, aimed to scientifically prove that Negroes were a human species different from the white people species; that the rulers of Ancient Egypt were not African; and that mixed-race offspring (the product of miscegenation) tended to physical weakness and infertility. After the Civil War, Southern (Confederacy) physicians wrote textbooks of scientific racism based upon studies claiming that Black freemen (ex-slaves) were becoming extinct, because they were inadequatee to the demands of being a free man— implying that Black people benefitted from enslavement. In 1850, Louis Agassiz commissioned a series of daguerreotypes of slaves of Columbia South Carolina for studying of races; four portraits are available at:

South African Apartheid

Scientific racism played a role in establishing Apartheid in South Africa. In South Africa, white scientists, like Dudly Kidd, who published *The Essential Kafir* in 1904, sought to understand the African mind. They believed that the cultural differences between whites and blacks in South Africa might be caused by physiological differences in the brain. Rather than suggesting that Africans were overgrown children, as early white explorers had, Kidd believed that Africans were misgrown with a vengeance. He described Africans as at once hopelessly deficient, yet very shrewd. The Carnegie Commission on the Poor White Problem in South Africa played a key role in establishing Apartheid in South Africa. According to one memorandum sent to Frederick Keppel, then president of the Carnegie Corporation, there was "little doubt that if the natives were given full economic opportunity, the more competent among them would soon outstrip the less competent whites". Keppel's support for the project of creating the report was motivated by his concern with the maintenance of existing racial boundaries. The preoccupation of the Carnegie Corporation with the so-called poor white problem in South Africa was at least in part the outcome of similar misgivings about the state of poor whites in the American South.

The report was five volumes in length. At the turn of the century, white Americans, and whites elsewhere in the world, felt uneasy because poverty and economic depression seemed to strike people regardless of race. White poverty contradicted notions of racial superiority, and hence it became the focus of 'scientific' study. Though the ground work for Apartheid began earlier, the report provided support for this central idea of black inferiority. This was used to justify racial segregation and discrimination in the following decades. The report expressed fear about the loss of white racial pride, and in particular pointed to the danger that the poor white would not be able to resist the process of 'Africanisation'.

Although scientific racism played a role in justifying and supporting institutional racism in South Africa, it was not as important in South Africa as it has been in Europe and the United States. This was due in part to the 'poor white problem', which raised serious questions for supremacists about white racial superiority. Since poor whites were found to be in the same situation as natives in the African environment, the idea that intrinsic white superiority could overcome any environment did not seem to hold. As such, scientific justifications for racism were not as useful in South Africa.

Eugenics

In his *The Passing of the Great Race* (1916), Madison Grant describe eugenics as the most influential tract of American scientific racism. In the 1920s-30s, the German racial hygiene movement embraced Grant's Nordic theory. Alfred Ploetz (1860–1940) coined the term Rassenhygiene in Racial Hygiene Basics (1895) and founded the German Society for Racial Hygiene in 1905. The movement advocated selective breeding, compulsory sterilization, and a close alignment of public health with eugenics. Racial hygiene was historically tied to traditional notions of public health, but with emphasis on heredity— what philosopher and historian Michel Foucault has called state racism.

In 1869, Francis Galton (1822–1911) proposed the first social measures meant to preserve or enhance biological characteristics, and later coined the term 'eugenics'. Galton, a statistician, introduced correlation and regression analysis and discovered regression toward the mean. He was also the first to study human differences and inheritance of intelligence with statistical methods. He introduced the use of questionnaires and surveys to collect data on population sets, which he needed for genealogical and biographical works and for anthropometric studies. Galton also founded psychometrics, the science of measuring mental faculties, and differential psychology, a branch of psychology concerned with psychological differences between people rather than common traits.

Like scientific racism, eugenics grew popular in the early 20th century, and both ideas influenced Nazi racial policies and Nazi eugenics. In 1901, Galton, Karl Pearson (1857–1936) and Walter F. R. Weldon (1860–1906) founded the Biometrika scientific journal, which promoted biometrics and statistical analysis of heredity. Charles Davenport (1866–1944) was briefly involved in the review. In Race Crossing in Jamaica (1929), he made statistical arguments that biological and cultural degradation followed white and black interbreeding. Davenport was connected to Nazi Germany before and during World War II. In 1939 he wrote a contribution to the festschrift for Otto Reche (1879–1966), who became an important figure within the plan to remove populations considered 'inferior' from eastern Germany.

Interbellum to World War II

Scientific racism continued through the early twentieth century, and soon intelligence testing became a new source for racial comparisons. Before the Second World War (1939–45), scientific racism remained common to anthropology, leading to programs of eugenics, compulsory sterilization, anti-miscegenation laws, and immigration restrictions in Europe and the United States. The war crimes and crimes against humanity of Nazi Germany (1933–45), discredited scientific racism in academia — but racist legislation based upon it remained in some countries until the late 1960s.

Nazi Germany

The Nazi Party and its sympathizers published many books on scientific racism, seizing on the eugenic and anti-Semitic ideas with which they would later become associated, although these ideas had been in circulation since the 19th century. Books such as *Rassenkunde des deutschen Volkes* ("Ethnology of the German People") by Hans F. K. Günther and Rasse und Seele ("Race and

Soul") by Dr. Ludwig Ferdinand Clauss attempted to scientifically identify differences between the German, Nordic, or Aryan people and other, supposedly inferior, groups. German schools used these books as texts during the Nazi era. In the early 1930s, the Nazis used racialized scientific rhetoric based on social Darwinism to push its restrictive and discriminatory social policies. During World War II, Nazi racialist beliefs became anathema in the United States, and Boasians such as Ruth Benedict consolidated their institutional power. After the war, discovery of the Holocaust and Nazi abuses of scientific research (such as Josef Mengele's ethical violations and other war crimes revealed at the Nuremberg Trials) led most of the scientific community to repudiate scientific support for racism.

United States

In the US, eugenicists such as Harry H. Laughlin, and Madison Grant sought to 'scientifically' prove the physical and mental inadequacy of certain ethnic groups to justify compulsory sterilization and restrict immigration, per the Immigration Act of 1924; compulsory sterilization continued until the 1960s and later. Lothrop Stoddard published many racialist books on what he saw as the peril of immigration, his most famous being The Rising Tide of Color Against White World-Supremacy in 1920. In this book he presented a view of the world situation pertaining to race focusing concern on the coming population explosion among the 'colored' peoples of the world and the way in which 'white world-supremacy' was being lessened in the wake of World War I and the collapse of colonialism.

Stoddard's analysis divided world politics and situations in to 'white', 'yellow', 'black', 'Amerindian', and 'brown' peoples and their interactions.Stoddard argued race and heredity were the guiding factors of history and civilization and that the elimination or absorption of the 'white' race by 'colored' races would result in the destruction of Western civilization. Like Madison Grant, Stoddard divided the white race into three main divisions: Nordic, Alpine, and Mediterranean. He considered all three to be of good stock, and far above the quality of the colored races, but argued that the Nordic was the greatest of the three and needed to be preserved by way of eugenics. Unlike Grant, Stoddard was less concerned with which varieties of European people were superior to others (Nordic theory), but was more concerned with what he called 'bi-racialism', seeing the world as being composed of simply 'colored' and 'white' races. In the years after the Great Migration and World War I, Grant's racial theory would fall out of favor in the U.S. in favor of a model closer to Stoddard's.

After 1945

By 1954, 58 years after the Plessy v. Ferguson upholding of racial segregation in the United States, American popular and scholarly opinions of scientific racism and its sociologic practice, had evolved. Subsequent to the Supreme Court's desegregation of American public schooling, in 1960 there appeared the Mankind Quarterly journal as a venue for scientific racism. It is criticized for extremist right-wing politics, anti-Semitic bent, and espousing academic hereditarianism. The magazine was founded in 1960, partly in response to the socially liberal Brown v. Board of Education legal decision. In April 1966, Alex Haley interviewed American Nazi Party founder George Lincoln Rockwell for Playboy. Rockwell explained why he believed blacks were inferior to whites, citing a study by G.O. Ferguson that showed black people, who were part white outperformed 'pure-black niggers' (Rockwell's words) on a test. Rockwell's use of these statistics is a textbook example of a statistical fallacy used to propagate scientific racism. Following the United States Civil Rights Movement, many scientists who previously studied racial differences moved to other fields. For example, Robert Yerkes, who previously worked on the World War I Army intelligence testing, moved to the field of primatology.

International bodies such as UNESCO attempted to draft resolutions that would summarize the state of scientific knowledge about race and issued calls for the resolution of racial conflicts. In its 1950 The Race Question, UNESCO declared that "A race, from the biological standpoint, may therefore be defined as one of the group of populations constituting the species Homo sapiens", which were broadly defined as the Mongoloid, Negroid, and the Caucasoid 'divisions' but stated that "It is now generally recognized that intelligence tests do not in themselves enable us to differentiate safely between what is due to innate capacity and what is the result of environmental influences, training and education." To this day, the statement is controversial among some scientists who disagreed with its accuracy (such as R. A. Fisher), or its purpose (as a political declaration of scientific consensus). In 1978, the UNESCO Declaration on Race and Racial Prejudice proclaimed no race was superior to any other, but, in contrast to the 1950 statement, relied more on "moral and ethical principles of humanity" rather than science. The corresponding 2001 statement by UNESCO, Universal Declaration on Cultural Diversity does not mention race at all, and does not justify its views on cultural diversity with science. Views, or at least the language, of racial discourse, have clearly evolved over the half-century. In 2007, James Watson, pioneer of DNA, was criticized after being quoted as saying that Africans were of different intelligence from other races.

Today, the term 'scientific racism' is used to refer to research seeming to scientifically justify racist ideology. The accusation of scientific racism often is cast upon researchers claiming the existence of quantifiable differences in intelligence among the human races, especially if said differences are partly genetic in origin. Contemporary researchers include Arthur Jensen (The g Factor: The Science of Mental Ability); J. Philippe Rushton, president of the Pioneer Fund (Race, Evolution, and Behaviour); Chris Brand (The g Factor: General Intelligence and Its Implications); Richard Lynn (IQ and the Wealth of Nations); Charles Murray; and Richard Herrnstein (The Bell Curve), among others. Thc critics of these authors, such as Stephen Jay Gould and Richard Lewontin, write that their works are motivated by racist presumptions unsupported by available evidence. The authors in turn reply that their work is objective and that criticisms are motivated by professional prejudice, political correctness, and censorship. Publications such as the Mankind Quarterly, an anthropology journal, are accused of scientific racism for publishing articles on controversial interpretations of human evolution, intelligence, ethnography, language, mythology, archaeology, and race subjects.

Racial Legacy of Orientalism

The orient has traditionally been considered to be the negation of the West, *i.e.*, the other side of rationality, science, development, economic growth, prosperity, and so forth. In other words, everything that was prized as the elements of superiority of the occident was lacking in the orient. Accordingly, the field of social scientific and sociological research has mainly neglected conducting research on the complexity, heterogeneity, and major transformations of what was called 'the orient'. The concepts of an Islamic civil society, Islamic political ideologies and modern Islam have been controversial and rejected by many classic and contemporary scholars of social sciences. The Orient could not have its own existence; as Said puts it; the Orient was a product of the West and therefore it existed according to the wishes of the West. By now, we know that Max Weber's vision of a 'value-free-sociology' remains just a vision yet to be realized. The field of production of knowledge is an inseparable part of the reproduction of power relations in the modern society. As Foucault (1977:27) mentioned: "Power and knowledge directly imply one another, that there is no power relation without the correlative constitution of a field of knowledge, nor any knowledge that does not presuppose and constitute at the same time power relations."

Foucault emphasizes that 'power produces knowledge'. They need each other for preserving and guaranteeing continuity of a system that serves both power and knowledge. Therefore the triumph of reason is the triumph of the alliance of power and knowledge. As Turner (1994:21) puts it, "the categories of 'criminal', 'insane' and 'deviant' are the manifestations of a scientific discourse by which the normal and sane exercise power along a systematic dividing of sameness and difference". The alliance of power and knowledge created whatever would be called 'the others'. It could be the 'insane', the 'criminal', the 'deviant' or the 'orient'. The modern reasonable man as the bearer of knowledge and power needed the deviance of unreason for preserving and defining the normality of reason. No matter if this 'man of reason' was as Foucault believe a modern construction or, according to Derrida a development of the old reasonable man with its roots in ancient Greece, unreason and reason have been and are inseparable. Following this line of discussion, one can say that the Western image of itself, the occident, was directly and necessarily connected to the discursive construction of 'the other', the orient.

The creation the paradigms of Orient and Occident is a manifestation of Western dominance and colonial intentions and politics. Orientalism is a discourse constituted of a network of categories, tables, and concepts by which the Orient is simultaneously defined and controlled, 'To know is to subordinate' (Turner, 1994: 21) The role of colonialists and imperial politics has been especially decisive in the constitution of Western image of Islam and the analysis of 'oriental societies' (Daniel, 1960; Southern 1962). Edward Said in his influential work, *Orientalism*, insightfully presents the Western anti-Islamic and colonial policies formulated in the typology of Orientalism, and how it was used as a subordinating discourse on the part of westerners. Europe, who defined the Orient, has itself been imprinted by what was called the Orient and therefore had a double-sided relation to it. This was not only depended on the fact that the Orient is situated very close to Europe, but also because it is there that Europe finds its best, richest and the oldest colonies, the sources of its civilization and language, its rival in cultural sphere, and one of its most usual picture of 'the others', as Said (1978) puts it.

Europe began its sociopolitical project of creation of a European or western identity since the eve of seventeenth century. Everything, rationalism, political democracy, individualism, and in short, Europe was supposed to begin at Greece's border against the Orient – a constructed geographical line with great socio-cultural and political consequences for the whole world. All properties that came to identify the West against the rest of the world, such as science, philosophy, democracy, were presented to have their roots in the ancient Greece. The influences of non-western – and in western tradition of the philosophy of science, the Orient – on Greek culture were intentionally ignored (Said, 1978; Bernal, 1991; King, 1999). As King (1999: 29) puts it:

Histories of Western philosophy invariably begin with the Greeks and avoid the issue of African and Oriental influences upon ancient Greek though. What is of particular interest is the absence of reference to the role played by Egyptian and Oriental 'mystery tradition' in the formulation of Greek philosophical ideas and approaches. The creation of a western imagined world and the spreading of its joined universalistic ideas were highly Eurocentric attempts. The universal was nothing more than the particular experiences of the western European understanding and socio-culturally embedded construction of themselves and 'the others'. Since, as Grace Jantzen (1995) arguments, the idea of a neutral, objective, and universal stance is a fiction. She means that there have never existed neutral views or believes separated from a particular place, because: "there are no views from nowhere and there are no views from everywhere. There are only views from somewhere, and the particular place will have an inescapable effect on what can be seen. If one assumes the contrary, then what is happening is that one is falsely universalizing a particular perspective.:

Not only the universalistic 'value-free' ideas about the world in general and the 'Orient' in particular is imagination and impossibility, but also the "myth of value-free sociology", as Gouldner (1973) puts it, remains just a myth for academic inner-circle discussions. Sociology, as many other sciences, has been used in overall domain of sociopolitical and military power exercises in creating the colonial and post-colonial world order. As mentioned earlier, the role of colonial and imperialistic politics has been especially decisive in the constitution of Western images of Islam and the analysis of so called 'oriental societies'. 'Oriental societies' was generalized and categorized through classical meta-theories, such as those of Marx and Weber, as societies with distinct properties that are completely different from the West. The main driving force for understanding 'the Orient' and establishing the tradition of Orientalism came from controversies between Western countries' religious rivalries and economic and military conflicts with the powerful empires of 'the Orient', such as Ottoman and Persian empires. Therefore, as Turner (1994:37) mentions, "knowledge of the Orient cannot, therefore, be separated from the history of European expansion into the Middle East and Asia".

The mutual relationship and influences between 'knowledge' and 'power' can be understood by the Western powers' imperialistic occupations during the Nineteenth and the beginning of Twentieth centuries. By 1878, Europe controlled about 67 percent and by 1914, 84 percent of the landed surface of the world (Headrick, 1977:3). After World War I, the percentage rose even higher when England and France established mandates over some of the succession states to the Ottoman Empire in the Middle East (Gordon, 1989:3). This made the West an influential actor in the uneven development of other parts of the world and also an enemy. The enmity of the West against other nations and peoples were not an imaginary construction, but a real phenomenon that highly influenced both the intellectual and the indigenous groups of many non-Western countries.

Although Orientalism came during the Middle Ages to include even the non-Muslim countries, such as China and India, it always has related to what was territorially called the 'Muslim World' and religiously Islam. The foundation of Orientalism was laid by John of Damascus (d. 748), a Christian scholar who was a great friend of the Ummayad Caliph, Yazid (Sardar, 1999). His declarations that Islam was a pagan cult, the Ka'ba in Makkah an idol, and the prophet Muhammad an irreligious and licentious man, became the classical source of all Christian writings on Islam (Sardar, 1999:18). The attitudes of the Christian world towards Muslim countries have historically been very negative and full of prejudices. Such a negative attitude made one of the very crucial bases in mobilizing simple European peasants for crusades. The crusades had in its turn reinforced the dogmatic Orient/Occident categorization. The anti-Islamic attitudes and understandings have consequently become a very part of western colonialism and self-perception. Following the example of animus towards Islam on the part of the West, 'even eminent scholars of the field', presented by Gordon (1989: 94) is highly illustrative:

> "The Lebanese historian Marwan Buheiry observes that at the turn of the century, to take only one example, a symposium was conducted in the fortnightly review Questions diplomatiques et colonials (15 may 1901) to consider prospects of Islam in the coming century. Speaking for many vof the Western scholars represented was the eminent Orientalist Baron Carra de Vaux, who wrote that, except for Persia with its 'Aryan' spirit, the prospects for progressive change among the Muslims was minimal. 'Islam is today vanquished', he went on to declare, "its political decadence was inevitable ... and in regard to its temporal destiny, Islam is finished as a religion." To destroy any threat from Pan-Islamism, he then advised one need only play Muslims against one another by encouraging Muslim heresies and the Sufi Orders against the mainstream and use nationalism to divide the various Muslim ethnic groups from one another."

Islam and Islamic societies were considered as 'the others' or the other side or counterpart of reason. Consequently, Islam and modernization were considered as two incompatible phenomena. Therefore, modernizing the Islamic countries was not possible without eliminating or 'destroying' Islam as a religion and as a political ideology and doctrine. The West was the motherland of modernization and had the prophetic mission to change the world according to a blueprint created by Western intellectuals, social scientists, and of course its superior military power. The West was the model and, as Aziz al-Azmeh (1981) formulates it, the Orient was and is reduced to 'the mirror image of the West' and so is defined and disfigured. In addition, the close connection of the 'Orient' with Islam, consequently, led to creation of an imagined 'Muslim world' that has specific common properties, of course essentially different from the West. A large part of the globe with different socioeconomic and cultural differences is encapsulated under a religious umbrella. Islam is a religion, like many other religions, highly depended on theological interpretations on the one side, and on its social embeddedness on the other. Islam has during one and half millennium of its existence gone through many theological and social transformations. The expansion of Islam as religion to far reaching areas with different socio-cultural structures in Asia, Africa, and Europe, forced the Islamic conqueror and theologian to adjust both themselves and Islam to the new societies' traditions, history and institutional arrangements.

The mutual adjustment of Islam and the new societies helped to create very diverse societies such that the Islamic dimension was just one of many different properties that separated every single 'Islamic' society from each other. How one can compare the Islamic Iran, Arabic peninsula, and Spain as the same component of a 'Muslim world'? One does not need to compare these remote areas to gain understanding of many differences between these countries. The simple comparison of countries very closed to each other, such as Iran, Turkey and Afghanistan, give us enough reason to put in question the imagined construction of the 'Muslim world'. Furthermore, the internal differences, such as urban/rural, elite/popular, diverse religious and ethnic groups, and different socioeconomic and cultural classes, in Muslim countries make the concept more problematic. Denying these internal and external diversities has been a part of Western Orientalists' and social scientists' 'value-free' attempts to construct Muslims as 'the others' who crystallizes 'backwardness', 'the traditional', 'the failure', 'the irrational', etc.

The 'Muslim world' along with the problematic Orient and the 'mirror image of the West' do not belong to the past of the modern 'Western world'. The Orient as 'the others' is an inseparable part of the self-perception of the West. The process of reconstruction and vitalization of the 'Orient' as the place of the category of 'the others' is highly modern and taking place outside our awareness. There are two agents keeping this process alive: one is the Western Orientalists (including many social scientists) and the other group is Western oriented, educated and influenced intellectuals (including many social scientists) in Muslim countries themselves. The first group is continuing its efforts more efficiently with the help of new communication technology and mass entertainment industry. The old and new Orientalists are obtaining help from Internet, CNN, CBS, BBC among others, Hollywood and other mass communication technologies to rewrite the history, change the facts, and simply reproduce the evil 'Oriental' guys. Unnecessary to enter the discussion about 'world community's' reaction against Iraq, and its 're-action' against Palestinians, and the picture that is presented of the despotic Oriental Saddam and Arafat, and the 'democratic Israel'. It is, however, not only the so called 'serious' new agencies that are engaging in *Orientalization* of the 'Orient', but also the entertainment industry contributes to an efficient way. There is innumerable movies, tv-programs, and popular books that are highly engaged in reproducing and reinforcing the image of the Oriental bad guys. Leaving many tv-series and show-talks aside, Hollywood's film industry just during the last twenty years accelerated its production of movies directly engaged in reinforcing prejudices about the bad guys of the 'Orient' and creating the pure image of the good Western and in particular American guys. Sardar (1999:102) provides an illustrative example from such movies:

In *Aladdin* (1992), it is the genie's 'phenomenal cosmic power' that needs to be tamed and brought into the service of America. Aladdin is perhaps the most culturally violent of all Disney animations. At the beginning of the film, our hero is simply Aladdin, the servant of God, but by the end of the story, having realized truth and beauty, he says, "just call me Al". The only thing that finally separates Aladdin from a normal mid-western Caucasian boy is his slight brown colouring. The film is totally steeped in Orientalism. The good guys are all clean-shaven, the bad guys have facial hair typically associated with Easterners and other civil characters. The Streets are lined with bartering Arabs and Hindu fakirs and 'Araby' is the land of the exotic. Women are portrayed as erotic, swaying about, wearing the briefest of harem costumes. Even though the genie was trapped in the Arab world, he only knows Western culture, and sings with all the inherent prejudices of Orientalism:

Oh I come from a land, from a faraway place,
Where the caravan camels roam;

Where they cut off your ears if they don't like your face;

It's barbaric, but hey, its home.

Films, TV- and radio programs, journals and newspapers contain negative attitudes to Muslims and are highly responsible in maintaining Orientalism and reproducing prejudices about Muslims. Orientalism does not exist somewhere out of the daily life of western societies; it is reproducing through socio-cultural and institutional arrangements. In other words, we do not *have* Orientalism, we are living it.

Cultural Racism

Since the defeat of Nazi Germany in the WWII, it seems that the racial biological racism has largely disappeared from the public and scientific arena in favor of a growing cultural essentialism that increasingly leads to categorization of people in different 'cultural boxes' and national societies. Social scientists and in particular anthropologists and ethnologists constructed imagined and abstract cultural entities and presented different societies as homogenous cultural systems. Culture in singular form hardly exists and as Tomlinson (1999) mentions, there is no single culture, but cultures. If it is a crucial mistake to reduce the complexity of national societies—as a tradition of 'container sociology' (Beck, 1997)— to singular national cultures and encapsulate different socioeconomic and ethnic groups under a culture, it is much worse to reduce the concept of culture in purely western or eastern or Oriental. Actually the West's understanding of the Greek philosophy was based on Islamic translations and interpretations of Greek philosophy, since 'the philosophy of Aristotle which became the major Christian framework for the philosophical formulation of Christian beliefs was transmitted by Islamic scholars – Averroes, Avicenna, al-Kindi and al-Razi. Here, therefore, is an area of common experience and historical development, where medieval Christian culture was dependent on Islam' (Turner, 1994:46). He also criticized those who consider Islam as the only mediator between the Greek and the Christian culture. Islam has highly influenced not only the Christian culture, but also the secular western philosophers who used Islam in their critique of irrational Christianity. Furthermore, and may be more important, is the fact that no society is essentially different from another one. This is a fact that have been denied by both the western and indigenous Orientalists who have during centuries tried to theoretically construct the great distinction of "West and the rest" and cultural relativists who equally have tried to line out essential cultural differences between different countries and societies. The problem of cultural relativism is traced far back to the Greek philosophers, Herodotus and Aristotle who confronted the fact that "fire burns both in Hellas and Persia, but men's ideas of right and wrong vary from place to place".

This cultural essentialism is not just somewhere an abstraction, but a part of daily life of many western countries. To consider 'ourselves' as modern individuals and social products of a high modern culture on the one side, and non-westerners or 'the others' as completely different and products of low cultures is a common understanding institutionalized in educational, judicial, political and bureaucratic systems of many European countries. This becomes obvious in the face of growing heterogeneity resulting, in part, from immigration from non-western countries to Europe. Many European countries are facing increasing immigration and growing demands of first and second generations immigrants for participation in these countries' socioeconomic and cultural life. The traditional negative attitudes towards 'the other' and in particular Muslims in Europe is demonstrating itself through implicit and explicit discrimination and racism in the European labour market, schools, judicial system, and mass media, among other spheres of social life. In addition to the extreme right groups and parties of European countries, the cultural racism has been reproducing by two active groups of agents:

1. Governmental and municipality agents,
2. The self-elected immigrants with 'cultural competence'.

The legacy of Orientalism and the superiority of the West over all other cultures, that is well established and institutionalized, demonstrate itself in governmental and communal policies for integration of immigrant groups in host societies. The assumption is that 'they' are different and culturally the opposite of 'us'. 'Knowing is to subordinate', therefore, 'we' must understand 'them' in order to be able to change them and make them adjusted to our society. We already know that they are different and strange, since they come from 'the Orient.' They are individuals who can be identified by their strange and deviant culture. All those coming from Muslim countries possesses the same 'code-of-morality' and has the same 'way-of-action'. They are Muslims, therefore, collectivists/holists, patriarchal, anti-modern and as such anti-western. They can kill for the sake of honor to defend their families and rape European girls and women because they are not Muslims. They are the fifth column of Muslim countries in Europe and, therefore, must be supervised for the risk they pose of political, social, and economic espionage.

Mass media of many western countries are full of illustrations of prejudices about Muslims. The frustration of many marginalized Muslim immigrants and the severe discrimination against them in many European countries, and the ways they are institutionally considered as 'the other' motivate some of them to go to mosques and religious circles as a compensation for the crisis of identity and the need for belonging. This is used by many European states and mass media as a sign of difference and enmity to European 'values' and ideals. The history of 'honor-killing' in Sweden, which has become an established paradigm in the image of the 'Oriental man', is illustrative. The mass media report that a Kurdish man has planned to kill his daughter, accusing her of becoming 'Swedish' and harming the father's honor. This becomes news much more important than any other national and international news in Swedish mass media, and the investigation and the following trial is step by step covered by mass media.

Governmental representatives, different political parties, and experts, are discussing the 'problem' of immigrants and seek discussions and cooperation with immigrant associations for implementing preventive policies and changing this traditional cultural property of 'immigrant cultures'. This engages of course the second class of agents who are winning economic advantages in defining immigrants as 'deviant cultural entities' whom nobody but 'cultural competent' persons from the same culture can understand. They make a cultural alliance for changing the immigrant cultures. The Kurdish men from rural areas in South Eastern Turkey, who would probably have the same problems of adjustment in Ankara or Istanbul as well, become the symbol of the 'Oriental man'.

The exclusion of 'the others', be them Muslims or immigrants, from non-western countries, are a part of daily social life and reproduction in many European countries. Individuals with immigrant backgrounds in general, and Muslims in particular, are institutionally constructed as 'cultural beings', belonging to traditional and low-ranking cultures. The 'cultural beings', however, are divided into two categories: gatekeepers and victims. The first group is constituted of male immigrants, who are patriarchal, aggressive, offender, and incompatible with the modern humanist western societies and values. Immigrant girls and women are, on the other hand, considered and treated as 'poor victims' of traditional cultures who are passively forced in living within these cultures.

Generalization and categorization of new social groups with immigrant backgrounds living in Western European countries of today – even those born in these countries – as 'the others' and different is reinforcing the sense of 'we' and 'they' and creates obstacles to immigrant groups democratic participation in all aspects of social life. 'They' are presented as a category for themselves in for instance statistics over crime, as if their 'cultural backgrounds' would have to do with a criminal act. The segregated residential areas of larger European cities are increasingly filling by individuals and families with immigrant backgrounds. It is not only residentially that many people with immigrant backgrounds are being marginalized and segregated, but also, socioeconomically and culturally. On the other side, gathering people who are considered and institutionalized as 'the others' and as the out-groups of European societies, force many immigrant groups to accept their otherness and make it a part of their identities. Institutionalized Orientalism and socio-cultural production of 'the others' by educational, political and judicial systems of European countries not only contributes to multiple exclusion of 'the others' but reinforces racism and Islam-phobia.

Institutionalized Discrimination and Islam-phobia

Orientalism is not only a question for discourse analyses, but must be studied in much broader context than the intellectual spheres of European societies. Many European institutions, such as those of education, the judiciary, and government are highly engaged in the process of reproduction of conceptions of Other and strategies of disempowerment and exclusion of 'them'. The increasing segregation and spatial, cultural, and open racism, indicate problems of discrimination and exclusion on the part of European institutions. Sweden used to be considered and, as Olof Palme said in one of his speeches during the early 1980s, want to be understood as 'the stronghold of tolerance', and a country with a strong and inclusive welfare state. But this image of Sweden is highly exaggerated and actually, in the face of a continued high level of racism and segregation of immigrants, seems more and more unreal. Following examples illustrate how cultural racism works in different institutions:

Schools: Cultural racism is working in different ways in Swedish schools. Without entering the otherwise important discussion on the fact that today in Sweden one is developing A-level and B-level schools, through which pupils with Swedish background are dominating the A schools with relatively high quality and pupils with immigrant background are gathering in B schools. This is a further serious segregation that reinforces racism in Swedish society.

Schoolbooks: The schoolbooks about history, social sciences, literature, and religion are highly ethno- and Eurocentric. One example is the world-history books. According to Swedish history books, the whole human history begins in Greece and ends in Sweden. One can find a strong attempt to (re)create a European identity for Swedes, which automatically excludes all other civilizations from the world history. One can find a few lines in history books mentioning the wars between Greece and Persians, for instance. But the way the wars and the Persian Empire are presented is very illustrative. When you read about the Persians success in wars against Greece, it says: "Persians forced themselves in Greece" and on the contrary, when Alexander, for instance, succeeded in defeating

Persians, it stays that: "Greeks won the war and conquered Persia". Furthermore, there is not a single word about Persian culture, but that "they were a warrior people" living in a geographic area between two mountain chains. In a Religion book used in Swedish high schools, one can, for instance read about Islam being also a warrior religion (recall Weber's understanding of Islam) and defining Jihad as "Muslims wars against non-Muslims," suggesting that non-Muslim includes also Christians, Jews, Zaraostrians. We know that this definition is highly provocative for many Muslims and unreal (Jihad is against 'infidels' and not non-Muslims). Furthermore, one can find in the book much praise of Christian ethics.

Teachers: Teachers working in Swedish schools have almost completely Swedish background, trained in Swedish schools and themselves have gone through Swedish education, convincing them that Sweden is a part of Europe, the modern and rational world, and all others, and in particular Muslims, are traditional, irrational, and very different from 'us'.

School curators: In Swedish schools there is usually a social worker called a 'curator', whose duty is to help pupils in different matters, such as individual difficulties, psychosocial health of pupils, and in some cases cooperating with municipal authorities when a pupils "development and health is in danger", as the 70 § Socialtjänstlagen (Social security act) puts it. The curators have in many cases become a person who sues very often immigrant pupils to municipal authorities. It happens often that the contact between school and immigrant families does not work properly and transfers into conflicts. Schools, like many other institutions working with immigrant families, very soon disqualify parents with immigrant background as suitable counterpart and as 'real parents'.

Social authorities: Another institution engaged in discrimination and exclusion of immigrants from the Swedish mainstream society and reinforcing cultural racism consists of the social authorities (social work, social benefits, etc.). A traditional and in many cases ethnocentric education make many social worker incompetent for working with immigrant families. Social workers consider immigrant families as 'culturally deviant' and in need of 'help' from social authorities. Many immigrants living in segregated areas are also long term 'clients' of social offices and are either depended on 'social allowances' from municipalities, the section called 'försörjningsenheter' (Sections of social allowances) or clients of 'familjesektioner' (Section on family problems). The following example illustrates how social authorities discriminate against immigrants: "A Swedish women contacts social authorities accusing her husband with Turkish background for planning to kidnap their children and take them to Turkey. She says that the children "are scared and do not make it to meat their father". Social authorities send the children to psychiatry and ask for "a basic investigation of the children's mental and physical health."

Mass media: One of the most important agent in reproduction of the image of Others as completely different and deviant is mass media. The Swedish mass media is highly and daily engaged in discursive differentiation and exclusion of immigrants. TV, radio, and major newspapers are daily reporting the crimes committing by immigrants, problems associated with immigrants, cultural differences, immigrants forcing their daughters to be married with a man that the family chose, and so forth.

Muslims in Swedish mass-media are presented in two different ways: Swedish newspapers and TV-channels show Muslims, who are out of Sweden, as aggressive, often armed, men in group shouting Allah-o akbar (God is great); meanwhile in Sweden they are illustrated as women with black scarf on their head who symbolize exploited females by their Muslim husbands or a patriarchal culture. Such pictures are daily reinforced even by using immigrant 'experts' for discussing such 'problems' that Muslims have both internationally and in Sweden. These are 'dirty tricks' (Preed, 2000) reproducing Islam-phobia, as well as presenting Orientalism has been institutionalized and is reinforcing in daily life of many European countries. The new way of reproducing Muslims as 'the absolute others' and as a group essentially incompatible with modernism is establishing the new ideas of multiculturalism, which has come to mean, "they live among us". They are Muslims, and of course essentially different from 'us', and 'we' as the good liberal or social democrat states has to accept the 'difference' and if possible help them to maintain their 'cultural specificity'. It seems to me that the pure existence of Muslims as 'the others' has become an inseparable part of the 'western identity'. They may fill the same function for Europe today, that the 'insane' did for the rational man in nineteenth century. As long as the radical measures for "undermining of central practices and power relations", reframing and changing of mass media, political, educational, and business-sector discourses, and changing of Eurocentrism and institutionalized Orientalism and Islamphobia have not taken place, we can not come to term with problems of exclusion and segregation. Cultural racism makes the main basis of exclusion of 'the others' and (re)creation of neo Nazism and Xenophobia in Europe.

Summary

Scientific racism is a pejorative term used against controversial works dealing with race and often its relationship to intelligence. The term implies that the claims of such works are motivated more by political opinions than scientific observations. Often when works purporting to be scientific examinations of racial questions are put out, there is debate over whether or not they are works of legitimate science or are simply scientific racism: the former implying that they contain objective, non-politically motivated research, and the latter implying that they do not. Often the line between scientific racism and legitimate science can be exceptionally blurry at the time of initial controversy.

As a term, it originated primarily to describe historical works which purported to be scientific in nature but were often simply veneers of objectivity placed over personal political beliefs. In the USA, works by early 20th century eugenicists are often labeled with this term, as are the theoretical justifications of the 20th century racial hygiene movement which flourished in Germany under the Nazis. Some regard the entire concept of race as having little use in modern science; see the article Race for the arguments for and against this position.

When the term is applied to modern works, it is often in reference to previous works which are generally agreed upon to be manipulations of statistical or scientific data in order to justify prejudices, such as much of the work done by Cesare Lombroso and Madison Grant. To call much earlier works in science 'scientific racism', however, runs the risk of ahistoricism. Some of the work of Charles Darwin, for example, contains many statements which would be considered racist (or 'scientific racism') in the current scientific and cultural context, but in their time were only to be expected, historically, from a 19th-century British scholar.

Cultural racism is one of several terms that scholars have coined to describe and explain new racial ideologies and practices that have emerged since World War II. The postwar era has seen the demise of overt forms of racism in Europe, North America, Australia, and the global postcolonial world. Reeling from the horrors of Nazism, Europe and other Western nations formally rejected racist values and established antiracism legislation. The world community, through the 1966 United Nations International Convention on the Elimination of All Forms of Racial Discrimination, put itself on record as opposing racism. There is general agreement that these new forms are both complex and subtle and that they operate in ways that do not require the formal assistance of educational, legal, and other institutions. Several terms have emerged to characterize what is sometimes called 'the new racism' or, perhaps, racisms. These include laissez-faire racism, cultural fundamentalism, unmarked racisms, neoracism, color-blind racism, and cultural racism. Cultural racism is not yet a standard label in the race and racism literature. It is virtually absent in the anthropological literature and has only recently appeared in the U.S. sociological literature (Bonilla-Silva 2003).

4

Assessment of Racial Discrimination

There are many different methods for assessing racial discrimination. We review three types of methods that are widely used in various literatures: controlled laboratory experiments and field experiments; analysis of observational data and natural experiments; and measures of reported perceptions and experiences of discrimination from surveys and administrative records. It is important to note that no one method allows researchers to address all of the measurement issues listed above. For example, laboratory experiments help researchers to identify the mechanisms that may lead to different forms of racial discrimination and the factors that mediate the expression of discriminatory attitudes and behaviours. Because of experimental control over relevant variables, researchers are able to identify whether race or the interaction of race and other factors triggers an expression of racial discrimination. Laboratory experiments are useful for drawing causal inferences at the individual level and important for identifying subtle mechanisms of discrimination; however, they do not directly address disparities in the aggregate. That is, laboratory effects do not often generalize to the broader population and can rarely tell us the extent to which naturally observed disparities are the result of discrimination.

The results of field experiments, on the other hand, are often more generalizable than the results of laboratory experiments. Although field experiments may involve less experimental control, researchers can use them to measure the extent of discrimination in a particular domain, such as the housing or labour market. For instance, audit studies in the housing or employment arena can provide useful information about the possible occurrence of discrimination by real estate agents against homebuyers or by employers against job applicants from disadvantaged racial groups. Some ability to generalize may also be gained by using nonexperimental approaches. Researchers can use statistical modeling and estimation to analyze observational data and draw causal inferences. Statistical models are useful for identifying associations between race and different outcomes while controlling for other factors that may explain the observed outcomes. Simply identifying an association with race, however, is not equivalent to measuring the magnitude of racial discrimination or its contribution to differential outcomes by race. In most observational settings, the lack of experimental control and the inability to manipulate 'treatment' variables make it difficult to dismiss alternative explanations of causation without relying on strong and often untestable assumptions.

One problem is that observational data often contain only a small set of characteristics and may not include variables that are important for explaining an observed effect or for modeling the process by which discrimination could occur. For instance, a finding of a large discriminatory effect within a domain (*e.g.*, differential treatment in hiring leading to wage disparities) may be erroneous if it is not possible to control for other explanatory variables, such as motivation or skill level, or to develop an accurate statistical model of the decision process. Alternatively, a finding that discrimination at a certain point within a domain contributes little to an observed disparity may ignore the possible effects of how earlier discrimination may have accumulated over time; for example, discrimination in secondary education can affect skill levels, and thereby affect subsequent wages.

Surveys also provide observational data to measure racial attitudes and reported experiences and perceptions of racial discrimination. But again, these data are rarely sufficient to establish causality, statistically or substantively. The most detailed observational studies are collections of case studies, which contain large amounts of information on small numbers of individuals or organizations. Such collections of case studies can produce the kinds of information on underlying behavioural processes needed to draw valid causal inferences, although their results may be limited in generalizability. Longitudinal survey data can be particularly helpful for understanding trends in racial attitudes and reported experiences and perceptions of discrimination and the extent to which racial disparities are a function of discrimination that occurs over time and across domains.

Determining how much of an observed outcome is an effect of racial discrimination is difficult. Translating effects from experimental data to what is observed in real situations is not easy. Moreover, it is much easier to assess the occurrence of discrimination at one point in a process than to identify effects of discrimination that occur earlier in a process or across relevant domains. A feasible solution to these difficulties may be to combine methods, using data and results from multiple sources. In the following five chapters, we describe issues and methods for research design, measurement, and analysis that together may allow researchers to identify and assess racial discrimination. When appropriate, each chapter contains conclusions and recommendations.

We begin by introducing a general framework for inferring causation between race-based discrimination and outcomes of interest. Racial disparities are often substantial and widely observed, but only rarely do researchers directly observe discriminatory behaviour. To establish a causal relationship between race and discrimination, one would ideally vary the race of a single person and measure any differences in outcomes. Because doing so is impossible, researchers typically observe a disparate outcome and trace back through the process that generated it to determine whether racial discrimination had a causal effect. In other words, they attempt to answer retrospectively the counterfactual question of whether the outcome for a nonwhite individual would have been different if he or she had been white. In this chapter we discuss how accumulated scientific evidence from both experimental and observational research may support causal conclusions and allow researchers to determine whether racial discrimination contributes causally to an observed racial disparity.

Controlled experiments, whose strengths are direct manipulation of experimental conditions and randomization, are ideal for drawing causal inferences and come closest to addressing the above counterfactual question.

We critically review the issues that must be addressed to draw valid causal inferences about racial discrimination from analyses of observational data. We first review the primary descriptive approach used in the literature on racial discrimination—decomposition of racial disparities. We then discuss the limitations of such descriptive analysis and the challenges of moving from description to inference by using statistical models (particularly regression models). We focus on the assumptions underlying statistical models and possible approaches to the problems of using such models to infer discrimination, one of which is to take advantage of natural experiments, which occur when a policy change targets discrimination in a particular domain or set of domains.

Our primary intent in this chapter is to consider the use of observational data from surveys, in-depth interviews, and administrative records to measure the occurrence of racially discriminatory attitudes and behaviours and people's reported perceptions of and experiences with discrimination. We provide extended reviews of major large-scale surveys of racial attitudes and reported perceptions and experiences of racial discrimination by white and black Americans. Finally, we provide an example of the challenges of measuring racial discrimination in an important area of current concern, which is racial profiling by law enforcement officials in which race alone or in combination with other variables is used to select individuals for further investigation (*e.g.*, to stop motorists to search for illegal drugs). Profiling is a form of statistical discrimination. We discuss some of the methodological challenges of determining when racial profiling may be occurring, although these challenges are such that we are not able to identify the best measurement approaches.

CAUSAL METHOD OF ASSESSMENT

Because discriminatory behaviour can rarely be directly observed, researchers face the challenge of determining when racial discrimination has actually occurred and whether it explains some portion of a racially disparate outcome. Those who attempt to identify the presence or absence of discrimination typically observe an individual's race (*e.g.*, black) and a particular outcome (*e.g.*, earnings) and try to determine whether that outcome would have been different had the individual been of a different race (*e.g.*, white). In other words, to measure discrimination researchers must answer the counterfactual question: What would have happened to a nonwhite individual if he or she had been white? Answering this question is fundamental to being able to conclude that there is a causal relationship between race and discrimination, which, in turn, is necessary to conclude that race-based discriminatory behaviours or processes contributed to an observed differential outcome.

To illustrate the problem, we turn to a classic Dr. Seuss book, *The Sneetches* (published in 1961), which describes a society of two races distinguished by markings on their bellies. In the story, one race of Sneetches is afforded certain privileges for having stars on their bellies, and the other race, lacking these markings, is denied those same privileges. There are, however, Star-On and Star-Off machines that can alter the belly and therefore the race of both Plain-Belly and Star-Belly Sneetches. Thanks to these machines, an individual Sneetch's racial status and various outcomes could be observed more than once, both as a Plain-Belly and a Star-Belly Sneetch.

In *The Sneetches*, belly-based discrimination is evident in the society; the causal relationship between race and discrimination can be ascertained because stars can be placed on or removed from any belly by a machine, and multiple outcomes can be observed for a single Sneetch. Therefore, one could readily answer the counterfactual question, saying with certainty what would have happened to a Plain-Belly Sneetch had he or she been a Star-Belly Sneetch (or vice versa). The phenomenon of a black individual passing as white (or vice versa) is an example of how race can be manipulated in this way in our society; thus, it is potentially interpretable causally. However, almost all the information on passing is anecdotal and there are few attempts to measure it systematically. Except under these circumstances, it is nearly impossible in the real world to observe the difference in outcomes across race for a single person; one must instead draw causal inferences.

Drawing Causal Inferences

In the context of measuring racial discrimination, researchers have developed alternative methods to answer the above counterfactual question and assess the incidence and effects of racial discrimination. A formal account of the counterfactual approach to causal inference provides a foundation for evaluating alternative solutions. Counterfactual analysis, combining elements of counterfactual and manipulability theories, is the dominant causal paradigm in recent literature in statistics. The past two decades have witnessed a growing literature formalizing the assumptions and the deductive process needed to draw cause-and-effect inferences from statistical data (Freedman, 2003; Holland, 1986, 2003). The counterfactual approach to causal inference underlies work in sociology, appearing in both methodological discourse and substantive applications (Gamoran and Mare, 1989; Lucas and Gamoran, 1991, 2002; Morgan, 2001; Sobel, 1995, 1996; Winship and Morgan, 1999; Winship and Sobel, 2004). Central to such cause-and-effect inferences is the notion of the manipulability of the potential causal variable, such as race. Because race cannot be directly manipulated or randomly allocated to study participants, researchers must be able to translate experimental results into a framework that allows them to address, in some form, causal statements regarding evidence of discrimination. Holland (2003) makes this point in detail and reiterates his earlier (1986) argument that one cannot have causation without manipulation. However, Holland also argues for the careful study of the interactions of race with manipulable variables. See Marini and Singer (1988) for a different perspective on causation.

As suggested above, causal questions are counterfactual questions. The causal effect of racial discrimination is the difference between two outcomes: the outcome if the individual were black and the outcome if the individual were white. Rubin (1974) describes the fundamental problem—the inability to simultaneously observe different outcomes for the same person—as a missing data problem: Each individual has potential outcomes under each set of circumstances, but only one of these outcomes is observed (or realized). The causal effect of interest is the difference between these potential outcomes—that is, the effect of racial discrimination. The entire enterprise of causal inference is centered on alternative approaches for overcoming our inability to observe both of these outcomes for a single individual. Imagine we want to estimate the effect of discrimination on earnings as experienced by a black person. At the individual level, the unit causal effect of racial discrimination (here, discrimination against a black individual) is

$$Y_b - Y_w,$$

where Y_b represents the black individual's potential earnings, and Y_w repre- sents the potential earnings if the same individual were white. However, we observe only Y, one of the two potential outcomes (Y_b or Y_w), depending on whether the individual is, in fact, black or white. To draw a causal inference about the incidence and effect of racial discrimination, the researcher reframes the question at the population level and then exploits knowledge of population averages of outcomes among aggregates of members of a racial group to estimate the average effect of racial discrimination.

Study Design and Statistical Methods

Research design is critical to the ability to draw causal inferences from data analysis. For purposes of causal inference, there is a hierarchy of approaches to data collection. As one moves from meticulously designed and executed laboratory experiments through the variety of studies based on observational data, increasingly strong assumptions are needed to support the claim that *X* 'causes' *Y*. The more careful and rigorous the design and control, the stronger are the inferences that can be drawn, provided that the design and control are used to address the causal question of interest.

Experimental Designs

The randomized controlled experiment is typically found at the top of the hierarchy of methodological approaches in terms of rigor and control. Such experiments involve direct manipulation of experimental treatments and random assignment of participants to treatments, which is believed to result in a balancing over unmeasured (and sometimes measured) variables whose effects must be controlled for if one is to infer causation. Controlled experiments have *internal validity* associated with inferences about causation for the units of study in the experiment (*i.e.*, the participant sample). But additional or extra-experimental information is required to achieve *external validity* whereby researchers can generalize from the units in the experiment to some larger population.

One way to achieve external validity is to draw experimental participants from the population of interest. Another is to carry out a series of replications designed to allow for generalization from the set of experiments. Many researchers argue for the 'universality' of the causal phenomenon measured in their experiment (*i.e.*, the effect holds more generally, independently of both the other variables and context), but there is serious uncertainty about this claim in the absence of replications or other extra-experimental information. Many experimenters also argue for the role of experiments as demonstrations of the plausibility of particular causal processes, that is, as an existence proof that a particular phenomenon can, under at least some circumstances, occur in a particular manner. But this demonstration of plausibility does not address the issue of external validity. In any well-designed and well-executed experiment, randomization allows researchers to dismiss competing explanations as highly unlikely, but they are not entirely eliminated. For this reason, independent replication is important.

Holland (2003), in addressing related issues of causation and race, attempts to distinguish among three types of causal questions: (1) identifying causes, (2) assessing effects, and (3) describing mechanisms. Identifying causes is often a form of speculative postmortem. Randomized experiments are used to assess effects, but Holland argues that they can rarely be used to measure the effects of discrimination. On the other hand, Holland's notion of describing mechanisms relates to what this report refers to as understanding the process whereby discrimination may be occurring. He argues that to conduct an experiment one does not need to fully describe mecha- nisms. This report views the effort to measure the unobserved counterfactual usually associated with experiments as necessarily being linked to a detailed understanding of the process.

The Roles of Randomization and Manipulation

Researchers justify the substitution of population-level expectations for individual-level outcomes by designing experiments that incorporate ele- ments of randomization and manipulability. Experiments allow us to distinguish more readily between prediction (or association) and causation (or intervention or manipulation). To predict a random variable Y from the variable X, we attempt to measure or estimate expected values or probabilities like

$$\Pr(Y = y \mid \text{Observe } X = x),$$

which is the probability that an outcome Y is equal to y, given that we have observed that some characteristic X is equal to x (*e.g.*, lung cancer is more frequent among cigarette smokers). In contrast, to infer that smoking cigarettes *causes* an increase in the risk of lung cancer, we attempt to measure or estimate

$$\Pr(Y = y \mid \text{Set } X = x),$$

which is the probability that an outcome Y is equal to y, given that we have an assigned value of x for the random variable X. That is, in experiments designed to demonstrate causation, researchers manipulate X, setting its value for each experimental unit. By using different values of the quantity X for different units in the study, researchers are able to compare outcomes conditional on each value of *X*; thus, they are able to estimate causal effects. In the first case, one estimates an association; in the second case, one estimates an effect.

To infer a causal relationship, researchers must eliminate alternative explanations. This is an omitted variable bias problem: Researchers must account for systematic effects of potentially omitted factors that both affect the outcome and are associated with the 'cause' of interest. For example, in objecting to the hypothesized causal relationship between smoking cigarettes and lung cancer, noted statistician R. A. Fisher (1935) suggested that people's genetic makeup might predispose them both to smoking and to developing lung cancer. This alternative explanation for the association between smoking and lung cancer was dismissed only after studies of identical twins revealed that a smoking twin was more likely to develop lung cancer than a nonsmoking twin (see further discussion below).

Randomization addresses the omitted variable problem by introducing a new random quantity, R, that identifies which treatment is assigned to the unit. Thus, for those units that are randomized according to the value $R = x_1$, we set $X = x_1$, and for those units that are randomized according to the value $R = x_2$, we set $X = x_2$. By introducing the new random quantity, we set the value of X and at the same time balance (on average) both observed and unobserved covariates across values of X. That is, random assignment makes treatment status independent of the other covariates, both observed and unobserved. Here, manipulation allows us to identify the direction of the causal relationship and determine whether *X* causes *Y* or *Y* causes *X*. Together, randomization and manipulation legitimize the direct causal inferences from *X* to *Y*.

This result can be formalized within the counterfactual framework described above; here, we ask what would have happened to a unit for which we set $X = x_1$ had we instead set $X = x_2$ for that unit. Again, the problem is that in the randomized experiment the unit can take only one of these values. Once we have assigned $X = x_1$, we cannot go back and investigate what would have happened had we set $X = x_2$ under the identical circumstances. Therefore, we cannot identify a causal effect for a specific unit. Note that this parallels the problem of identifying, at the individual level, the effect of racial discrimination. What we can infer, however, is the value of

$$\alpha = E(Y \mid X = x_1) - E(Y \mid X = x_2)$$

using averages across the distribution of Y. That is, we can infer the value of α, the average effect, from the difference in the expected values of Y when X is equal to x_1 and when X is equal to x_2. Randomization actually allows us to do this by using the $X = x_1$ group to measure $E(Y \mid X = x_1)$ and the $X = x_2$ group to measure $E(Y \mid X = x_2)$. That is, as alluded to above, we exploit knowledge of population averages of outcomes among multiple groups to estimate the causal effect. Because randomization has balanced the distribution of potential confounding variables across each group, this is an unbiased estimate of the average causal effect of X. Rubin (1976, 1978) provides a careful explication of this result, although different aspects of the result are implicit in the early descriptions of randomization in Neyman (1923) and Fisher (1935). As we have shown, counterfactuals go hand in hand with the notion of manipulation, but in practice they are rarely acknowledged as integral parts of the randomized controlled experiment.

Weighing Evidence from Multiple Studies

How is causality established in the absence of a perfectly designed and implemented experiment? It is possible to provide a stronger argument for causal inference by combining methods—from laboratory studies of proposed mechanisms, to field experiments demonstrating external validity, to natural experiments demonstrating policy relevance and efficacy. Researchers can learn how the accumulation of evidence from multiple sources with a variety of research designs contributes to causal inference by examining a widely cited example of inferring causation in nonexperimental settings—the connection between smoking and lung cancer. The case of smoking and lung cancer illustrates how researchers can draw causal inferences in the absence of any single study that alone would have conclusively demonstrated a causal relationship. This causal link was not accepted until findings to that effect had consistently been produced in multiple settings and in varied study designs, both observational and experimental.

EXPERIMENTAL METHODS OF ASSESSMENT

As we discussed in above, at the core of assessing discrimination is a causal inference problem. When racial disparities in life outcomes occur, explicit or subtle prejudice leading to discriminatory behaviour and processes is a possible cause, so that the outcomes could represent, at least in part, the effect of discrimination. Accurately determining what constitutes the effect of discrimination, personal choice, and other related and unrelated factors requires the ability to draw clear causal inferences. In this chapter, we review two experimental approaches that have been used by researchers to reach causal conclusions about racial discrimination: laboratory experiments and field experiments.

Experimental Design

To permit valid causal inferences about racial discrimination, the design of an experiment and the analytic method used in conjunction with that design must address several issues. First, there are frequently intervening or confounding variables that are not of direct interest but that may affect the outcome. The effects of these variables must be accounted for in the study design and analysis. In controlled laboratory experiments, the investigator manipulates a variable of interest, randomly assigns participants to different conditions of the variable or treatments, and measures their responses to the manipulation while attempting to control for other relevant conditions or attributes. As described in the previous chapter, randomization greatly increases the likelihood of being able to infer that an observed difference between the treatment and control groups is causal. Observing a difference in outcome between the groups of participants can be the basis for a causal inference. In controlled field experiments, researchers analyze the results of a deliberately manipulated factor of interest, such as the race of an interviewer. They attempt to control carefully for any intervening or confounding variables. Random assignment of treatments to participants is frequently used to reduce any doubts about lingering effects of unobserved variables, provided, of course, that one can actually apply the randomization to the variable of interest.

In addition to the problem of credibly designing an experiment that supports a causal inference, a common weakness of experiments is a lack of external validity. That is, the results of the experiment may not generalize to individuals other than those enrolled in the experiment, or to different areas or populations with different economic or sociological environments, or to attributes that differ from those tested in the experiment. Despite these problems, the strengths of experiments for answering some types of questions are undeniable. Even if their results may not be completely generalizable and even if they do not always capture all the relevant aspects of the issue of interest, experiments provide more credible evidence than other methods for measuring the effects of an attribute (*e.g.*, race) in one location and on one population.

Using Experiments to Measure Racial Discrimination

Use of an experimental design to measure racial discrimination raises important questions because race cannot be directly manipulated or assigned randomly to participants. Researchers who use randomized controlled experiments to measure discrimination, therefore, can manipulate race by either varying the 'apparent' race of a target person as the experimental treatment or can manipulate 'apparent' discrimination by randomly assigning study participants to being treated with different degrees of discrimination.

In the first case, the experimenter varies the treatment, namely, the apparent race, by such means as by providing race-related cues on job applications (*e.g.*, name or school attended) or by showing photographs to participants in which the only differences are skin color and facial features. The experimenter then measures whether participants respond differently under one race treatment compared with another (*e.g.*, evaluating black versus white job applicants or associating positive or negative attributes with photographs of blacks versus whites). In such a study, the experimenter elicits responses from the participants to determine the effect of apparent race on their behaviour (*e.g.*, whether the participants engage in discriminatory behaviour toward black and not white applicants). That is, they measure the behaviour of potential discriminators toward targets of different races. If successful, then finding a difference in behaviour would indicate an effect of race.

In the second instance, experimenters randomly assign participants to be treated differently, that is, either with or without discrimination. This type of experiment attempts to measure the response to discrimination rather than directly measure the expression of discrimination—that is, it measures the behaviour of potential targets of discrimination. Because race cannot be experimentally manipulated, an explicit specification of the behavioural process is needed that allows the translation of results from such experiments into causal statements about the actual discrimination mechanism measured in the experiment (*i.e.*, the extent to which the experimenter can manipulate some other factor related to race, such as perception). To our knowledge, no one has attempted to carry out such formal reverse reasoning, and we believe that doing so is especially crucial when arguing for the external validity of experimental results.

One of the few examples of attempts to perform similar inferential reversals is the special case of understanding odds ratios (and adjusted odds ratios) in the context of comparing retrospective and prospective studies on categorical variables. In retrospective studies, the data are collected only after the treatment has taken place, whereas in prospective studies the data are collected on possible covariates before treatment and on outcomes after the treatment. If one has both categorical explanatory and categorical response variables, one can estimate their relationship in the prospective study based on a retrospective sample. If the logistic causal model is correct, the inference about the key causal coefficient from the retrospective study is the same as if one had done a prospective sampling on the explanatory variable. Those results, however, do not generalize to relationships among continuous variables.

Laboratory Experiments: Design

Laboratory experiments, like all experiments, include the standard features of (1) an independent variable that researchers can manipulate (*i.e.*, assign conditions or treatments to participants); (2) random assignment to treatment conditions; and (3) control over extraneous variables that otherwise might be confounded with the independent variable of interest, potentially undermining the interpretation of causality. Laboratory experiments occur in a controlled setting, chosen for its ability to minimize confounding variables and other extraneous stimuli.

Laboratory experiments on discrimination would ideally measure reactions to the exact same person while manipulating only that person's race. As noted above, while strictly speaking one cannot manipulate the actual race of a single person, experimenters do typically either manipulate the apparent race of a target person or randomly assign subjects or study participants to the experimental condition while attempting to hold constant all other attributes of possible relevance. One common method of varying race is for experimenters to train several experimental confederates—both black and white—to interact with study participants according to a prepared script, to dress in comparable style, and to represent comparable levels of baseline physical attractiveness (Cook and Pelfrey, 1985; Dovidio *et al.*, 2002; Henderson-King and Nisbett, 1996; Stephan and Stephan, 1989). Another common method of varying race involves preparing written materials and either incidentally indicating race or attaching a photograph of a black or white person to the materials (Linville and Jones, 1980).

Effects of race occur in concert with other situational or personal factors, called 'moderator variables', that may increase or decrease the effect of race on the participants' responses. In addition to manipulating a person's apparent race, for example, investigators may manipulate the person's apparent success or failure, cooperation or competition, helpfulness, friendliness, dialect, or credentials (Cook and Pelfrey, 1985; Dovidio *et al.*, 2002; Henderson-King and Nisbett, 1996; Linville and Jones, 1980; Stephan and Stephan, 1989). Even more often, experimenters will manipulate features of the situation expected to moderate levels of bias toward black and white targets; examples involve anonymity, potential retaliation, norms, motivation, time pressure, and distraction (Crosby *et al.*, 1980). Finally, the study participants frequently are black and white college students (Crosby *et al.*, 1980; Correll *et al.*, 2002; Judd *et al.*, 1995).

Strengths of Laboratory Experiments

Laboratory experiments, if well designed and executed, can have high levels of internal validity for causal inference—that is, they are designed to measure exactly what causes what. The direction of causality follows from the manipulation of randomly assigned independent variables that control for two kinds of unwanted, extraneous effects: systematic (confounding) variables and random (noise) variables. Laboratory experiments are the method of choice for isolating a single variable of interest, particularly when fine-tuned manipulation of precisely defined independent variables is required. Laboratory studies also allow precise measurement of dependent variables (such as response time or inches in seating distance). The laboratory setting gives experimenters a great degree of control over the attention of participants, potentially allowing them to maximize the impact of the manipulation in an otherwise bland environment.

Because of these fine-grained methods, laboratory experiments on discrimination are well suited to examining psychological processes. Both face-to-face interactions and processes in which single individuals react to racial stimuli are readily studied in such experiments. The most sophisticated experiments show not only the effect of some variable (*e.g.*, expectancies) on an outcome variable (*e.g.*, discriminatory behaviour) but also the mechanism or process that mediates the effect (*e.g.*, biased interpretations, nonverbal hostility, stereotypic associations). That is, when an experiment manipulates the apparent race of two otherwise equivalent job candidates or interaction partners Dovidio *et al.*, 2002; Word *et al.*, 1974), the experiment ideally should also measure some of the proposed explanatory psychological mechanisms (such as emotional prejudices and cognitive stereotypes, either implicit or explicit), as well as the predicted discrimination. A hallmark of the better laboratory experiments is that they not only test useful theories but also show how important, compelling phenomena (*e.g.*, the automaticity of discrimination) can and do occur. Laboratory studies often show that very small, subtle alterations in a situation can have substantial effects on important outcome variables.

Measuring Racial Discrimination

Experimenters measure varying degrees of discrimination. Laboratory measures of discrimination begin with verbal hostility (*e.g.*, in studies of interracial aggression), which can constitute discrimination, when, for example, negative personal comments result in a hostile work environment . At the next level are disparaging written ratings of an individual member of a particular group (Talaska *et al.*, 2003). If unjustified, such negative evaluations can constitute discrimination in a school or workplace. At the subtle behavioural level, laboratory studies measure nonverbal indicators of hostility, such as seating distance or tone of voice (Crosby *et al.*, 1980). Related nonverbal measures include coding of overt facial expressions, as well as measurement of minute nonvisible movements in the facial muscles that constitute the precursors of a frown. Experimenters study these nonverbal behaviours because they, too, could result in a hostile environment.

Moving up a level, laboratory measures of discriminatory avoidance include participants' choice of whether to associate or work with a member of a racial outgroup, volunteer to help an organization, or provide direct aid to an outgroup member who requests it (Talaska *et al.*, 2003). In a laboratory setting, segregation can be measured by how people constitute small groups or choose leaders in organizational teams (Levine and Moreland, 1998; Pfeffer, 1998). Finally, aggression against outgroups can be measured in laboratory settings by competitive games or teacher–learner scenarios in which one person is allowed to punish another—an outgroup member—with low levels of shock, blasts of noise, or other aversive experiences (Crosby *et al.*, 1980; Talaska *et al.*, 2003).

A review of laboratory studies as of the early 1980s (Crosby *et al.*, 1980) summarized the findings as follows. Experiments on unobtrusive forms of bias and prejudice showed that white bias was more prevalent than indicated by surveys. Experiments on helping, aggressive, and nonverbal behaviours indicated that (1) whites tended to help whites more often than they helped blacks, especially when they did not have to face the person in need of help directly; (2) under sanctioned conditions (*e.g.*, in competitive games or administration of punishment), whites acted aggressively against blacks more than against whites but only when the consequences to the aggressor were low (under conditions of no retaliation, no censure, and anonymity); and (3) white nonverbal behaviour displayed a discrepancy between verbal nondiscrimination and nonverbal hostility or discomfort, betrayed in tone of voice, seating distance, and the like.

Since the 1980s, laboratory experiments on discrimination have concentrated more on measuring subtle forms of bias and less on examining overt behaviours, such as helping others. This shift occurred precisely because of the discrepancy between some people's overtly egalitarian responses on surveys and their discriminatory responses when they think no one is looking, or at least when they have a nonprejudiced excuse for their discriminatory behaviour.

Limitations of Laboratory Experiments

Laboratory experiments usually are limited in time and measurement, so they generally do not aim to answer questions about behaviour over long periods of time or behaviour related to entire batteries of measures. The purpose of a laboratory experiment may include one or more of the following: (1) to demonstrate that an effect indeed can occur, at least under some conditions, with some people, for some period of time; (2) to create a simulation or microcosm that includes the most important factors; (3) to create a realistic psychological situation that is intrinsically compelling; or (4) to test a theory that has obvious larger importance.

Laboratory experiments are also at risk for various biases related to the settings in which they occur. For example, they may be set up in such a narrow, constraining way that the participants have no choice but to respond as the experimenters expect (Orne, 1962). Crafting more subtle manipulations and providing true choice in response options can sometimes be used to limit the potential biases in such cases. In addition, the experimenter may inadvertently bias presentation of the manipulations and measures, so that participants are equally inadvertently induced to confirm the hypotheses (Rosenthal, 1976). This problem can often be addressed using double-blind methods, in which experimenters as well as participants are not aware of the treatment assigned to them. Participants may also worry about whether their behaviour is socially acceptable (Marlow and Crowne, 1961) and fail to react spontaneously. Nonreactive, unobtrusive, disguised measurement can avert this problem. It is worth noting that not all of these issues are unique to the laboratory. Many of the potential biases and artifacts of laboratory experiments also occur at least as often in other kinds of experiments (*e.g.*, field experiments, which we turn to next), as well as with nonexperimental methods (natural experiments and observational studies, such as surveys).

BOX -1

The Effect of Psychological Mechanisms on Measures of Discriminating Behaviour

Laboratory experiments can create working definitions of manipulated race, randomly assign participants to interact with black or white confederates, and measure a variety of proposed psychological mechanisms (implicit and explicit attitudes) to determine their effect on various types of discriminatory behaviour. For example, Dovidio *et al.* (2002) conducted a multiphase experiment on how whites' explicit and implicit racial attitudes predict bias and perceptions of bias in interracial interactions. At the beginning of the term, white college students completed a 20-item standardized measure of prejudice, the Attitudes Toward Blacks Scale. Later in the semester, 40 students

(15 male and 25 female) participated in what they believed to be two separate studies. In the first, a decision task required participants to respond as quickly as possible—after the letter P or H was displayed on a computer screen—as to whether a given word displayed for each trial could ever describe a person or a house. Unbeknownst to them, on critical trials versus practice trials the letter P was preceded by a standardized schematic sketch of a black or white man or woman, presented at subliminal speeds (0.250 seconds). This level of presentation has been shown repeatedly to prime relevant associations in memory and, in particular, stereotypes. As in countless other studies (*e.g.*, see Fazio and Olson, 2003), the findings in this study revealed subtle forms of stereotypic association when people responded more quickly to negative words ('bad', 'cruel', 'untrustworthy') preceded by a black face and to positive words ('good', 'kind', 'trustworthy') preceded by a white face, and more slowly to the converse combinations. As is typical with this method, no participant reported being aware of the subliminal faces. Such studies show how researchers can measure automatic and unconscious racial bias, regardless of expressed levels of prejudice (Devine, 1989). At this point, then, the experimenters had access to two kinds of attitudes—the explicit ones expressed on the questionnaire and the implicit ones suggested by the participants' speed of stereotypic associations. These are the psychological causes of different kinds of discrimination hypothesized in the next step.

In what participants assumed to be a separate study focused on acquaintance processes, the participants met separately with two inter- action partners—one white and one black—for a 3-minute conversation about dating in the current era. Five white and four black student confederates, trained to behave comparably to each other, played the role of interaction partners. All were unaware of the study's hypotheses and the participants' levels of implicit and explicit prejudice. After each interaction, both the participant and the confederate (in separate rooms) completed scales assessing their own and each other's perceived friendliness (pleasant and not cold, unfriendly, unlikable, or cruel). Two coders used the same scales to rate, separately, participants' verbal and nonverbal behaviour, respectively, from audiotapes and from videotapes on which only the participant was visible. Two more coders rated participants' overall friendliness from audio and video information combined. Analyses compared the differences in the participants' responses to the white and black confederates as rated by the participants themselves, the confederates, and the observers.

Two patterns of response emerged: one an explicit and overt sequence of processes, and the other an implicit and subtle sequence of processes. The explicit sequence involved overt measures of verbal behaviour. White participants' scores on the attitudes questionnaire and their self-reported friendliness (both measures of explicit, overt prejudice) correlated with each other; that is, whites' self-reported attitudes predicted bias in verbal friendliness toward black relative to white confederates. These measures also correlated with verbal friendliness as rated by observers from audiotapes (a measure of explicit, overt discriminatory behaviour).

In contrast, the implicit sequence of processes was indicated by responses to subliminal primes (an implicit, subtle measure of prejudice), which correlated significantly with a series of implicit, subtle forms of discriminatory behaviour: nonverbal behaviour rated by observers from silent videotapes, confederate perceptions of participants' friendliness, and overall friendliness rated by other observers, which also correlated significantly with each other. In other words, whites' implicit attitudes predicted their bias and others' perceptions of bias in nonverbal friendliness. None of the explicit and implicit measures correlated significantly with each other, indicating that the implicit and explicit sequences are independent. Each sequence is important: Effect sizes were moderate to large by social science standards.

Translating Experimental Effects

Laboratory experiments are useful for measuring psychological mechanisms that lead to discriminatory behaviour (*e.g.*, implicit or explicit stereotypes), but they do not describe the frequency of occurrence of such behaviour in the world. They cannot, by their nature, say how often or how much a particular phenomenon occurs, such as what proportion of a racial disparity is a function of discriminatory behaviour. Thus, they can be legitimately criticized on the grounds of low external validity– -that is, limited generalizability to other samples, other settings, and other measures. Laboratory experimenters can sometimes make a plausible case for generalizability by varying plausible factors that might limit the applicability of the experiment. For example, if there are theoretically or practically compelling reasons for suspecting that an effect is limited to college sophomores, one might also replicate the study with business executives on campus for a seminar or retirees passing through for an Airstream conference. But laboratory experiments rarely randomly sample participants from the population of interest. Thus by themselves they cannot address external validity, and it is an empirical question whether or how well their findings translate into discrimination occurring in the larger population. In well-designed and well-executed experiments, the effects of confounding variables are randomized, allowing researchers to dismiss competing explanations as unlikely, but they are not entirely eliminated. For this reason, replication is important. In the study of discrimination, there are many laboratory experiment results that do not generalize in field settings. Findings either may diminish or not hold up over time. However, many other effects tested both in the laboratory and in the field have been consistent, some showing even stronger effects in the field (Brewer and Brown, 1998; Crosby *et al.*, 1980; Johnson and Stafford, 1998).

Field Experiments: Design

Field experiments have many of the standard features commonly found in laboratory experiments. The term *field experiment* refers to any fully randomized research design in which people or other observational units found in a natural setting are assigned to treatment and control conditions. The typical field experiment uses a two-group, post-test-only control group design (Campbell and Stanley,

1963). In such a design, people are randomly assigned to treatment and control groups. An experimental manipulation is administered to the treatment group, and an outcome measure is obtained for both treatment and control groups. Because of random assignment, differences between the two groups provide some evidence of an effect of the manipulation. However, because no preexperiment measure for the outcome is obtained (which is an option in laboratory experiments), one cannot be altogether sure whether the groups are similar prior to the experiment. Nonetheless, randomization protects against this problem because it ensures that, on average, the two groups are similar except for the treatment.

Field experiments are attractive and often persuasive because, when done well, they can eliminate many of the obstacles to valid statistical inference. They can measure the impact of differential treatment more cleanly than nonexperimental approaches, yet they have the advantage of occurring in a realistic setting and hence are more directly generalizable than laboratory experiments. Furthermore, for measuring discrimination, they appear to reflect the broader public vision of what discrimination means—the treatment of two (nearly) identical people differently. The social scientific knowledge necessary to design effective field experiments is stronger in some areas than in others. For example, our knowledge of the mechanisms and incentives underlying real estate markets is arguably more advanced than our knowledge of the incentives underlying labour markets (Yinger, 1995). Hence, our ability to use field experiments is correspondingly stronger for measuring behaviour in housing markets than in other areas. We, therefore, focus our discussion below on a common methodology—audit or paired testing—used particularly to assess discrimination in housing markets as well as in other areas.

Audit or Paired-Testing Methodology

Audit or paired-testing methodology is commonly used to measure the level or frequency of discrimination in particular markets, usually in the labour market or in housing (Ross, 2002; Bendick *et al.*, 1994; Fix *et al.*, 1993; Neumark, 1996; Riach and Rich, 2002).

Auditors or testers are randomly assigned to pairs (one of each race) and matched on equivalent characteristics (*e.g.*, socioeconomic status), credentials (*e.g.*, education), tastes, and market needs. Members of each pair are typically trained to act in a similar fashion and are equipped with identical supporting documents. To avoid research subjects becoming suspicious when they confront duplicate sets of supporting documents, researchers sometimes vary the documents while keeping them similar enough that the two testers have equivalent levels of support.

As part of the study, testers are sent sequentially to a series of relevant locations to obtain goods or services or to apply for employment, housing, or college admission (Dion, 2001; Esmail and Everington, 1993; Fix *et al.*, 1993; National Research Council, 1989; Schuman *et al.*, 1983; Turner *et al.*, 1991a, 1991b; Yinger, 1995). The order of arrival at the location is randomly assigned. For example, in a study of hiring, testers have identical résumés and apply for jobs, whereas in a study of rental housing, they have identical rental histories and apply for housing. Once the study has been completed, researchers use the differences in treatment experienced by the testers as an estimate of discrimination. To the extent that testers are matched on a relevant set of nonracial characteristics, systematic differences by the race of the testers can be used to measure discrimination on the basis of race. Propensity score matching is sometimes used when there are too many relevant characteristics on which to match on every one. In propensity score matching, an index of similarity is created by fitting a logistic regression with the outcome variable being race and the explanatory variables being the relevant characteristics on which one wishes to match. Subjects of one race are then paired or matched with subjects of the other race having similar fitted logit values—the pro-pensity score index (Rosenbaum, 2002).

Paired-testing studies use an experimental design in natural settings to obtain information on apparently real outcomes and to assess the occurrence and prevalence of discrimination. An advantage to using paired tests is that individuals are matched on observed characteristics relevant to a particular market. Effective matching decreases the likelihood that differences are due to chance rather than discrimination because many factors are controlled for. Paired testing is used in audit studies, such as the U.S. Department of Housing and Urban Development's (HUD's) national study of housing discrimination, to estimate overall levels of discrimination against racial and ethnic minorities. Audit studies can be highly effective enforcement tools for assessing treatment or detecting unfavorable treatment of members of disadvantaged groups (Ross and Yinger, 2002). Studies in the housing market (Wienk *et al.*, 1979; Yinger, 1995) and in the labour market (Bendick *et al.*, 1994; Cross *et al.*, 1990; Neumark, 1996; Turner *et al.*, 1991b) using the paired-testing methodology provide evidence of discrimination against racial minorities (Ross and Yinger, 2002). In the case of housing, these studies might involve selecting a random sample of newspaper advertisements and then investigating the behaviour of real estate agencies associated with these advertisements (Ross and Yinger, 2002). Employment audits are similarly based on a random sample of advertised jobs. While providing the generality valued by researchers, these studies also make it possible to observe the behaviour of individual agencies or firms. This approach has been applied to other areas as well.

Much of the use of audit or paired-testing methodology to study discrimination flows primarily from federal investigations concerning housing discrimination. National results of the 2000 Housing Discrimination Study (2000 HDS), conducted by the Urban Institute for HUD, show that housing discrimination persists, although its incidence has declined since 1989 for African Americans and Hispanics. Non-Hispanic whites are consistently favored over African Americans and Hispanics in metropolitan rental and sales markets (Turner *et al.*, 2002b); similarly, Asians and Pacific Islanders in metropolitan areas nationwide (particularly homebuyers) face significant levels of discrimination (Turner *et al.*, 2003). In another example, Yinger (1986) studied the Boston housing rental and sales markets in 1981. In the rental market, whites discussed 17 percent more units with a rental agent and were invited to inspect 57 percent more units than blacks. In the sales market, whites discussed

35 percent more houses and were invited to inspect 34 percent more houses; moreover, the difference in treatment was larger for low-income families and families with children. Yinger also found substantial variation in treat- ment across neighborhoods. Taken together, these results document significant discrimination in the housing market.

Limitations of Audit Studies

Ross and Yinger (2002) discuss two main issues raised by researchers concerning the use of paired-testing methodology. They are (1) the accuracy of audit evidence and (2) its validity, particularly with respect to the target population. It is also worth noting that such studies typically require extensive effort to prepare and implement. They can be very expensive.

The Accuracy Issue

Many claim that the designs of audit studies are not true between-subjects experiments because research subjects (*e.g.*, employer or housing agent) are not assigned to treatment or control groups but are exposed to both treatment and control. Also, although the order of exposure for each subject is randomized so that it should balance out, the time lapse between exposures makes it possible for the difference to be unrelated to the concept of focus (*i.e.*, discrimination). In the time between two visits to an establishment, for example, someone else other than a tester may take the job or apartment of interest.

In the housing market, newspaper advertisements are used as a sampling frame (National Research Council, 2002b), but they may not accurately represent the sample of houses that are available or affordable to members of disadvantaged racial groups. Newspaper advertisements can be limiting because the sampling frame is restricted to members of disadvantaged racial groups who respond to typical advertisements and are qualified for the advertised housing unit or job. This limited sample may lead to a very specific interpretation of discrimination. For example, members of the sample may not be aware of alternative search strategies or know of other available housing units or jobs of interest. The practical difficulties associated with any sampling frame other than newspaper advertisements (and the associated steps of training auditors and assigning characteristics to them) are difficult to overcome.

The Validity Issue

Inferential target: estimating an effect of discrimination. Researchers have also debated the validity of audit studies (see the discussion in Ross and Yinger, 2002). Heckman and colleagues criticize the calculation of measures of discrimination (Heckman, 1998; Heckman and Siegelman, 1993). They argue that an estimate of discrimination at a randomly selected firm (or in an advertisement) does not measure the impact of discrimination in a market. Rather, discrimination should be measured by looking at (1) the average difference in the treatment of disadvantaged racial groups and whites or (2) the actual experience of the average member of a disadvantaged racial group, as opposed to examining the average experience of members of disadvantaged racial groups in a random sample of firms (*i.e.*, the focus should be on the average across the population of applicants rather than the population of firms). Both of these proposed approaches to measuring discrimination are valid, but each has limitations.

Researchers typically determine the incidence of discrimination by mea- suring (1) the proportion of cases in which a white tester reports more favorable treatment than a nonwhite tester reports (gross adverse treatment) or (2) the difference between the proportion of cases in which a white tester reports favorable treatment and the proportion of cases in which a nonwhite tester reports favorable treatment (net adverse treatment) (for further discussion of these measures, see Fix *et al.*, 1993; Heckman and Siegelman, 1993; Ondrich *et al.*, 2000; Ross, 2002). Because statistical measures are 'model-based' aggregates, net measures correctly measure the parameters in those models conditional on important stratifying variables. The gross measure may provide useful supplemental information to the net measure if the balancing disparities are large.

Ross and Yinger (2002) note that it would be valuable to know the true experiences of members of disadvantaged racial groups on average, but such information could not reveal the extent to which these individuals change their behaviour to avoid experiencing discrimination. As a result, discrimination encountered by averaging over members of a disadvantaged racial group is not a complete measure of the impact of racial discrimination (Holzer and Ludwig, 2003). It is valuable to determine how much discrimination exists before such behavioural responses take place—which is the amount estimated using paired testing—and whether discrimination arises under certain circumstances.

The key observation of Murphy (2002) relates to the inferential target: Are we interested in estimating an overall or a market-level discrimination effect? Several distinct effects might be estimated, and they need to be distinguished because the estimates that result will not necessarily be identical. What is the appropriate population of real estate agents or ads from which to sample? Do we want to use only those agents that minorities actually visit? If past discrimination affects choice of agent, this population may vary from the population of agents selling houses that members of a nonwhite population could reasonably afford. Thus, the estimated effect of discrimination will be different under these alternative sampling strategies. Would it make sense to sample from agents or ads that could not reasonably be expected to be appropriate for most members of the nonwhite population? Murphy recommends ascertaining "discrimination in situations in which Blacks are qualified buyers" (2002:72).

Auditor heterogeneity, Heckman and colleagues (Heckman, 1998; Heckman and Siegelman, 1993) also argue that average differences in treatment by race may be driven by differences in the unobserved characteristics of testers (*i.e.*, auditor heterogeneity) rather than by discrimination. Such characteristics (*e.g.*, accent, height, body language, or physical attractiveness) of one or the other member of the pair may have a significant impact on interpersonal interactions and judgments and thus lead to invalid results (Smith, 2002). The role of these characteristics cannot be eliminated because of the paucity of observations of the research subjects. Ross (2002) addresses the problem by suggesting that, instead of trying to match testers exactly (which is virtually impossible), one can train testers to ensure that their true characteristics, as opposed to their assigned characteristics, have little influence on their behaviour during the test.

Murphy (2002) addresses most of the issues raised by Heckman (1998) and discussed above. She lays out a framework showing that "as long as audit pairs are matched on all qualifications that vary in distribution by race, audit results averaged over realtors, circumstances of the visits, and auditors can be viewed as an unbiased estimate of overall-level discrimination" (Murphy, 2002:69). Murphy formally delineates the circumstances under which an estimate of discrimination will be erroneous if the researcher fails to account for individual auditor characteristics that do not vary in distribution by race and therefore were not used in the matching process.

The problem is the effect of the heterogeneity among applicants and agents. The strategy of matching on all characteristics that vary in distribution by race––including observed, unobserved, and unobservable character- istics—substitutes for randomization. The problem, of course, is that we do not know whether we have in fact matched on all characteristics that vary by race. If all unmatched characteristics have the same distribution across racial groups and if the auditors were selected to be representative of the distribution of these characteristics, we will have managed to balance the covariates across racial groups and can estimate an unbiased effect of race. But as Heckman and others note, there are a variety of reasons to believe that this goal of matching is elusive.

Heckman and Seigelman (1993) make the point that the problem of auditor heterogeneity poses a challenge particularly for employment audits, as well as for studies of wage discrimination, because the determinants of productivity within a firm are not well understood and are difficult to measure. Ross and Yinger (2002:45) note: "Heckman and Siegelman argue that matching may ultimately exacerbate the biases caused by unobserved auditor characteristics because those characteristics are the only ones on which [testers] differ; however, the direction and magnitude of this type of bias

[are] not known." Heckman and his colleague further argue that the factors that employers use to differentiate applicants are not well known; thus, equating testers on those factors can be difficult, if not impossible. This lack of knowledge may make experimental designs particularly problematic for labour market behaviours. However, it does not affect designs in areas with a well-known or identifiable set of legitimate cues to which establishments or authorities may respond (*e.g.*, the rental market).

There are several other problems associated with paired testing. First, paired testing cannot be used to measure discrimination at points beyond the entry level of the housing or labour market. Examples are job assignments, promotions, discharges, or terms of housing agreements and loans. Second, the assignments and training provided to testers may not correspond to qualifications and behaviours of members of racially disadvantaged groups during actual transactions. Third, actual home or job seekers do not randomly assign themselves to housing agents or employers but select them for various reasons. Finally, different employees in the same establishment may behave differently. If a rental office has more than one agent who shows apartments, different experiences of the members of the pair may be traceable to differences in the behaviour of the agent with whom they dealt.

Addressing the Limitations of Audit Studie

Ross and Yinger (2002) offer several options for addressing the limitations of audit studies. Three of the approaches they identify to address the problem of accuracy are (1) broaden the sampling frame to encompass methods other than newspaper advertisements (*e.g.*, searching neighborhoods for rental or help-wanted signs); (2) examine whether the characteristics of the specific goods or services involved (*e.g.*, housing unit) instead of the characteristics of the testers affect the probability of discrimination (Yinger, 1995); and (3) use actual characteristics—as opposed to assigned characteristics—of testers and determine whether controlling for these characteristics influences estimates of discrimination.

To address validity concerns, Ross and Yinger (2002) suggest a strategy of sending multiple pairs to each establishment, which would allow researchers to obtain the data needed to reduce the effects of the idiosyncratic characteristics of single pairs of testers. Testers could then be debriefed after each experience to determine the agent with whom they had dealt. Doing so would not remove the potential effect of different agents on the results obtained, but it would allow researchers to assess that effect. Use of additional pairs of testers would also address issues regarding the calculation of outcome measures. Using multiple pairs might help in distinguishing systematic from random behaviours of an establishment and should, at the very least, tighten the bounds one might calculate on the basis of different mathematical formulas. Of course, care would need to be taken to avoid sending so many pairs of confederates that the research would become obvious.

Another approach to addressing the limitations of omitted variables is to collect extensive information on the actual characteristics of testers, as opposed to assigning their characteristics, and to determine whether controlling for these characteristics influences estimates of discrimination. HUD's national audit study of housing discrimination, conducted in 2000, explicitly collected information on many actual characteristics of testers, such as their income (as opposed to the income assigned to them for the study), their education, and their experience in conducting tests.

STATISTICAL ANALYSIS OF OBSERVATIONAL DATA

In the absence of experimental design, causal inference, applying statistical models to observational data can be useful for understanding causal processes as well as for identifying basic facts about racial differences. Indeed, observational studies are the primary tool through which researchers have explored racial disparities and discrimination. The main goals of this section are to delineate the strengths and problems associated with measuring discrimination using observational studies and to identify methodological tools that are particularly promising for application in certain areas of research on discrimination. In the next section, we continue with an outline of the fundamental issues that must be addressed to draw causal inferences about racial discrimination from statistical analyses of observational data. We illustrate the main issues by laying out a statistical model that can be used to measure discrimination in hiring decisions. As we see it, the hiring example is robust in the sense of surfacing all of the conceptual issues that hamper research on discrimination across domains, including the five domains on which we focus in this report (labour markets, education, housing, criminal justice, and health care). We discuss the strengths and limitations of existing approaches to measuring discrimination across these domains and suggest how approaches prevalent in one domain might usefully be employed in others.

Even a cursory review of the literature on labour markets, education, housing, criminal justice, and health care reveals that it is quite common for researchers to employ statistical models when addressing questions of racial discrimination. Given the range of domains we examine, we do not attempt to be exhaustive in our presentation. Instead, we provide examples from individual studies in particular domains to illustrate particular methodological issues. Our intent is to summarize what we see as the most important challenges that arise in using statistical models to study racial differences in outcomes. And although we make frequent use of labour market concepts as concrete examples throughout this chapter, the fundamental statistical issues underlie the measurement of discrimination in all domains. It should be noted that the style of exposition in this chapter is more mathematical than that in the rest of the report. This mathematical presentation is necessary to make clear what statistical decompositions of racial differences measure. It is also needed for precision regarding the role of models as descriptions of the ways in which outcomes are determined in the presence of discrimination, the role of models and assumptions in drawing causal inferences regarding discrimination from observational data, the nature of the biases that arise when those assumptions are violated, and the ways in which alternative study designs can reduce those biases.

Statistical Analysis for Research and Litigation

Before we proceed, a caveat is in order. This chapter attempts to illuminate state-of-the-art statistical methods that should be used by academic researchers attempting to detect the existence and magnitude of racial discrimination in a wide variety of domains. Statistical proof of racial discrimination may often be sought in other contexts in which the same degree of attention to methodological detail may be valued differently. In particular, courts are often called upon to decide discrimination cases in circumstances that are far less congenial to the detailed and sustained analysis of the academic researcher. Litigants often press for expert testimony based on something far short of state-of-the-art statistical practices that academic researchers might employ. In some instances, a straightforward analysis of the available data may appear to make a compelling case, but many outside the courts would argue for more details and alternative analyses to buttress the arguments.

Nelson and Bennett (2003) investigate the courts' use of statistics to make decisions in cases alleging racial discrimination in employment. They analyze published federal court opinions on racial discrimination in employment that refer to 'statistics' in some form. They compare practices in cases published in 2000–2002 (178 opinions) and in cases published in 1980–1982 (124 opinions) to evaluate changes over time. For cases published in 2000–2002, a preliminary analysis revealed that courts treat statistical data on racial discrimination conservatively; in other words, "they are reluctant to reject the null hypotheses of nondiscrimination and they are reluctant to hold that plaintiffs have met their burden of proof" (Nelson and Bennett, 2003:2). Most courts expect to see statistical evidence presented by plaintiffs in employment discrimination cases; Nelson and Bennett conclude, however, that in most cases courts are skeptical of statistics used to prove discrimination. Moreover, they do not appear very often to base opinions on statistical evidence in contrast to Supreme Court precedent or other judicial rulings. In fact, courts are relying on statistics less frequently now than they did in the 1980s, even though statistical techniques have improved.

Moreover, the interpretation of statistical evidence varies across courts and cases. Overall, the lack of credence given by courts to statistical evidence and the complexities of drawing inferences about racial discrimination from such data appear to be detrimental to plaintiffs. In both periods examined by Nelson and Bennett, plaintiffs lost to defendants more than three times to one, and it is becoming increasingly more difficult for plaintiffs to convince courts that their claims are valid.

The main reasons cited for not relying on statistical data in judicial opinions are (1) relatively small sample sizes, (2) difficulty in defining the comparison groups, (3) lack of relevant controls for nondiscriminatory explanations for disparities, and (4) the use of aggregated data across multiple job levels in a class action suit. These statistical issues (particularly the first three) were prominent in the cases examined within each time period. Moreover, although there have been many sophisticated advances in statistical analyses, the analyses used in court cases typically involve simple comparisons between the racial composition of an applicant pool or a potential promotion pool and a set of selection outcomes (such as hiring or promotion). Few cases involve rigorous assessment of the use of multiple regression and other multivariate analyses. Courts discount small samples without considering the probabilities of outcomes, displaying a lack of statistical knowledge and reasoning. Courts also have no consistent approach to dealing with these problems. A recent Supreme Court decision, however, appears to open the door to expanded use of statistical methods to support inferences of discrimination in legal proceedings.

Statistical Decompositions of Racial Differences

Two types of regression models have been used to decompose racial differences in outcomes. They are (1) regression models with race-specific intercepts, which assume that the effects of other variables (*e.g.*, education) are similar for race groups, and (2) race-specific regression models that allow for interaction effects between race and other variables. All such models pose problems for interpretation.

Regression Models with Race-Specific Intercepts

A standard way to explore the difference in an outcome between groups is to decompose the difference into 'explained' and 'unexplained' components. To illustrate, suppose the researcher is comparing outcomes of white and black men. The simplest formulation is captured by the regression model

$$Y_i = \beta_0 + \gamma R_i + X_i \beta + u_i \qquad (4.1)$$

where Y_i is the outcome of interest, such as a wage rate, with i indexing the individuals in the sample; R is an indicator variable that takes on the value 1 for blacks and 0 for whites; X_i is a set of variables that are believed to be relevant to the determination of Y_i; β_0 is the intercept; β is a vector of coefficients on the variables in Xi at a point in time; the coefficient γ captures the difference between groups in the average value of Y that is not accounted for by differences in X; and the error term u_i captures the effect of other factors that influence Y_i. The coefficients γ and β and u_i are defined so that the mean of u_i is unrelated to R_i and X_i. As we explain in detail below, unless the researcher is confident that he or she has measured all of the variables that are both correlated with R and relevant to the determination of Y, the model should be interpreted as descriptive rather than causal.

Let Y_b and X_b be the mean of Y and X for black men, and let Y_w and X_w be the mean of Y and X for white men. For concreteness, let Y be the wage rate. The average difference between the groups is

$$Y_w - Y_b \qquad (4.2)$$

This difference can be decomposed as

$$Y_w - Y_b = \gamma + \left(X_w - X_b\right)\beta. \qquad (4.3)$$

The term $(X_w - X_b)\beta$ is the contribution of group differences in the observed characteristics X to the race gap in Y. For example, studies of the wage gap almost always include a measure of education among the variables in X. The product of the difference between whites and blacks in the education measure and the coefficient relating education to Y is the contribution of the education difference to the gap. The parameter γ is the portion of the group difference in the means of Y that is not accounted for by the difference in X_w and X_b given the weights β that the X variables have for a given time period. This parameter is a 'catchall' that includes the effects of group differences in omitted factors that would influence Y in the absence of discrimination, as well as the effect of discrimination.

Everett and Wojtkiewicz (2002) provide a good example of this technique from the criminal justice literature and illustrate the fact that the technique is not restricted to linear regression models. They examine the racial and ethnic disparities in federal sentencing following implementation of guidelines that were intended to ameliorate past disparities in sentencing. They estimate ordinal logistic regressions to assess the relative odds of receiving a sentence within each successive quartile of the sentencing range for the committed offense. Adding various legal and extralegal factors to a baseline model including only indicators of race and ethnicity (black, Hispanic, Native American, and Asian, with white as the comparison group), they examine changes in the log-odds coefficient for each indicator. They find that significant racial differences in sentencing remain after accounting for legal factors (offense-related traits such as severity of the crime, as well as recidivism) and other, extralegal factors (such as age and education).

Race-Specific Regression Models

The above description covers a great deal of early research on discrimination that served as the basis for further work on measuring discrimination and explaining racial differences in a variety of social, political, and economic outcomes. For the past 30 years, however, researchers have used a more general statistical model of such differences (or gaps) that allows for the possibility that the slope coefficients β differ between groups (*e.g.*, an interaction between race and education; see Blinder, 1973; Duncan, 1968; Oaxaca, 1973). Suppose that Y_{wi} and Y_{bi} are determined by the equations

$$Y_i = \beta_{0w} + X_i\beta_w + u_i \text{ (for whites),} \qquad (4.4)$$

$$Y_i = \beta_{0w} + X_i\beta_b + u_i \text{ (for blacks)} \qquad (4.5)$$

where β_w and β_b are defined so that $E(u_{wi} \mid X_{wi}) = 0$ and $E(u_{bi} \mid X_{bi}) = 0$. Consequently, the means of Y_i for whites and blacks are $Y_w = \beta_{0w} + X_w\beta_w$ and

$$Y_b = \beta_{0b} + X_b\beta_b, \text{ respectively.}$$

The difference in the mean of the outcome can be written as

$$Y_w - Y_b = \left(X_w - X_b\right)\beta_w + \left[\left(\beta_{0w} - \beta_{0b}\right) + X_b\left(\beta_w - \beta_b\right)\right]. \qquad (4.6)$$

The first term in this decomposition is the portion of the total gap that is explained by average differences in characteristics of whites and blacks using the coefficients for whites $\left(\beta_w\right)$ as the weights. In other words, it is the portion of the gap in Y that would be eliminated if the gap in X were closed and if the dependence of Y on X were the same for blacks and whites. The second term is the 'unexplained' part of the gap in Y; that is, the difference that arises because the relationship between characteristics and outcomes, as summarized by the regression parameters including the difference in $\left(\beta_{0w} - \beta_{0b}\right)$ in intercept terms, differs between groups. Blau and Beller (1992) offer a good example of such a decomposition. Alternatively, the average outcome difference can be decomposed as

$$Y_w - Y_b = \left(X_w - X_b\right)\beta_b + \left[\left(\beta_{0w} - \beta_{0b}\right) + \left(\beta_w - \beta_b\right)X_w\right]. \qquad (4.7)$$

This alternative decomposition uses the coefficients from the model for blacks to determine the consequences for $Y_w - Y_b$ of the group differences in X and uses the mean of X for whites to determine the consequences of the difference $\left(\beta_w - \beta_b\right)$ in the slopes. The first term is the portion of the total gap that would be eliminated if the gap in X were closed and if the dependence of Y on X were the same for whites and blacks. The second term is the 'unexplained' portion of the gap in Y. This second decomposition sometimes produces quite different results from those produced by the first. Many authors report both results or (occasionally) the average of the two (see Oaxaca and Ransom, 1999, for references).

Interpreting the Decomposition

The share of the total difference due to the second component in equation (4.6) is sometimes referred to as the "share due to discrimination." This is misleading terminology, however, because if any important control variables are omitted, one or more of the β coefficients, including the intercept, will be affected. The second component therefore captures both the effects of discrimination and the unobserved group differences in factors that would be expected to determine Y in the absence of discrimination. If there is a gap in favor of whites (blacks) in most of the omitted variables that boost Y, the second component will tend to overestimate (underestimate) the effects of discrimination. On the other hand, omitted variables that are correlated with X will influence the coefficients β, potentially caus- ing the 'unexplained' portion of the gap to be either an overestimate or an underestimate of discrimination. Finally, the inclusion in X of variables that are themselves an outcome in a particular domain, such as occupation or position within a firm in a study of earnings differences, may cause the second component to underestimate or less often overestimate discrimination. It is also misleading to label only the second component as the result of discrimination. This is the case because discriminatory barriers in the labour market and elsewhere in the economy can affect the X variables, which are the characteristics of individuals that matter in the labour market.

Two Pitfalls in Statistical Decomposition

Many researchers further decompose the 'explained' gap into the contribution of subgroups of variables. For example, suppose that X contains sets of indicators for region of the country, for city size, and for educational attainment (less than high school, some high school, high school, some college, college, and some graduate school). One would like to know the contribution of each of these sets of indicators to the explained and unexplained portions of the gap. The contributions of each set of variables to the explained gap are identified and can be estimated separately. The problem, however, is that the contributions of the individual variables to the unexplained gap are not identified separately and depend on the choice of the reference category for each variable. That is, one cannot distinguish the contribution to the overall unexplained gap of racial differences in the coefficients on region of the country from the contribution of racial differences in the coefficients on city size. See Jones (1983) and especially Oaxaca and Ransom (1999) for a more extended discussion of this issue and citations of a number of studies that have included such detailed decompositions.

When the relationship between Y and the X variables is highly nonlinear and the racial difference in the distribution of X is large, a lack of overlap between the black and white distributions in the X variables may make it difficult or impossible to estimate the decompositions of equations (4.6) or (4.7) reliably. This problem may not be obvious if researchers use functional form specifications of equations (4.4) and (4.5) that are not sensitive to potential nonlinearities. Barsky *et al.* (2002) and Altonji and Doraszelski (2002) investigate the problem posed by lack of overlap in black and white income distributions in the context of studies of the black–white wealth gap, with differing conclusions. Barsky *et al.* (2002) standardize for the effects of income by reweighting the sample of whites to have the same income distribution as the sample of blacks.

Inferring Discrimination from Statistical Analysis of Observational Data

In this section, we discuss some of the more frequently encountered obstacles to causal inference in statistical studies of racial discrimination. As discussed in chapters, it could be relatively easy to estimate the degree of discrimination if only it were possible to manipulate a person's race. Except in very limited or special circumstances (*e.g.*, an audit framework), race cannot be randomly assigned. Statistical models are widely used in observational studies in an attempt to replace the experimental control that could ensure an 'all-else-equal' comparison. Again, the crucial problem that must be addressed to draw a causal inference from observa- tional data is that the researcher has no control over which subjects have which attributes. Essentially, the inference that race has a causal effect on an outcome (because of racial discrimination) is drawn by shaping a set of statistical correlations using other information and assumptions formalized in a model of how the process under study is determined. This approach is typical of statistical analysis of observational data and is not unique to the problem of discrimination. Sometimes, the most we can claim is that the evidence is consistent with a certain explanation, with the caveat that other plausible explanations cannot be excluded.

Below we identify and discuss common obstacles to causal inference and some of the solutions proposed in the literature. We begin with a brief introduction to the essential role of theoretically informed models and adequate data in drawing causal inferences from observational data. We then illustrate this point with an extended example involving hiring decisions in the labour market. Finally, we discuss two of the most important sources of bias in observation studies of discrimination—omitted variables bias and sample selection bias.

Developing Statistical Models

According to Sir Ronald Fisher, as quoted by Cochran (1965:252), "When asked in a meeting what can be done in observational studies to clarify the step from association to causation, [I] replied: 'Make your theories elaborate.'" To justify causal inference from observational data, we need a theoretically informed model that depicts, as accurately as possible, the specific process in which we are attempting to assess the presence and magnitude of racial discrimination. Depending on the particular process and context, one may have more or less information on which to base a theoretical model and then translate it into a statistical model. Laboratory experiments are designed precisely to test the plausibility of various detailed theoretical frameworks.

As discussed in detail in above chapter, there is a growing literature that formalizes the assumptions and the deductive process needed to draw cause-and-effect inferences from statistical data. The key idea underlying this literature is the hypothetical counterfactual introduced in above Chapter : What would have happened if the applicant for a job or rental housing had been white rather than nonwhite but nothing else had changed? Obviously, the counterfactual situation cannot be observed and compared with what actually occurred. Therefore, to draw a causal inference from experimental or observational data, it is necessary to specify assumptions and conditions under which the counterfactual logic can be applied. Assumptions from the causal literature are particularly important for justifying the use of regression methods for drawing causal inferences. To draw inferences from running regressions on observational data, substantial prior knowledge about the mechanisms that generated the data must be used to support the necessary assumptions. Studies vary substantially in the degree to which the necessary assumptions are adequately justified. Below we discuss some of the specific issues that must be addressed in such models and their assumptions to draw causal inferences.

Example: Hiring Decisions in the Labour Market

Here, we lay out a generic framework that underlies many statistical approaches to measuring discrimination. The example is from the labour market domain—in particular, hiring. However, the principles described here are quite general, and the issues raised apply across various domains. Our main purpose is to identify what a researcher must know about how an outcome is determined and what data must be available if discrimination is to be measured. We also discuss some of the most important limitations and issues of interpretation surrounding statistical studies of race differences based on observational data. To set the stage, suppose the researcher is interested in understanding an outcome variable, labeled y. In the labour market context, y might be the probability of getting hired by a particular firm for a particular job. In other contexts, such as housing or education, y might be the probability that a housing loan application will be approved or that a person will be admitted to a university. To develop an adequate model of the phenomenon, the analyst needs to have a good understanding of the process that would determine y in both the absence and the presence of discrimination. In this example, the researcher would want information about the legitimate criteria (*e.g.*, education or experience) used by the firm's recruiters to screen applicants for the position.

In the case of hiring, a rational, profit-maximizing, nondiscriminating firm would prefer to hire people who are the best suited to perform well in the jobs for which they are screening applicants. Let the variable P denote productivity in a particular position. To make the model of the decision process as realistic as possible, we distinguish among the variables that determine productivity on the basis of whether they are known to the researcher, the employer, both, or neither. Let X_1 be the factors that are known to both researcher and employer. Examples of X_1 factors might be years of education or labour force experience, or other criteria that are easily observable from an application form. Let X_2 be a set of factors known to the employer but not to the researcher. Examples of X_2 might be such factors as the performance of the applicant in an interview, which is likely to affect screeners' hiring decisions but unlikely to be observed by the researcher. Let Z be a set of variables known to the researcher but not to the employer. Such variables might comprise information collected as part of a survey of the applicants by the researcher. For example, the researcher but not the employer might know that the applicant's spouse works at the company. Finally, even the most diligent employers and researchers might not have access to all the factors likely to affect a person's productivity in a given job. Let Q be a set of factors that affect productivity but are observed by neither the employer nor the researcher.

For simplicity, we assume throughout that all relationships among the variables are linear, so that X_1, X_2, Z, and Q determine productivity according to

$$P = X_1B_1 + X_2B_2 + ZG_1 + QG_2, \qquad (4.8)$$

where $B1$, $B2$, $G1$, and $G2$ are weights capturing the importance of each set of factors in determining productivity in the job. For example, if the factors that are unknown to both the employer and the researcher (*i.e.*, Q) are not very important, G_2 will approach zero, and QG_2 will have little affect on productivity P. Similarly, if the Z factors are not very important as determinants of productivity, the weight G_1 will approach zero.

Two important points must be made about the framework summarized in equation (4.8). First, because this equation is a model of hiring in the absence of discrimination, we exclude the race (labeled R) of the individual from the list of X_1 factors, despite the fact that R might easily be observed by both the firm and the researcher. In this model, therefore, R has no effect on productivity, which is fully determined by X_1, X_2, Z, and Q. We relax this assumption below in discussing a case in which race does influence productivity as viewed by the firm because its customers are prejudiced.

Second, equation (4.8) has the virtue of specifying precisely what the decision criteria would be for a rational firm seeking to hire the most productive candidates. In particular, a rational firm will base its hiring decisions on the expected productivity of the applicants, given the information it has, X_1 and X_2. If the firm uses only X_1 and X_2 to make its productivity assessment, ignoring race, the firm's hiring decision will be a function of the expected value of P given X_1 and X_2. The firm's expectation of productivity conditional on the information it has (X_1 and X_2) can be denoted $E(P \mid X_1,X_2)$, which is a function of the information the firm has (X_1 and X_2), taking into account the expected value of the information it does not have (Z and Q). The expected values of Z and Q, conditional on X_1 and X_2, are $E(Z \mid X_1,X_2)$ and $E(Q \mid X_1,X_2)$, respectively. After weighting each of these terms by its importance as a determinant of productivity (B_1, B_2, G_1, and G_2, respectively), the rational firm's expectation of productivity will be

$$E(P \mid X_1,X_2) = X_1B_1 + X_2B_2 + E(Z \mid X_1,X_2)G_1 + E(Q \mid X_1, X_2)_{G2}. \qquad (4.9)$$

We assume throughout that all conditional expectations are linear functions, in which case equation (4.9) can be rewritten as

$$E(P \mid X_1, X_2) = X_1 B_1^* + X_2 B_2^*, \tag{4.10}$$

where

$$B_1^* = B_2 + \pi_1, B_2^* = B_2 + \pi_2,$$

and the equation

$$E(Z \mid X_1, X_2)G_1 + E(Q \mid X_1, X_2)G_2 = X_1\pi_1 + X_2\pi_2$$

defines π_1 and π_2.

The intuition behind π_1 and π_2 can be seen by rewriting equation (7.9) as

$$E(P \mid X_1, X_2) = X_1(B_1 + \pi_1) + X_2(B_2 + \pi_2).$$

The π_1 and π_2 terms, respectively, capture the ways in which X_1 and X_2 affect the firm's estimate of productivity indirectly via their associations with the unobserved factors Q and Z.

We now turn to the hiring decision itself. For a rational, nondiscriminating firm, the hire probability is an increasing function of $E(P \mid X_1, X_2)$. For simplicity, we assume that the relationship is linear, in which case

$$y = \text{constant} + \alpha_1\left[E(P \mid X_1, X_2)\right] + u; \alpha_1 > 0, \tag{4.11}$$

which, using equation (7.9) to substitute for $[E(P \mid X_1, X_2)]$, can be written as

$$y = \text{constant} + X_1(\alpha_1 B_1^*) + X_2(\alpha_1 B_2^*) + u. \tag{4.12}$$

The error term u captures random noise in hiring, as well as the fact that whether an individual with a particular set of characteristics will be hired at a given point in time will be affected by random variation in the quality of the other applicants at that time. We assume that both of these sources of variation are unrelated to race (*R*).

For a nondiscriminating firm, note that there is no role for *R* in the hiring equation even if *R* happens to be correlated with *Z* or *Q* and thus correlated with *P*. The reason is that the hiring decision *y* depends on $E(P \mid X_1,X_2)$, not on $E(P \mid X_1,X_2,Z,Q)$ or P itself. (The firm does not observe Z, Q, or P.) If R is added to the model of equation (4.12), it will enter with a coefficient of zero, and the researcher will typically find that for a nondiscriminating firm there is no evidence of a difference in the hiring rates of members of different racial groups who have the same values of X_1 and X_2. (To focus on the key ideas, we assume throughout this section that samples are large enough that we can ignore sampling error in estimates.)

Figure 4-1 depicts the model of the nondiscriminating firm. The arrows from the box containing the firm's information (X_1 and X_2) and other factors (Z, Q) to productivity capture the fact that all four variables determine productivity. However, there is no arrow from the box containing (Z, Q) to the firm's judgment about productivity or to the hiring outcome because the firm does not observe Z or Q. For the same reason, there is no arrow linking actual productivity P to the firm's judgment about P or to the outcome. Race can be correlated with X_1, X_2, Z, and Q, but the nondiscriminating firm makes no use of race in making a judgment about productivity or in deciding the outcome. Consequently, there is no arrow from race to the outcome.

Now we allow for the possibility that the firm discriminates and bases its decisions on both expected productivity and race. A simple way to capture this possibility is with the hiring rule

$$y = \text{constant} + (1-\alpha)\alpha_1 E(P \mid X_1 X_2) + \alpha R + u, 0 \le \alpha \le 1, \qquad (4.13)$$

where α is the relative weight placed on race by the firm's screeners, and $1-\alpha$ is the relative weight on productivity. This can be rewritten as

$$y = \text{constant} + X_1\left(dB_1^*\alpha_1\right) + X_2\left(B_2^*\alpha_1\right) + \alpha R + u, \qquad (4.14)$$

where $\alpha_2 = (1-\alpha)$. The parameter α is the difference in the hiring probability that is due to discrimination on the part of the firm. In contrast to the situation for a nondiscriminating firm, when adding R to equation (4.12) will yield a coefficient of zero, α will not be zero for a discriminatory firm when estimating equation (4.14). Figure 4-2 shows the model of a discriminating firm. In contrast with Figure 4-1, Figure 4-2 introduces an arrow from race to the outcome Y that represents the influence of discrimination. In this model, the strength of the link is α.

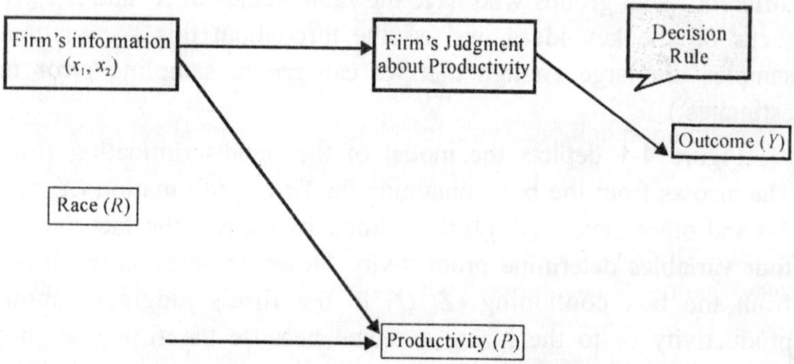

FIGURE 4-1: Model of a nondiscriminating firm

What should be obvious from this discussion is that to correctly estimate α, the researcher must have quite a bit of knowledge about how the firm behaves. First, the researcher must have a solid understanding of how the firm would behave in the absence of discrimination. The above model assumes that a nondiscriminating firm would hire on the basis of expected productivity in the firm. This presumption should guide the search for control variables (X_1, X_2). Second, the researcher must know how the firm predicts productivity and must have data used by the firm.

In the notation of the model, there must not be any X_2 variables—variables used by the firm of which the researcher is ignorant. Third, one must know that the firm does not use Z in its hiring decision. Otherwise, if Z were correlated with race and data on productivity were available, it would be easy to draw the wrong inference about α from a joint analysis of productivity and hiring decisions even if there were no omitted X_2 variables. (For example, the researcher might have data on performance on tests that were administered as part of a survey and would not be observed by firms.) A similar point applies to other variables the researcher happens to observe that have no relationship with P conditional on X_1, X_2, Z, and Q. Fourth, one must know enough about the relationship between P and X_1 and between y and $E(P \mid X_1)$ to be able to specify a functional form relating y to X_1 that is both a good approximation and estimable given the data at hand. In the above discussion, we have specified the relationships to be linear in the variables (which may include nonlinear transformations of a set of underlying variables). Even if they are in fact linear, the researcher will typically not know this to be the case and may have to use flexible functional forms or matching techniques or both.

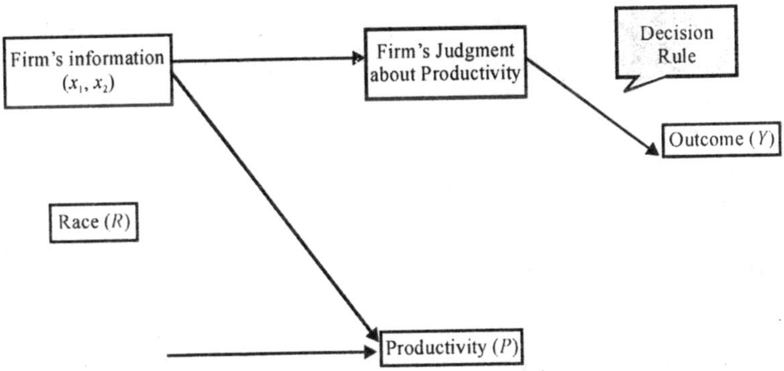

FIGURE 4-2: Model of a discriminating firm

What would the sources of such knowledge be? To continue with the hiring example, in some relatively rare situations the researcher may have deep knowledge of how hiring decisions are made and have access to nearly the same information as the firm (see the example in Box). In other cases, the researcher may have general knowledge of the most important determinants of P, based on, for example, case studies of similar jobs or interviews with employers or employees, or other knowledge about how the labour market works that is relevant to the problem. When data on P as well as y are available, the researcher can estimate the relationship between P and X_1 and so can draw inferences with weaker assumptions.

Munnell *et al.* (1996) study of discrimination in mortgage lending is an analysis in which the quality of the data used and the level of understanding of how outcomes should be determined in the absence of discrimination are sufficiently high that the results are informative about discrimination in mortgage markets. Munnell *et al.* previously interviewed lenders to identify the factors important to them in determining the suitability of an applicant for a loan, and, thus, their choice of variables to include in equations (4.10) and (4.14) was well motivated. They make a good case that they have measured the most important factors considered by lenders. They show that differences between blacks and whites and Hispanics and whites in such characteristics as income explain much of the higher rejection rates for minorities, but they also find that a substantial unexplained gap remains. Although some have raised questions about the study (see Harrison, 1998), the authors provide a strong foundation for their conclusion that "a serious [racial discrimination] problem may exist in the market for mortgage loans" (Munnell *et al.*, 1996:51).

Problems with Measuring Discrimination by Fitting Statistical Models to Observational Data

In addition to the concept of manipulability discussed, any causal analysis that fits multiple regression models to observational data must address several issues. One such issue is whether the structure of the regression model—the variables and their functional form—captures the causal mechanism with sufficient accuracy. If, as is frequently the case, the variables or their functional form are not specified in advance of the analysis, there is a danger of overfitting. Also, a purely exploratory 'fishing expedition' analysis may not be replicable. To address these issues, variables not appearing in a model but highly correlated with model variables could be substituted to evaluate whether alternative models based on these variables would fit as well. Also, cross-validation by examining the performance of the model on a subset of the data or on another data set could improve confidence in the robustness of the inference. A regression model would be suspect if the coefficients changed drastically when the model was fit to a subset of the data.

How to address these generic issues is described in many texts on multiple regression (Weisberg, 1985). There are two key limitations of statistical analysis of racial differences based on observational data that we discuss in more depth using the above framework. The first and most important of these is omitted variables bias; the second is sample selection bias.

Omitted Variables Bias

Before we discuss omitted variables bias in the context of the above model, we provide in Box 7-4 a simple illustration of this type of bias involving a study of graduate school admissions (Bickel and O'Connell, 1975), which is an example of what has come to be called 'Simpson's paradox'. The hypothetical data in the example involve a case in which the gender disparity in admissions reverses sign when an additional relevant variable is introduced—hence, the term omitted variable bias. Precisely the same phenomenon can occur in regression studies of racial disparities.

Omitted variables bias poses a serious problem for the large share of studies of racial differences in surveys (*e.g.*, the Current Population Survey or decennial census long-form sample) having only a limited set of the characteristics that may reasonably factor into the processes under study. In such circumstances, it is possible to measure the extent of the difference in the outcome that is associated with race, but it is not possible to decompose that difference into a portion that reflects discrimination and a portion that reflects the association between race and omitted variables that also affect the outcome. Because researchers generally do not know whether or what critical variables have been omitted, they must be very careful in making the leap from statistical decompositions in a statistical accounting exercise as discussed above to conclusions about the role of discrimination.

Turning back to the specific regression model of hiring outlined above, if elements of X_2 are correlated with R and are important for productivity, failure to control for them when estimating the discrimination parameter α will lead to bias in estimates of the extent to which race has an independent effect on hiring probabilities.

The model laid out above in equations 4.8 through 4.14, however, allows us to be more precise about ways in which the omitted variables threaten an inference about discrimination. The discussion below provides a foundation for possible solutions to the problem of omitted variables bias.

Omitted variables affect the estimation of α as follows. The researcher attempts to estimate α by regressing y on $X1$ and R. Given equation (4.13), the coefficients of the regression are estimates of the regression model y = constant ·:· $d\alpha_1 E[E(P \mid X_1, X_2) \mid X_1, R] + \alpha R + u^*$, where u^* is uncorrelated with $X1$ and R by definition of $E[E(P \mid X_1, X_2) \mid X_1, R]$ and because of the properties of the error term u in equations (4.12), (4.13) and (4.14).

Because we are assuming that expectations are linear, we can write

$$E[E(P \mid X_1, X_2) \mid X_1, R] = \left(B_1^* + \gamma_1\right) + R\gamma_2,$$

where γ_1 and γ_2 are the coefficients relating the mean of $X_2 B_2^*$ to X_1 and R, respectively. Then the regression of y on X_1 and R is

$$y = \text{constant} + X_1\left(B_1^* + \gamma_1\right)\alpha_1\alpha' + R\left[\left(\gamma_2\alpha_1\right)\alpha' + \alpha\right] + u^*, \qquad (4.15)$$

where u^* is uncorrelated with R and $X1$. The bias in the coefficient on R as an estimator of α is $\gamma_2\alpha_1\alpha'$. The bias is due to correlation between R and the omitted variables X_2. The bias will be positive if R is positively related to the index of omitted factors that raise productivity, controlling for X_1; it will be negative if the opposite is true.

Sample Selection Bias

Sample selection bias exists when, instead of simply missing information on characteristics important to the process under study, the researcher is also systematically (*i.e.*, nonrandomly) missing subjects whose characteristics vary from those of the individuals represented in the data. The classic example pertains to the study of the wages people could expect to get in the labour market (see

Heckman, 1979). In that context, the selection problem arises because wages are observed only for those who enter the labour market and find employment. People who have sought and managed to find work are likely to have better labour market opportunities than those who are observed not to be working.

In the context of our example, discrimination in hiring lowers the incentives of minorities with a given value of X_1 and X_2 to apply to a firm. Suppose that data are available only on applicants rather than on the entire pool of potential applicants. If the researcher observes all the information the firm uses in making its hiring decisions (X_2 has no elements) and if applicants know this is the information the firm uses, in addition to R, to make its decisions, then selection in who applies will not lead to bias when one uses equation (4.15) to estimate α. This outcome is extremely rare. Intuitively, discrimination may lower the probability that a black individual with a given value of X will apply, but estimation of equation (4.15) will still uncover the race difference in the hire probability between blacks and whites who are otherwise identical in the relevant characteristics.

Unfortunately, researchers seldom have as much information on applicant qualifications as the firm, in which case X_2 has elements, such as performance on an application test or in an interview. Then in the presence of discrimination, minorities with more favorable values of X_2 will choose to apply more frequently, conditional on X_1. Consequently, selection will tend to induce a positive relationship between R and the index α_1 that influences hiring but is omitted from the regression. (Again, it is omitted because the researcher *does not* observe X_2.) Estimates of the amount of discrimination on the basis of regressions of y on X_1 and R will bc understated as a result.

It is also important to note that, if discrimination in hiring influences the applicant pool, one cannot infer the consequences of discrimination in hiring from knowledge of α alone. One would need to know the effect of discrimination at the hiring stage on the racial mix of who applies.

Possible Solutions to Problems of Using Statistical Models to Infer Discrimination

There are many situations in the social sciences in which the researcher is confronted with an omitted variables problem that is parallel to that discussed above. The most common approach for dealing with omitted variables bias is to use an instrumental variables estimator, which amounts to isolating the relationship between the outcome and a particular source of variation in the explanatory variable of interest that is unrelated to the omitted factors. This strategy is not likely to be available in observational studies in the case of race because the sources of variation in race—race of parents and perhaps the social definition of race at a particular time and place—are likely to be related to the omitted variables.

Absent such so-called instrumental variables strategies, the best we are likely to be able to do with observational studies of racial discrimination is to specify the model as completely as possible. Consequently, it is critically important that the researcher understand how expected productivity is determined and obtain as rich a data set as possible. The most important variables to control for are ones that are likely to have strong effects on *P* and to be related to *R*. Because it is difficult to argue that any finite set of productivity-related factors is complete, this strategy will always yield findings vulnerable to the criticism that variables have been omitted.

Classic experimental designs employ random assignment to treatment as a way to ensure that the treatment is uncorrelated with other factors, omitted or not. If it were feasible to randomly assign people to race, then, in the context of equation (4.15), the $\gamma_2\alpha_1$ term would be zero, and estimating α would be a way of detecting whether a firm is discriminating on the basis of race. Similarly, random assignment of race to a pool of applicants could resolve the bias associated with sample selection. Indeed, despite their other complications, the big advantage of audit studies is their ability to manipulate race experimentally and thereby get around these problems. Given our inability to manipulate race in observational studies, what can be done about omitted variables and sample selection bias? In the following sections, we discuss some of the strategies that have been used to address these problems.

Using an Indicator of Productivity to Address the Omitted Variables Problem

In many situations in which people are screened, such as hiring, college admission, and mortgage approval, rational nondiscriminating screeners should base their decision on how well they expect a candidate to perform if hired, admitted, or approved. In this section, we use the hiring example to show that data on actual performance can be very useful in attacking the omitted variables problem when studying discrimination.

To illustrate how such data can be employed, we consider the problem of using equation (4.15) as a basis for assessing discrimination in our hiring example. We will consider two situations: one in which the firm knows enough about the worker to make statistical discrimination irrelevant and another in which race yields nonredundant information about productivity. Suppose that the indicator or proxy for productivity P^* is equal to

$$P^* = gP + \text{noise},$$

where the noise is unrelated to actual productivity P, X_1, X_2, and race indicator R. The researcher can then estimate $gE(P \mid X_1, R)$ from a regression of P^* on X_1 and R. In general,

$$E(P^* \mid X_1,R) = g_1\ E(P \mid X_1,R) = g_1[X_1B_1 + E(X_2 \mid X_1,R)B_2 + E(Z \mid X_1,R)G_1 + E(Q \mid X_1,R)G_2].$$

In the special case in which ZG_1 and QG_2 are unrelated to R conditional on X_1 and X_2, $E(P^* \mid X_1,R)$ can be written as

$$E(P^* \mid X_1,R) = E(P^* \mid X_1,X_2) \mid X_1,R = g_1 + \left[X_1\left(B_1^* + \gamma_1\right) + R\gamma_2\right]. \tag{4.16}$$

This is the special case in which the firm knows enough about the worker to make the information in R redundant. Consequently, the firm has nothing to gain from resorting to statistical discrimination on the basis of R. If, after conditioning on X_1 and X_2, R is still correlated with the productivity determinants Z and Q that are not observed by the firm, then equation (4.16) will not hold. Furthermore, the firm would have an incentive to resort to statistical discrimination. To see this point, note that in general

$$E(P \mid X_1, X_2, R) = X_1 B_1 + X_1 B_2 + E(Z \mid X_1, X_2, R)G_1 + E(Q \mid X_1, X_2, R)G_2].$$

and in this situation both R and X_1 and X_2 are useful for predicting Z and Q and thus P.

Now recall that if the firm uses only X_1 and X_2 to judge productivity, then from equation (7.14),

$$E(y \mid X_1, R) = E\left[E(y \mid X_1, X_2) \mid X_1, R\right] = \text{constant} + \alpha'\alpha_1\left[X_1\left(B_1^* + \gamma_1\right) + R(\gamma_2)\right] + \alpha R.$$

We can identify the discrimination coefficient α by estimating equation (7.15) and then regressing y on the resulting estimate of $g1$ and on R:

$$y = \text{constant} + \alpha'(\alpha_1 / g_1) g_1\left[X_1\left(B_1^* + \gamma_1\right) + R\gamma_2\right] + \alpha R + \text{error}. \tag{4.17}$$

If equation (4.16) holds—the case in which the firm has no incentive to statistically discriminate—the coefficient on R is an unbiased estimate of α. Thus, under these circumstances, expanding the model to incorporate actual productivity permits one to solve the omitted variables problem.

If race yields nonredundant information about productivity, equation (4.16) fails. If the firm chooses to use race as a predictor and statistically discriminate, the estimate of α will be an unbiased estimate of the extent to which the hiring rate depends on R independently of the firm's belief about productivity. However, the analysis will not reveal whether the firm statistically discriminates when forming its belief about productivity.

In other circumstances, productivity data do not solve the omitted variables problem. If the firm does not statistically discriminate and the special condition of equation (4.16) fails, an estimate of *á* based on equation (7.16) will be biased. The reason is that the relationship between P and R and X_1 will be different from the relationship between $E(P \mid X_1,X_2)$ and R and X_1, and hiring is based on $E(P \mid X_1,X_2)$. If the firm statistically discriminates on the basis of incorrect stereotypes about how R is related to performance conditional on X_1 and X_2, it is easy to show that the estimation of equation (4.17) will also produce biased estimates of α. The bias in α stems from the fact that actual hiring will reflect the incorrect weights placed by the firm on X_1, X_2, and R in forming its expectation of P, rather than the relationships the researcher will uncover when estimating $E(P^* \mid X_1,R)$. That is, the estimate of α will mix two forms of discrimination—the overt or subtle preference for whites given beliefs about productivity and the use of incorrect stereotypes to judge the productivity of blacks or other minority groups.

Sample selection will also influence estimates of the effect of R on productivity P if the researcher leaves X_2 out of the model. The bias in α based on the estimation of equations (4.16) and (4.17) will depend on the same considerations raised in the discussion of these two equations above. Unfortunately, few studies have enough information about productivity to attempt to estimate an equation such as (7.17). Altonji and Blank (1999) survey a few papers examining wage differentials using a methodology that fits into the above framework, including Hellerstein and Neumark (1998, 1999) and a series of papers looking at compensation for professional athletes. A much simpler strategy is available if the researcher actually observes the firm's belief about P. In this case, one may estimate α by regressing y on R and the firm's belief. Identifying whether the firm is statistically discriminating is more difficult, particularly in the absence of data on the firm's beliefs. Progress can be made using variants of the approach of Altonji and Pierret (2001), although strong assumptions are required.

Matching and Propensity Score Methods

Matching methods provide an alternative to multivariate linear regression as a way to control for variables that are likely to matter for an outcome in observational studies. Matching consists of comparing outcomes of two paired individuals (or groups) who are comparable on relevant observed attributes except for race. Matching attempts to mimic the experimental setting in the same way as paired testing. To the extent that (1) the observed factors capture the relevant variables affecting the outcome and (2) the comparability is close, racial differences in the outcome variable in a matching study can be attributed to discrimination. Matching has been the subject of considerable research, and relatively sophisticated methods, such as propensity score matching, have been developed.

The objective in matching is to construct matched sets or strata using relevant nonracial covariates that are available. Analogous to overfitting in specifying a multiple regression, the analyst doing the matching must make the trade-off between matching on too few variables with the result of poor comparability within matched sets and matching on too many variables with the result of poor statistical power and problems with interpretation (*i.e.*, overmatching). A common way to manage this trade-off is to combine matching on a small number of variables that are proven to have large effects together with matching on propensity scores (described below) derived from a larger set of additional variables thought to be relevant.

Propensity score matching addresses the problem that, as the number of covariates increases, it becomes increasingly difficult to find matched sets with similar values of the covariates. Even if each covariate is binary, there will be $2p$ possible sets of covariate values leading to very fine-grained strata for large p. The propensity score is a device for constructing matched sets or strata when there are many covariates. It is typically estimated by fitting a logistic regression to minority versus nonminority group membership using the covariates as the explanatory variables. Subjects with similar propensity scores are grouped into the same strata to create matched sets.

As compared with multiple regression, matching methods reduce the risk of imposing an inappropriate functional form on the relationship between the outcome y and the observed covariates.

Multiple regression models use all the data. In matching, on the other hand, each minority-race individual is typically matched to one or more nonminority individuals. The pool of unmatched nonminority individuals is not used in a matched analysis. Matching is most effective when the minority group is very small as compared with the nonminority group. In this situation, the loss in precision from discarding the nonmatched members of the nonminority group is low. Choosing between matching and regression methods often involves weighing the trade-off between reduced sample size from matching and the functional-form assumptions needed for regression. See Rosenbaum (2002) for an excellent review of these methods and a discussion of the advantages and disadvantages of matching versus multiple regression in various situations. As noted above, matching techniques are beginning to be used as an alternative to multiple regression in statistical decompositions of racial differences. However, these methods do not help with the key problems of omitted variables bias or sample selection bias because matching is performed on the basis of observed variables only.

In the same spirit as matching, stratification on relevant variable(s) can also be used to achieve some measures of control on nonracial factors. Stratification approaches include (1) pre- and poststratification of the data for analysis purposes and (2) adjustment of strata to a standard population. Because stratification methods are widely used in the epidemiology literature but not in the statistical discrimination literature, we simply refer the reader to Sarndal *et al.* (1992) for further information.

Panel Data Methods

Another strand of research using observational data has proceeded by exploiting features that become available with longitudinal data. People do not change race, but one can learn about changes in the consequences of race by following individuals over time. If unobserved characteristics are relatively stable, but outcomes and factors that are related to discrimination do change over time, then the unobserved factors can be partialed out of analyses comparing racial groups over time. (Hsiao, 1986.) In the labour market context, following individuals over time enables one also to examine the differences across regions, industries, sectors (private versus government) and occupation in racial differences in outcomes. The assumption that unobserved factors are not changing over time is a strong one, however and that assumption typically cannot be approximated well enough to be usable unless the time frame is relatively short. Furthermore, people do not switch regions, change industries, and so on at random, which suggests that longitudinal designs comparing the consequences of changes for whites and minorities are subject to selection bias.

Natural Experiments

Another approach to addressing the problem of omitted variables and limited understanding of how a nondiscriminating firm would make decisions is to exploit so-called natural experiments. As discussed above, using the experimental approach in a controlled setting makes it easy for an experimenter to directly ascertain the effects of explanatory variables on some outcome of interest. If the experimenter could force some firms to be nondiscriminators, their behaviour could be compared with that of a control group of firms, and discrimination could be measured as the difference. When an experimental design is not practical, researchers can use natural experiments to observe the natural variations that occur both before and after a specified time period during which an intervention is introduced. Thus, the researcher observes some exogenous intervention, such as a policy change that affects procedures governing hiring or college admission. Instead of random assignment, treatment and comparison groups are defined, and naturally occurring events are used for comparisons.

Social scientists have used a 'differences-in-differences' approach (*i.e.*, the racial difference in some outcome of interest both before and after an intervention) to test the effects of changes occurring at some specified time period that affect some firms or other actors but not others (see, *e.g.*, Card and Krueger, 1994; Tyler *et al.*, 1998). In the language of causal modeling, the policy change is a formal manipulation, which is applied to some actors (*e.g.*, firms in a particular industry or state) but not others. (In some studies, the policy change affects all actors and the comparison is done before and after the change.) The pre-policy-change data are used to estimate the counterfactual condition of what would have happened had the policy change not occurred. Such designs are also sometimes termed quasi-experiments. Because there is some degree of control, the assumptions made for natural experiments to support a causal inference need not be as strong as those required for uncontrolled observational studies; however, natural experiments fall short of randomized controlled experiments. (For more detail on natural experimental designs, see Campbell and Stanley, 1963; Meyer, 1995; and Shadish *et al.*, 2002.)

The key idea in the context of discrimination is to find settings in which there is an exogenous source of variation in the weight that firms, schools, lenders, and other actors could place on *R* that can be plausibly thought of as being independent of the unobservable factors. In the hiring case, the idea is to contrast hiring policy before and after a change in procedure that restricts or eliminates the extent to which the firm can use race in hiring decisions.

Examples of Natural Experiments to Study Discrimination: Below we provide several examples of natural experiments that were used to study racial discrimination in the labour market, education, and health care domains.

Labour market. Holzer and Ludwig (2003) discuss the empirical research using natural experiments in the labour market domain to test the effectiveness of antidiscrimination laws (Freeman, 1973; Heckman and Payner, 1989) and the effects of a policy change on different racial and ethnic groups (Chay, 1998; Neumark and Stock, 2001). The basic approach is to determine whether the law has had the result of forcing á to be zero, or at least closer to zero than was the case before the law. By comparing employment rates before and after the change in the law, one can draw inferences about the extent of reduction in discrimination after the change.

Another source of variation in employment policy to examine could be changes at the firm level within an industry that are not necessarily mandated by changes in the law. Goldin and Rouse (2000), for example, focused on an interesting setting for an attempt to measure discrimination in hiring—a professional orchestra. Even though they considered discrimination against women, the methodology they used applies to other groups as well. In the 1970s and 1980s, many orchestras began to hide the auditioning musician from the jury by using a screen or other device. The representation of women in orchestras, especially among new hires, increased dramatically over this period, and the question investigated was the extent to which this increase was attributable to the change in audition practices. Goldin and Rouse obtained data for a number of years on the auditions for a set of nine orchestras; some of these auditions took place with the screen, while others did not.

Basically, Goldin and Rouse used regression models to estimate whether an individual advanced from one round of auditions to the next and whether an individual was hired in the final round as a function of three things: (1) type of audition (blind versus not blind), (2) the interaction between gender and type of audition, and (3) controls for characteristics of the individual and the audition. By construction the weight on gender in the blind audition was 0, because the gender was unknown to those judging the musicians. Because the researchers had multiple observations of the orchestras, they were able to include orchestra-specific constants to control for unobserved differences among orchestras that might have been associated with adoption of a screen. They were also able to include person-specific constants to control for unobserved differences in the quality of the musicians to guard against the possibility that the use of a screen influences the relative quality of the men and women who audition, which made the results weaker.

Overall, Goldin and Rouse found that women were much more likely to advance and be hired when auditions were blind and concluded that the introduction of a screen led to reduced discrimination against women. Their work provides an example of a case in which a change in policy made discrimination at a key stage of the hiring process much more difficult than it had previously been. Moreover, the increase in the rate of hiring of women after the change demonstrated that discrimination existed prior to the change. The obvious limitation of this work is that it is dangerous to draw broad conclusions about discrimination in hiring from the orchestra case. Yet another source of variation in employment policy to examine could be changes in wages in an industry in response to competitive pressure. The idea is that prejudiced firms may indulge biases when economic rents (excess profits) are available. Competitive pressure may reduce the rents, forcing firms to either reduce discrimination (hire the best people) or go out of business. This situation would lead to a reduction in *á*, the weight placed on race.

Limitations of Natural Experiments

In the context of the study of discrimination, as well as in other arenas, natural experiments have limitations.

First, the change under study may be endogenous. That is, it may be a reaction to particular circumstances that warranted a policy change or intervention. As a result, one may not be able to generalize from the results of a study to estimate the average amount of discrimination prior to the change. For example, suppose one is trying to measure discrimination by comparing hiring rates in a particular firm before and after an intervention by the Equal Employment Opportunity Commission (EEOC) with those of firms in the same industry around the same time period. Assuming that the EEOC responds to the most serious cases, the estimated effect would tend to overstate the amount of discrimination in the industry at large prior to the intervention.

Second, the effects of policy interventions may spill over into the control groups used in the study. For example, the effects of heightened EEOC activity involving a particular set of employers in a given industry might influence the behaviour of other firms and industries even though they have not been targeted. This phenomenon would reduce estimates of the effect of EEOC enforcement based on a 'differences-in-differences' design.

Third, differences in trends in other factors that affect outcomes cannot always be addressed adequately even in differences-in-differences designs, particularly when the policy intervention takes place over a period of time, as is the case with civil rights policy.

Fourth, a change in one domain, such as school desegregation orders, may be accompanied by changes in another domain, such as housing, or by a change in attitudes. Consequently, it may be difficult to use a change in policy in one domain to identify the amount of discrimination in that domain prior to the change.

Fifth, only in rare circumstances (such as the Goldin and Rouse orchestra study) can one be sure that the change in policy under study has eliminated a role for discrimination in the decision under study. In most cases, the best one can hope for is that a comparison of groups affected by the change in policy will identify the reduction in discrimination induced by the policy (the change in *á*), rather than the level of discrimination that existed prior to the change.

Sixth, in some cases, changes in policy that lead to positive effects in one dimension may induce negative effects in others. A major concern in the literature on the effects of antidiscrimination policy in the labour market, for example, is that positive effects on wage rates for blacks have been offset in part by negative effects on employment (see Altonji and Blank, 1999, for discussion and references).

Finally, natural variation in the data may be insufficient to identify the effects of interest or may be correlated with other, unmeasured factors that may bias the results. (See Holzer and Ludwig, 2003, on the use of natural experiments to study discrimination; see Shadish *et al.*, 2002, and Meyer, 1995, for a general discussion of the strengths and weaknesses of these designs.)

Summary of Possible Solutions to Problems

It should be obvious that more accurate and complete data collection efforts are critical to reducing the key problem of omitted variables bias. Of course, the data needed must pertain to the particular domain of analysis. Data on performance (*e.g.*, productivity in the hiring context, default rates in the lending context) and detailed knowledge of how an outcome depends on performance can solve the problem of omitted variables bias in some cases. However, situations in which the researcher will possess the data and detailed knowledge needed to support specification of an appropriate model are relatively scarce, at least in the labour market setting. Matching and propensity score methods are useful as a means of relaxing assumptions about the functional form relating the variables *X*1 and *X*2 to productivity and to hiring decisions. However, they do not solve the omitted variables bias problem.

Panel data are useful as a way of identifying differences in the amount of discrimination across types of institutions, regions, or time. However, this approach requires the assumption that time-varying unobserved characteristics of the individual are not related to mobility, which is a strong assumption. Natural experiments in which a legal change or some other change forces a reduction in or the complete elimination of discrimination for some groups provides leverage in assessing the importance of discrimination prior to the change and for groups not affected by the change.

Additional Issues

Thus far we have discussed prospects and problems for measuring discriminatory treatment of persons who are identical except for race. In the context of our hiring example, the parameter *á* measures discriminatory treatment of blacks and whites with the same values of *X*1 and *X*2, the variables known to a firm to determine productivity. The model developed above, however, also sheds light on other discriminatory processes.

Effects of Past Labour Market Discrimination on Factors in Hiring

Discrimination by a firm or elsewhere in the labour market may influence some of the elements of *X*1 and *X*2, the (nonracial) characteristics used by the firm to make hiring decisions. For example, some studies of hiring are based on whether the person was referred by an existing employee (Fernandez and Weinberg, 1997; Fernandez *et al.*, 2000; Petersen *et al.*, 2000). Current labour market discrimination against minorities by the firm will lead to a discrepancy in the probability that minority applicants will know people who work in the firm because personal networks tend to run along racial lines. Even if the use of referrals in hiring is justified by productivity considerations, the total effect of current discrimination will be understated if one holds constant whether a person was referred to the firm. In particular, the parameter *á* will understate current discrimination.

Alternatively, suppose that in the past a firm discriminated against disadvantaged racial groups but no longer does. Continuing with the referral example, again suppose that the firm makes use of referrals in hiring decisions. If the researcher is simply interested in whether the firm treats applicants with a given set of characteristics differently at the present time and if the researcher observes all the variables the firm uses to assess productivity (there are no *X*2 variables that the researcher does not observe), the researcher will draw the correct conclusion of no such differential treatment. In this case, *á* will be zero. However, if the researcher wants to know the total effect of both past and current discrimination on the part of the firm on the racial composition of current hires, it is incorrect to take as given whether employees were referred. The reason is that past discrimination led disadvantaged racial groups to be underrepresented among the pool of potential referrers, thus reducing the chances of attracting disadvantaged racial groups through referrals. To measure the effect of both past and current discrimination on current outcomes in this dynamic context, the researcher must model the effect of past discrimination on current *X* variables.

To give another example, it is standard practice for many types of jobs—and in many situations defensible from a productivity standpoint— to consider past work experience when trying to predict productivity. However, past experience will be influenced by discrimination in the labour market. Consequently, the coefficient on *R* will provide an estimate of the effect of discrimination on the firm's behaviour, given X_1 and X_2. But because discrimination in the labour market leads to a racial gap in the experience-related components of X_1 and X_2, the coefficient on R will understate the total effect of all discrimination that has taken place in the labour market.

Furthermore, discrimination in the labour market may influence the choices of X_1 and X_2 that people make before they enter the labour market. For example, if African Americans know they are discriminated against for white-collar positions and college has little value in the blue-collar world, they will have less incentive to pursue a college education. If one uses a model such as equation (4.14) to measure labour market discrimination against blacks in white-collar positions holding education (one of the X_1 variables) constant, one will underestimate the total effect of discrimination on the racial composition of such jobs. Similarly, if firms develop a reputation of having a hostile work environment for racially disadvantaged groups and if such applicants avoid seeking employment at those firms, a model such as equation (4.14) will underestimate the total effect of discrimination in hiring decisions. This will be the case even if the researcher observes all of the variables used by firms to choose employees. Developing measures of the discrimination that results from a process such as that described above is extremely challenging because of the much longer timeline and more complex environment that must be accounted for to reach statistically valid "all else being equal" conclusions.

Effects of Discrimination in Other Domains

To measure the total effect of discrimination in society on a particular outcome, such as the odds of getting hired, one needs to measure the effects of discrimination in other domains on elements of X_1 and X_2 that are determined outside of the labour market. In our example of hiring, if there is racial discrimination in 'pre-market factors' (Neal and Johnson, 1996), such as education, that are related to labour market success, discrimination in the educational sphere will also affect labour market success indirectly. Thus controlling for education in a hiring equation is reasonable in assessing whether a particular employer is discriminating. However, if there is racial discrimination in the educational domain, controlling education will understate the total effect of all racial discrimination in analyses of labour market discrimination alone. Developing and validating statistical models of these broader processes is one way to gain insight into the presence or absence of discrimination in these other areas. One's choice of control variables is influenced by whether one is trying to measure discrimination in a specific domain or the cumulative impact of discrimination.

Other Discriminatory Effects on the Productivity Equation

Another issue concerns whether discrimination on the part of customers, coworkers, or suppliers leads characteristics of the worker, including race, to enter the productivity equation (7.9). Consider Becker's (1957) theory of customer discrimination, and consider sales positions. Suppose that white customers prefer to buy from white salespeople, and black or Latino customers are indifferent. In such a world, P is influenced by the match between the race (or ethnicity) of the job candidate and the racial composition of the customers. R will not appear directly in the equation for productivity, but the interaction between R and the racial composition of the customer base will. If the firm obeys the law, it will not apply the interaction variable in making decisions about hiring, and the interaction variable will not enter significantly into hiring decisions. (The interaction will show up in a productivity regression.) If the firm disobeys the law, the interaction term will influence hiring and show up in a hiring regression. One will then conclude correctly that firms discriminate for or against black or Latino salespeople as a function of the customer base. If one excludes the interaction term but adds R to the hiring equation, one will likely find evidence that the firm discriminates against minorities if most of the markets for which the firm is hiring happen to be heavily white. But one will not detect the fact that the nature of the discrimination is related to the match between customers and the sales agent. If there are data that can be used to estimate the effect of the interaction between race and customer composition on productivity, one can see whether hiring decisions appear to reflect such considerations. A number of studies of professional sports take this approach (see Altonji and Blank, 1999, and Kahn, 1991, for examples).

A somewhat different example involves the possibility that discrimination in social institutions that are extraneous to the firm or the labour market influences the form of the productivity equation. Consider again a marketing position. Suppose that social connections play a critical role in marketing. In such a world, sales productivity may well depend on club memberships, where one lives, the schools one attended, and the like. Variables measuring such social connections belong in *X*1 and *X*2. *R* may have no relationship to productivity or to hiring decisions if one conditions on these variables. Now suppose that societal discrimination (including housing discrimination) influences social connections. In this case, discrimination outside the labour market will lead to a race gap in some elements of *X*1 or *X*2 or both, as well as in hiring, even though the variable *R* will not have an independent effect on hiring conditional on *X*1 and *X*2. Finally, note that the recruiting strategies chosen by the firm are likely to influence the importance of social networks. Strategies that place more emphasis on personal contacts and less on advertising may not be race neutral. A discriminating firm may consciously choose a recruiting strategy in which social networks are important and then exclude minorities who lack them. It will be difficult to determine whether the firm's recruitment strategy is really the profit-maximizing one or in fact is shaped at least in part by the goal of discrimination.

Summary

Racial discrimination is difficult to measure. Researchers rarely observe discriminatory behaviour directly. Instead, they attempt to infer from disparate outcomes whether racial discrimination has occurred. Establishing that racial discrimination did or did not occur requires causal inference. Identifying a racial disparity and determining that an association between race and an outcome remains after accounting for plausible confounding factors is a relatively straightforward task. The real difficulty lies in going beyond the identification of an association to the attribution of cause. Insights drawn from social science theory about types of discrimination and mechanisms through which discriminatory behaviour and processes may operate can play an important role here, informing research design and models and assisting researchers in identifying and testing alternative explanations. Ultimately, researchers usually must rely on the evaluation of evidence from multiple studies—considering the strength of association, consistency, and plausibility of each study's research design and findings—to draw causal conclusions. All research methods have particular strengths and weaknesses with respect to measuring racial discrimination, particularly concerning the extent to which they support causal inferences. In particular, experimental designs facilitate causal inference but limit generalization, whereas observational designs facilitate generalization while limiting causal inference. In any research design, drawing a valid causal inference from a study requires careful specification of the assumptions and the logic underlying the inference.

True experiments involve manipulation of the variable hypothesized to be causal, random assignment of participants to the experimental condition, and control of confounding variables. Experimental methods potentially provide the best solution to addressing causal inference (*e.g.*, assigning disparate racial outcomes to discrimination per se) because well-designed and well-executed experiments have high levels of internal validity. In the language of contemporary statistics, experiments come closest to addressing the counterfactual question of how a person would have been treated but for his or her race, although they do not do so in a form that is easily translatable into direct measurement of the discriminatory effect.

The experimental method faces challenges when applied to race, which cannot be randomly assigned to an actual person. Experimental researchers frequently manipulate racial cues (*e.g.*, racial designations or photographs on a résumé) or train black and white confederates to respond in standard ways. In both approaches, an attempt is made to manipulate apparent race, while holding all other variables constant, and to elicit a response from the participants. Although the experimental method has uncovered many subtle yet powerful psychological mechanisms, a laboratory experiment does not address the generalizability or external validity of its effects. Therefore, it is unable to estimate what proportion of observed disparities is actually a function of discrimination.

Over the past two decades, laboratory experiments have focused more on measuring subtle forms of bias and nonverbal forms of discriminatory behaviour and less on examining overt behaviours, such as assisting others. If laboratory studies were to be more focused on real-world-type behaviours, they could help analysts who use statistical models for developing causal inferences from observational data (see Chapter 7). Thus, the results of real-world-oriented laboratory studies could provide more fully fleshed-out theories of discriminatory mechanisms to guide the modeling work. In turn, real-world studies based on laboratory-developed theories could be usefully conducted to try to replicate, and thereby validate, laboratory results.

Because laboratory experiments have limited external validity, researchers turn to field experiments, which emphasize real-world generalizability but inevitably sacrifice some methodological precision. Field audit studies randomly assign experimental and control treatments (*e.g.*, black and white apartment hunters) to units (*e.g.*, a rental agency) and measure outcomes (*e.g.*, number of apartments shown). Aggregated over many encounters and units of analysis, audit studies come closer than laboratory experiments to assessing levels of discrimination in a particular market. Both the accuracy and the validity of audit studies on discrimination have been questioned, however. Advocates of paired-testing and survey experiments have responded that all these limitations can be remedied. Although generally limited to particular aspects of housing and labour markets (*e.g.*, showing of apartments or houses and callbacks to job applicants), audit studies to measure racial discrimination in housing and employment have demonstrated useful results. It is likely that audit studies of racial discrimination in other domains (*e.g.*, schooling and health care) could produce useful results as well, even though their use will undoubtedly present methodological challenges specific to each domain.

The use of multivariate regression and related techniques to decompose racial differences in some outcome of interest into a portion due to differences in the distribution of observed characteristics and a portion not explained by those characteristics is an essential tool for describing racial differences. The most informative studies use explanatory variables that both measure the most important determinants of the outcome under study and are likely to have different distributions by race. But the residual race differential may include not only any effect of discrimination but also the effect of other omitted factors that would generate different outcomes by race even in the absence of discrimination. Hence the unexplained gap may overestimate or underestimate the effects of discrimination.

The main purpose of this chapter has been to review the strengths and limitations of various approaches to dealing with the challenges of measuring discrimination with statistical methods using observational data. This review leads to several conclusions. Our first conclusion relates to the uses and limitations of statistical decomposition of gaps in outcomes among racial groups: "The statistical decomposition of racial gaps in social outcomes using multivariate regression and related techniques is a valuable tool for understanding the sources of racial differences. However, such decompositions using data sets with limited numbers of explanatory variables, such as the Current Population Survey or the decennial census, do not accurately measure the portion of those differences that is due to current discrimination." Matching and related techniques provide a useful alternative to race gap decompositions based on multivariate regression in some circumstances. More generally, we will often be hampered in our ability to infer discriminatory behaviour on the basis of regression decompositions because we can never be sure we have included all the relevant controls in the model. We must be able to control for the relevant variables well enough to approximate closely the hypothetical counterfactual in which only race has been changed.

5

Attitudinal and Behavioural Indicators of Discrimination

In this chapter, we consider the challenges of collecting direct evidence of the incidence, causes, and consequences of discrimination from sample surveys, governmental administrative data, nongovernmental data, and in-depth interviews. We also review in some detail the scale measures of racial attitudes used in surveys. Survey and administrative records data do not provide direct observations of actual discrimination, but they can measure reported experiences, perceptions, and attitudes that involve discrimination. Used in addition to statistical methods for drawing causal inferences, these data can help researchers better understand the nature and likely occurrence of racial discrimination. Several parts of this chapter are drawn from a paper commissioned by the panel by Thomas Smith, director of the General Social Survey (GSS), on various approaches to measuring racial discrimination and their strengths and weaknesses (Smith, 2002). The approaches he assesses include administrative counts of discriminatory incidents reported to governmental and nongovernmental authorities, in-depth interviews about past experiences with discrimination, and survey-based studies in which representative samples of randomly selected respondents report on their experiences with discrimination and prejudice. Some approaches (*e.g.*, large-scale surveys) assess aggregate knowledge about the incidence of discrimination, while other approaches (*e.g.*, information obtained from in-depth interviews) assess knowledge of such occurrences in a particular instance.

Perceptions of Discrimination

At the end of the twentieth century, open support for principles of racial discrimination had fallen to very low levels among whites, with only 10 to 15 percent endorsing discriminatory actions or policies. Although whites may have come to support a nondiscriminatory society in principle, however, they remain substantially uneasy about its implications in practice. White respondents, for example, continue to express reservations about racial mixing in social institutions where such mixing formerly did not occur, and racial segregation generally remains high in schools, churches, neighborhoods, and marriages (see Emerson and Smith, 2000; Farley, 1996; Massey and Denton, 1993; Orfield and Eaton, 1996). For instance, although most whites now agree that blacks should be able to live wherever they choose, they still want blacks to choose to live somewhere else.

Racial attitudes of individual Americans may not correspond with their views about or support for public policies or practices. Loury (2002) draws a useful distinction between the 'social meanings' associated with racial classification and the 'racial attitudes' held by individuals. Social meanings refer to the unexamined beliefs that influence how citizens understand and interpret the images they glean from the larger social world. For example, the meaning of a policy regarding job preference may be sensitive to the race of those affected: Veterans have been seen as acceptable beneficiaries, whereas the application of such a policy for blacks has been thought to violate meritocratic principles (Skrentny, 1996). Likewise, views about welfare policies may depend on the race of local recipients, so that more blacks being on the local rolls is associated with greater hostility toward recipients (Luttmer, 2001).

Sniderman and Piazza (1993) illustrate the difference between racial attitudes and racial meanings in their 'mere mention' experiment. As noted by Loury (2002), these survey researchers found that 'the mere mention' of affirmative action, in the context of soliciting from white respondents their views about racial stereotypes, made those whites more likely to agree with negative racial generalizations (*e.g.*, most blacks are lazy). Compared with two groups of similar whites, the ones to whom affirmative action was 'merely mentioned' showed a significantly higher tendency to affirm negative stereotypes about blacks than did those to whom affirmative action was not mentioned at all. The researchers concluded that the respondents' expression of these anti-black sentiments had been 'caused' by their dislike of affirmative action, and not the other way around. That is, whites were expressing primarily their ideological views about policy, which, when affirmative action was mentioned, then spilled over to affect their views about race.

Regardless of how it is conceptualized, the discrepancy between the acceptance of nondiscrimination in principle and the discomfort about its implications in practice can be traced, at least in part, back to the persistence of anti-black stereotypes. In the mid-1980s, 61 percent of whites nationwide said that blacks on welfare could get a job "if they really tried," 42 percent said that black neighborhoods are more rundown because blacks "don't take care of their property," and 43 percent endorsed the view that blacks would be as well off as whites "if they would just try harder" (Sniderman and Piazza, 1993; Loury, 2002). As of 1991, moreover, 34 percent of whites described blacks as 'lazy' and 21 percent labeled them as 'irresponsible' (Sniderman and Piazza, 1993). Likewise, according to the 1993 Multi-City Study of Urban Inequality, whites perceived blacks to be significantly less intelligent, less rich, less self-supporting, and less easy to get along with than Asians, Hispanics, or whites (Bobo and Massagli, 2001) and whites perceived African Americans as the least desirable potential neighbors (Charles, 2001).

Black Perceptions of Discrimination

Prior to the passage of civil rights legislation, blacks perceived the United States to be a highly prejudiced and discriminatory society.

In 1963, more than three-quarters of a nationally representative sample of black Americans perceived significant racial discrimination in U.S. job markets (Schuman *et al.*, 1997). Asked whether they had as good a chance as whites to get jobs for which they were qualified, a resounding 77 percent said 'no'. In the following years, the percentage of black respondents perceiving employment discrimination fell, reaching 64 percent in 1978 and 55 percent in 1989. As late as 1997, more than half (53 percent) of all African Americans said that blacks still did not have as good a chance as whites to get jobs for which they were equally qualified. Moreover, in 1996, 63 percent of African Americans nationwide continued to view discrimination as a primary cause of disadvantage among blacks (Schuman *et al.*, 1997).

Between 1997 and 2001, the Gallup Organization and Princeton Survey Research Associates public opinion polls asked nationally representative samples of African Americans to report any discrimination or unfair treatment they had experienced within the past 30 days (Smith, 2001). On an average, 26 percent of respondents said they had experienced discriminatory treatment while shopping, 16 percent at the workplace, and 16 percent while on public transportation. A national survey of African Americans sponsored by the *Washington Post* during 2000 found that 30 percent had at least sometimes been "called names or insulted" and 17 percent had been "physically threatened or attacked" because of their race. Rates for non-blacks were substantially lower, with only 18 percent of the general population reporting a racial or ethnic insult and 11 percent a physical threat or attack. Clearly, African Americans, more than other Americans, still perceive significant discrimination in public life and view it as a significant barrier to their social and economic advancement.

In the Multi-City Study of Urban Inequality, each respondent was asked: "In general, how much discrimination is there that hurts the chances of blacks to get good-paying jobs?" In Atlanta, 60 percent of black respondents answered 'a lot', compared with 57 percent in Boston, 62 percent in Detroit, and 69 percent in Los Angeles. When respondents who answered 'some' to the same question were added, the percentage of African Americans who perceived racial discrimination in job markets rose to well over 90 percent in each metropolitan area (Kluegel and Bobo, 2001). Of course, the implicit definition of discrimination used by respondents may not be the same as the legal definition currently recognized by U.S. courts.

White Perceptions of Discrimination

Not long ago, white respondents were willing to admit their support for racial discrimination to survey researchers. In the early 1940s, for example, 68 percent of whites nationwide said they thought blacks and whites should attend separate schools, 55 percent said whites should have priority over blacks in hiring, and 54 percent agreed that separate sections should be reserved for blacks and whites on buses and streetcars. By the 1960s, such segregationist attitudes had moderated considerably, with 30 percent of whites still favoring racially separate schools and 11 percent approving of white preferences in hiring. In 1970, 12 percent of whites admitted to favoring racial segregation in public transportation (Schuman *et al.*, 1997).

In the years since the civil rights era ended, these percentages have fallen even further; fewer and fewer whites are willing to express open support for racial discrimination. By 1995, only 4 percent reported they believed that blacks and whites should attend separate schools, just 13 percent said there should be laws against black–white intermarriage (as late as 1963 the percentage was still 62 percent) and over 90 percent of whites endorsed the principle that blacks have a right to live wherever they can afford to live (Schuman *et al.*, 1997). Although white support for racist principles had fallen to low levels, it had not disappeared entirely. As late as 1993, 15 percent of whites agreed that blacks should respect the rights of whites to exclude blacks from their neighborhoods if they so desire (Schuman *et al.*, 1997).

Moreover, while fewer whites openly support principles of racial discrimination, many remain ambivalent in their attitudes about race. For instance, surveys show that only 13 percent of whites support a ban on black–white intermarriage, whereas 33 percent still disapprove of the practice personally. A mere 2 percent object to sending their children to a school where 'a few' students are black, while 19 percent object to sending their children to one where half are black. Likewise, just 2 percent of whites said they would move out of their home if black neighbors moved in next door, but 25 percent said they would leave if blacks entered their neighborhood 'in great numbers'. As of 1995, nearly a quarter of whites (23 percent) said they would object to having a black dinner guest (Schuman *et al.*, 1997).

Challenge of Direct Measurement of Discrimination

Prior to 1964, many forms of racial discrimination were legal. Although a few states had passed civil rights laws, there was no national prohibition on discriminatory treatment. Many Americans were regularly denied access to jobs, housing, accommodations, and services on the basis of their race or ethnicity. Under these circumstances, the incidence, causes, and consequences of discrimination could be assessed by surveying employers, landlords, and business establishments about their racial policies or by surveying minority group members about the frequency and circumstances under which they were denied access to jobs, housing, or accommodations because of their race. The civil rights legislation passed in 1964 made open discrimination on the basis of race or ethnicity illegal, and perpetrators could be prosecuted under both criminal and civil law. In succeeding years, overt discrimination was prohibited progressively in various markets in the United States—first in markets for labour, goods, and services (in 1964); later in housing markets (in 1968); and finally in mortgage lending (in 1974, 1975, and 1977). Overtly denying nonwhites a job or apartment because of their race would invite prosecution and, if admitted in court, would virtually guarantee conviction. Although readily observable acts of discrimination declined, the persistence of high levels of residential segregation along racial lines and large racial gaps with respect to income, wealth, and other societal outcomes indicate the continued existence of racial discrimination, at least at some level. Rather than being open and readily observable, however, discrimination was more often subtle in nature, assuming new forms that are not as easily identified but may be damaging nonetheless.

Under these circumstances, assessing the extent of racial discrimination directly from observational studies, such as asking black Americans whether they have been denied housing or employment because of their race, can be complicated. Those surveyed may suspect that they have been victims of discrimination, but ambiguity in such a situation can make proving discrimination—or sometimes even recognizing it—difficult. On one hand, the true incidence of discrimination may be underestimated because a person may not realize that it has occurred or be uncertain about whether it was actually present. On the other hand, the true incidence of discrimination may be overstated because, in an ambiguous situation, respondents may falsely attribute the denial of work or housing to discrimination that is in fact due to some other reason, such as qualifications, timing, or even chance. Likewise, asking white Americans whether they intend to discriminate or whether they support discriminatory policies is unlikely to provide a good indication of the prevalence of racial discrimination in American society (Bonilla-Silva and Forman, 2000).

Respondents to social surveys are understandably reluctant to admit to socially sanctioned behaviour, particularly if it is illegal (Sudman and Bradburn, 1982). Thus, whites will tend to underreport discriminatory attitudes and behaviours and be unwilling to admit to perceptions or feelings that might appear to be prejudiced (a phenomenon known as social desirability bias). Much of the information on racial attitudes and perceptions of discrimination comes from sample surveys and other observational studies (as distinct from experimental studies). It is, therefore, important to be cognizant of what such data sources can and cannot do. Survey measures capture reported experiences, perceptions, or attitudes about discrimination. These measures may provide some indication that discrimination is occurring, as well as what its causes and consequences may be. Nonetheless, evidence from surveys and other observational studies is not statistically valid in terms of causality. In such studies, it is not discrimination per se that is being directly measured but reports of experiences of discrimination or discriminatory attitudes.

We discussed the difficulty of using observational data to assess the extent to which racial differences in outcomes are the result of discrimination, as opposed to some other observed or unobserved variable that is correlated with race. Unknown characteristics or process-related differences in treatments (*e.g.*, processes occurring before a reported incident) can bias observed effects. Because only a small set of characteristics is often available in any data set, other unobserved characteristics that may affect the outcome of interest are omitted, biasing the observed effect of racial discrimination. Thus, we again see how lack of experimental control can hamper the ability to draw causal inferences from observational data. To the extent that members of disadvantaged racial groups report being discriminated against and whites admit to racist attitudes and discriminatory behaviours, these data likely represent lower-bound estimates of the actual occurrence of discrimination in society, although evidence on this issue is far from clear. The only validation of reported discrimination comes from credible descriptions of discriminatory incidents and from instances in which self-reports, matched-pair studies, and counts of complaints yield similar results, particularly similar intergroup differentials (Smith, 2002). Indeed, direct measures of experiences and perceptions of discrimination are probably best used to support valid findings from other kinds of studies to estimate the contribution of discrimination to observed disparities in outcomes among racial groups. Longitudinal data in particular can provide useful information about process-related differences across racial groups, such as changes in perceptions and experiences (as well as outcomes) over time. Thus, despite our caveats, we conclude that it is informative to consider directly reports of levels and changes in discrimination and prejudice.

Sources of Observational Data

Probably the most extensive data on experiences and perceptions of racial discrimination come from survey research. We therefore begin this review of sources of observational data on discrimination by discussing in detail the content, uses, advantages, and limitations of surveys of interpersonal relations and racial discrimination. We then examine more briefly three additional data sources: governmental administrative data, nongovernmental data, and in-depth interviews.

Surveys of Interpersonal Relations and Racial Discrimination

Surveys of interpersonal relations use interviews or questionnaires to collect detailed information about respondents' perceptions of and experiences with discrimination. Researchers use this information to better understand the causes and consequences of various forms of discrimination and to investigate relationships among racial attitudes and beliefs, on the one hand, and perceptions and experiences of discrimination on the other. The surveys are typically administered on a regular basis, either cross-sectionally or longitudinally, so that researchers can observe changes over time in attitudes and perceptions and in the relationships between them.

In his review of survey research methods, Fowler (1993) describes three key methodological components—sampling, interviewing, and question design—that are necessary for designing quality surveys and collecting credible data. First, survey researchers use probability methods to randomly draw large representative samples from specified populations in order to ensure statistical generalizabilty. Second, they rely on multiple interviewers rather than a single investigator to reduce bias, and they use structured interviews or standardized questionnaires to ensure consistency of data collection and measurement. Third, they design survey questions to gather objective information or to measure subjective phenomena, often by using scale measures. It is essential that the survey questions be reliable and consistent with what the researchers are trying to measure.

When developing survey content, researchers consider the general data collection approach (*e.g.*, personal interviews, computer-assisted telephone interviewing, or mail questionnaires), as well as such factors as question order, content, wording, and type (*e.g.*, open-ended versus fixed responses). As demonstrated by Bobo and

Suh (2000; see also Suh, 2000) and Smith (2001), the use of open-ended questions in surveys is particularly valuable for obtaining detailed descriptions of incidents of discrimination. Such questions combine some of the best strengths of surveys (*e.g.*, generalizability and standardized data collection) and in-depth interviews (*e.g.*, narrative richness and detail). Open-ended questions yield specific details about the nature and circumstances of discriminatory behaviour that can often validate (or indicate inaccuracies in) direct, self-reported accounts, thereby providing useful information for understanding discrimination.

Imperfect Relationship of Attitudes to Behaviours

Smith (2002:14) notes that "many of the questions on intergroup relations in the holdings of the Roper Center or on the GSS provide important information on the state of intergroup relations and help one to understand the context and causes of discrimination, public support for policies to combat discrimination, and related matters." However, relatively few surveys attempt to measure the incidence of discrimination directly at either the individual or the collective level. Smith continues: "Given that only a moderate correlation exists between intergroup beliefs and attitudes (*e.g.*, stereotypes and prejudice) and discriminatory actions (Dovidio, 1993; Dovidio *et al.*, 1996; Fiske, 2000), studying the former is not the same as measuring the latter."

In most studies of attitudes and behaviours, the correlation is typically moderate (Eagly and Chaiken, 1993) and the intergroup domain is no exception. The methodological solutions in the racial discrimination area are the same as in other areas:

- Investigators must create a careful match between the attitude and the behaviour. For example, some intergroup experiments indicate that subtle attitudes best predict subtle (but powerful) behaviours, whereas overt attitudes predict more overt behaviours (Dovidio *et al.*, 2002). As another example, there is evidence that whites' general attitudes toward blacks predict patterns of discrimination, not necessarily any one randomly chosen behaviour; by the same token, there is evidence that whites' attitudes toward a specific racial policy or practice (such as busing in a particular school district, housing in a particular neighborhood, or affirmative action in a particular employment or education context) predict their specific behaviour in that regard. This elementary point is often missed (Ajzen, 2001).

- The racial attitude–behaviour match will depend on moderator variables relating to the type of person involved. Some people act on their attitudes more reliably than do others (Snyder and Swann, 1976).
- The racial attitude–behaviour match will also depend on the situation in which the attitude and the discrimination are measured. Social norms strongly affect both what is reported and what is enacted (*e.g.*, Ajzen, 1991), so they can override the ability of attitudes to predict behaviour.
- The strength of the attitude itself affects related behaviour (Petty and Krosnick, 1995).

Survey Limitations

Smith (2002) describes a number of limitations of surveys. These limitations encompass both methodological factors and reporting biases.

Methodological factors. As noted above, surveys cannot directly measure discrimination; they capture self-reported evidence on perceptions and experiences of discrimination that is not validated. Moreover, such factors as target group, data collection mode, interviewer race, venue, and time of occurrence, as well as question format (*e.g.*, explicit or implicit, phrasing, order), mode (*e.g.*, survey or in-depth interview) and context, can affect the accuracy and completeness of reported perceptions and experiences of discrimination. Discrimination that is subtle or indirect, for instance, may not be readily detected using explicit items. Respondents may also use different meanings for discrimination from one reported account to another (*e.g.*, individual, group, or structural discrimination).

Reporting biases. As the leading historical targets of discrimination in the United States, African Americans may be in the best position to assess the ongoing reality of race in public life. Some scholars, however, suggest that African Americans may have become more sensitive to discrimination because of their socialization since the passage of civil rights legislation, leading them to notice prejudicial actions now more than in the past and producing an upward reporting bias over time (Bobo and Suh, 2000; Brown, 2001; Gary, 1995; Gomez and Trierweiler, 2001; Sigelman and Welch, 1991; Suh, 2000). This reporting bias may also occur if respondents attempt to support a personal conviction that America is a racist society or to explain unfavorable situations and outcomes in their own lives (Harrell, 2000; Lucas, 1994).

Given that blacks are likely to have been well attuned to racial discrimination both before and after the civil rights legislation, however, such upward reporting biases are not likely to be severe. Coleman *et al.* (2002) actually find that blacks sharply underreport exposure to discrimination when such reports are compared with separate statistical estimates of wage discrimination. In general, researchers have found direct self-reports of discrimination to be accurate and reliable when cross-validated against other data sources (Bobo and Suh, 2000; Essed, 1991; Landrine and Klonoff, 1996). For example, in one recent national survey and one local survey, items on racial discrimination were followed by open-ended questions asking people to describe the mistreatment they supposedly had experienced (Smith, 2000). Across all racial and ethnic groups, some 95 percent of respondents were able to describe specific, appropriate, and credible incidents of discrimination.

Whatever biases may stem from changes in sensitivities among blacks or other racial or ethnic minorities, they are likely to be small in comparison with shifts in white behaviour from fairly overt forms to more subtle forms of discrimination. As noted above, because most overtly discriminatory behaviours were declared illegal by the mid-1970s, continued differential treatment on the basis of race has had to become subtler and often may not be apparent even to its targets. Other things being equal, the shift from more overt to more subtle forms of discrimination by whites may actually increase underreporting by blacks because they may be less likely to perceive subtle forms of discrimination. To the extent that real shifts have occurred in white racial attitudes and behaviours, reported declines in discrimination by blacks will be accurate, but part of the decline may reflect the fact that discrimination has been declared illegal by the federal government with the consequence that public expressions of racial prejudice and overt forms of discrimination are widely considered to be socially unacceptable.

Means of Improving Survey Measures

Methodological improvements. Perhaps the most important area for methodological research to improve survey measures of discriminatory experiences and perceptions is research to help understand what aspects of survey and question design may affect levels of reported discrimination, such as the degree to which reports are influenced by race priming. To address this issue, Smith (2002) suggests investigating different approaches to the wording and placement of questions experimentally through random assignment on existing social surveys. If levels of reported discrimination vary by question wording and order, follow-up work will be needed to explain these variations and establish which wordings and placements yield the most accurate results. Another area for research is to use bounded and aided recall techniques in panel surveys to learn how cross-sectional reports may be distorted by errors of memory and telescoping. In addition, cognitive research is needed to understand what respondents specifically include and exclude when they hear such terms as 'discrimination' and 'unfair treatment.'

One fruitful avenue for improvement might be greater use of the factorial vignette method, in which stories are presented to respondents about people being questioned by the police, applying for a job, running for political office, and the like, with the race of the people in the vignette, along with other relevant factors (*e.g.*, age, gender, education, work experience, criminal history), being systematically varied by random assignment. This approach enables researchers to see experimentally how race influences respondents' reported perceptions and evaluations (for a recent example, see Emerson *et al.*, 2001).

Finally, more and better validation studies are needed to discover which approaches yield the most accurate reports of behaviour. One possible way of validating self-reports is to collect and compare information from representative samples on reported behaviours and practices that may be considered discriminatory (potential discriminators) and on reported experiences with discrimination (targets of discrimination). The former approach may not prove practical, however, if discriminators do not perceive their actions as unfair or biased (Dovidio, 1993; Essed 1991) or if self-recognized acts of discrimination are underreported because of social desirability bias. Nonetheless, the approach merits investigation, as incidents of reported discrimination necessarily have both perpetrators and targets. Studies of employers also show that it is possible to collect self-reports of prejudiced attitudes and biased actions against members of disadvantaged racial groups (see Kirschenman and Neckerman, 1991; Supphellen *et al.*, 1997).

Perhaps the most basic form of cross-validation is the use of multiple methods in measuring discrimination. For example, employment discrimination at a company might be studied by examining grievances filed, carrying out surveys of employees and bosses, conducting in-depth interviews, and analyzing employee records. Other improvements. Smith (2002) offers suggestions for improvements that do not involve additional methodological research.

First, surveys should include more target groups. In most surveys, statistically reliable results are available only for whites and blacks, yet Hispanics and Asians are rapidly increasing their shares of the U.S. population, and Arabs and Muslims have recently become prominent as potential targets of prejudice.

Second, surveys should elaborate and extend their measures of discrimination. Some surveys have used only a single measure. Questions need to be refined substantively as well as methodologically to capture subtle and not just explicit discrimination (Dovidio, 1993; Pettigrew and Meertens, 1995; Sears *et al.*, 1997). In this regard, Supphellen *et al.* (1997) find that projective measures of employment discrimination (*e.g.*, rating the attitudes or opinions of others) are more valid than direct self-reports.

Third, surveys should inquire about discrimination within specific venues and not rely on global questions that leave time and place unspecified. Typical venues included in surveys to date include work, restaurants, stores, interactions with police, schools, housing, public transportation, banks, and government agencies (Brown, 2001; Collins *et al.*, 2000; Gary, 1995; Newport *et al.*, 2001; Smith, 2000). An 'other' category might be included to capture incidents occurring outside these venues (Smith, 2000). Specific time periods should also be specified. Doing so would enable estimation not only of the incidence of discrimination but also of its frequency. Lifetime 'ever' questions are less than ideal because they demand recall over extended periods of time (which is cognitively difficult and leads to underreporting); they confound cross-sectional monitoring and time-series analysis (because some people report on events that occurred only in the distant past, and others do not); and they underestimate the frequency (as opposed to the incidence) of discrimination (Suh, 2000).

Fourth, not only is it important to measure discrimination, it is also important to assess racial preferment. In 1991, for example, 38 percent of black respondents to the GSS reported that their promotion opportunities were worse because of their race, but 18 percent indicated that their chances were better, yielding a net disadvantage of –20 points. In contrast, white respondents gave responses that yielded a net advantage of +19 points (Smith, 1998).

Governmental Administrative Data

After the passage of the various civil rights acts prohibiting racial discrimination, bureaucratic agencies were established and charged to investigate complaints, monitor compliance, and work to eliminate bias. For example, the National Fair Housing Alliance (NFHA) produces an annual report on the state of housing discrimination in the United States that is based on information from local fair housing groups, the U.S. Department of Housing and Urban Development, the U.S. Department of Justice, and numerous state and local government agencies. Discrimination is tracked in four different market sectors: rental markets, mortgage lending, home sales, and homeowner insurance. Complaints filed with NFHA and other agencies provide one source of data on the underlying trends in the frequency and incidence of housing discrimination. The NFHA data compiled for 2001 show that race continues to be the most commonly reported basis for discrimination, accounting for 32 percent of the 23,557 cases filed (National Fair Housing Alliance, 2002). Other potential sources of administrative data include antidiscrimination suits filed in state and federal courts (Garrett, 2001; National Research Council, 1989; Romero, 2000; Shivley, 2001) and registries of hate crimes maintained by state and local human rights commissions and race relations boards (Evans, 2001; Strom, 2001).

As noted by Smith (2002), administrative data have several advantages: They represent socially significant events, they are publicly accessible, and they are generally inexpensive to use because the costs of collection are borne by the enforcing agency. Using industry data from the Bureau of Labour Statistics, for example, Petersen and Morgan (1995) were easily able to document the skewed placement of men and women within occupational categories within firms. The data showed that women were far more likely to be in poorly paid jobs. This finding suggests that if one were to look for possible gender discrimination, it would be important to look not just at wage differences within jobs but also at the mechanisms that allocate men and women to occupations within the firm.

As Smith points out, however, relying on government reports also has serious limitations. First, the data are collected to meet legal requirements, not to facilitate social science research. In other words, coverage is defined by law, and the information is collected largely for administrative rather than scientific purposes. Second, willingness to report discriminatory treatment may depend on the ease of reporting and the vigor with which an agency deals with complaints (Lucas, 1994). As these conditions vary over time, trends may be biased (Shivley, 2001). Finally, not all discriminatory practices are illegal (and thus covered by government enforcement mandates) and many acts of discrimination that are now illegal were not so several decades ago (Romero, 2000). The Anti-Defamation League (2001), for example, includes acts of anti-Semitic speech in its annual report on anti-Semitism, even though such speech is legal. Because of problems with the quality and completeness of administrative data, the usefulness of these data sets for research purposes is limited.

Nongovernmental Data

In addition to government agencies, many private organizations maintain a record of discriminatory complaints. However, complaints in such cases are made to internal grievance boards governed by formal procedures within an organization; an example is complaints filed with an employer or labour union. Internal data from for-profit organizations have many of the same limitations as those from governmental agencies. Companies establish procedures to serve legal and business purposes, not to further a scientific research agenda. In addition, company reports are typically not made public, and their nature and specifics vary considerably across organizations.

Racial grievances may also be lodged with independent nonprofit organizations whose mission is to promote racial or ethnic equality, such as the Anti-Defamation League or the Mexican-American Legal Defense and Educational Fund. Reports to nongovernmental third parties have the advantage that they are publicly accessible, typically cover many different types of discrimination in various venues, and draw from across the nation. However, the resulting data are often compiled by highly self-interested organizations that are not scientifically motivated. Moreover, as with government and other organizational reports, these sources rely on targets of discrimination knowing where and how to report mistreatment and being motivated and able to do so.

In-Depth Interviews

In conducting in-depth or qualitative interviews, a researcher engages one or more subjects in an extensive, semistructured conversation, which is often audio recorded (Bonilla-Silva and Forman, 2000; Essed, 1997; Feagin, 1991; Feagin and Sikes, 1994; St. Jean and Feagin, 1998, 1999; Zweigenhaft and Domhoff, 1991). The advantages of such interviews are that they ask individuals about their actual experiences of discrimination and often elicit information that is richly detailed. Essed (1991), for example, claims that using unstructured interviews rather than highly structured ones allowed her to draw out more detailed accounts of people's experiences. She also notes that participants were able to express intuitive feelings regarding their experiences with prejudice and discrimination that might otherwise be difficult to articulate and to report events in ways that others might consider oversensitive.

In-depth interviews are generally based on small, usually unrepresentative samples that are often biased because participants are of higher status, more articulate, and more politically aware than most of the subject population (see Essed, 1991; Feagin, 1991; Zweigenhaft and Domhoff, 1991). The most frequently used method of selection is the chain referral method, also known as snowball sampling, in which respondents provide leads to other potential interviewees within their social networks. Because social networks tend toward homogeneity, snowball sampling can yield biased samples and findings that are difficult to generalize (Goodman, 1961). Moreover, the accuracy of self-reports may be affected by ways in which respondents react to interviewer probes for reports of discrimination or other behaviours, or if respondents provide vague and poorly detailed accounts (Smith, 2002).

Scale Measures Used in Surveys

As discussed above, although survey-based self-reports have been found to be reliable, accurate, and useful ways of measuring experiences of discrimination, the shift from overt to subtle forms of discrimination has made it more difficult to assess the occurrence of discrimination or to capture people's beliefs using survey questions. Many observers have noted an ongoing conflict between principle and practice regarding racial prejudice in the American psyche and have theorized the contradiction under a variety of conceptual rubrics (Fiske, 1998): modern racism (McConahay, 1986), symbolic racism (Kinder and Sears, 1981), ambivalent racism (Katz *et al.*, 1986), aversive racism (Dovidio and Gaertner, 1986), laissez-faire racism (Bobo *et al.*, 1997; Bobo and Smith, 1998) and subtle racism (Pettigrew and Meertens, 1995). Although individual survey questions may not capture such complex attitudes and ambivalence about race, scale measures, which combine information from multiple questions, can capture the sometimes contradictory mechanisms that lead to more subtle types of discrimination. We turn to these measures next.

Measures of Modern Racism

The psychological source of a conflict between racial equality in principle and practice results from people's assimilation of egalitarian laws and norms, along with their internalization of continued cultural messages that blacks are inferior to whites. For example, many whites, regardless of explicit individual prejudices, make rapid associations between whites and positive ascriptions and between blacks and less positive ascriptions (*e.g.*, Devine, 1989; Dovidio *et al.*, 1986; Gaertner and McLaughlin, 1983;. In part, these associations may reflect media coverage depicting blacks less favorably than whites in news reports and in entertainment. Many Americans resolve the conflict between these culturally influenced associations and the nation's egalitarian values by maintaining those values simultancously with subtle, automatic, or indirect forms of prejudice.

In survey settings, measures of modern racism examine reactions to black Americans as perceived threats to whites' traditional values and economic status (Duckitt, 2001). The single most commonly used measure since the mid-1970s has been McConahay's (1986) Modern Racism Scale—an outgrowth of work on symbolic politics (Kinder and Sanders, 1996; Kinder and Sears, 1981). Generally split into three parts, this scale typically encompasses modern (subtle) racism, old-fashioned (overt) racism, and filler items on irrelevant current events to disguise the measure. Items on modern racism include believing, for example, that the government and the media give blacks more respect than they deserve, that discrimination is no longer a problem, that blacks have gotten more economically than they deserve and that blacks are too demanding. In contrast, items on old-fashioned racism ask about open opposition to fair housing laws, integration, intermarriage, and having a black neighbor.

Scores on the Modern Racism Scale predict a variety of variables related to discrimination to varying degrees (Kinder and Sanders, 1996). Examples include conscious endorsement of stereotypes about black Americans (Devine, 1989), anti-black feelings, simulated hiring decisions, voting for white over black candidates (even after controlling for ideology) and opposing busing to achieve school desegregation (even after controlling for related variables). A variant of the scale (Pettigrew and Meertens, 1995) distinguishes subtle and explicit prejudice against immigrant minorities in Europe. Items on this scale include blaming minorities for being too pushy and intrusive but simultaneously not trying hard enough, as well as with-holding sympathy for their disadvantaged situation.

Although widely used, the Modern Racism Scale has provoked two kinds of scholarly debate. First, while few dispute the empirical correlates of the scale, their meaning is open to interpretation, either as a perceived threat to the situation of one's own group or as principled conservatism. For example, some argue that opposition to racial integration, school desegregation, affirmative action, and welfare programs reflects primarily opposition to government intervention (Sniderman, 1985); however, the role of such ideology appears to be empirically small (Kinder, 1998). Some argue that racial attitudes reflect narrow economic self-interest (Bobo and Kluegel, 1997); that is, people vote their own personal wallet. Yet perceptions of the economic standing of one's racial group, as a whole appear to be at least as strong a predictor of racial attitudes and voting behaviour as perceptions of one's own economic standing (Kinder and Kiewiet, 1981; Sears and Funk, 1991). This suggests that modern racism is based on the interests of one's group, not one's own self-interest. Moreover, consistent with the idea of modern racism, the importance that white Americans attach to equality of opportunity, relative to their other core values, correlates with their more specific racial attitudes and policy preferences (Kinder and Sanders, 1996). In other words, modern racism represents a syndrome of perceived own group interest, basic values, and specific attitudes toward policies—all of which disadvantage minorities.

Some common ground for this first type of debate—over the meaning of modern racism as group threat versus principled conservatism—appears in findings that modern, subtle forms of prejudice correlate with (a) subjectively perceived threats to group status (Bobo, 1983), (b) positive feelings toward one's own racial group, and (c) negative feelings toward racial outgroups (Wood, 1994). Group prejudice may not be the only factor predicting racial attitudes and policy preferences, but as one commentator notes, "it is always present, and of all the ingredients that go into opinion, it is often the most powerful" (Kinder, 1998:805).

A second form of scholarly debate has emerged more recently. The original items on the Modern Racism Scale were considered relatively nonreactive; that is, respondents did not necessarily interpret them as measures of discrimination and so apparently did not monitor their responses for social desirability. Over the past decade, however, growing evidence suggests that the items have become reactive (Fazio *et al.*, 1995). Modern racism scores now correlate with more explicit measures of deliberative discrimination, rather than with automatic or implicit measures (*e.g.*, Dovidio *et al.*, 1997), although correlations with more implicit, spontaneous measures of discrimination still occur (Wittenbrink *et al.*, 1997, 2001). More generally, various dimensions of prejudice matter to understanding both prejudiced attitudes and discriminatory behaviour. One dimension contrasts spontaneous, implicit, automatic, and subtle versus deliberative, explicit, and controlled reactions; another important dimension contrasts emotional, evaluative, and affective processes versus belief, conceptual, and cognitive processes; and a third dimension contrasts ingroup preference versus outgroup derogation.

One key component of measuring subtle racism is that it depends heavily on context. As an example, to the extent that white attitudes are ambivalent—encompassing both sympathy and rejection—people may act on different aspects of their attitudes under different circumstances. Racial ambivalence (Katz and Hass, 1988; Katz *et al.*, 1986) suggests the co-occurrence of blaming anti-black feelings (the perceived irresponsibility of black families, leaders, and values underlies the continuing disadvantage of black Americans) with paternalistic pro-black feelings (emphasizing obstacles, discrimination, and unequal opportunities). The work by Katz and colleagues demonstrated empirically that anti-black attitudes correlated with white perceptions that blacks violate values related to the Protestant work ethic and that pro-black attitudes correlated with humanitarian and egalitarian values. Whites can simultaneously possess both sets of attitudes. The implication for discriminatory behaviour is that reactions toward a single black individual can be affected by a small push in either a positive or negative direction (*e.g.*, slightly superior or slightly inferior credentials for a job applicant). Racially ambivalent whites then overreact, making excessively positive or excessively negative decisions as compared with their decisions about a comparable white individual. The Modern Racism Scale elicits a similarly exaggerated response, either overly positive or overly negative, in simulated hiring decisions.

The common thread of all the work on modern racism, symbolic racism, subtle prejudice, and ambivalent racism is that appearing racist has become aversive to many white Americans (Dovidio and Gaertner, 1986), creating more complex racial attitudes than in the past. Whatever their source, subtle, modern forms of racism predict avoidance of interactions with racial outgroups, and such passive rejection can result in discrimination. Survey research would be improved by a more explicit model of what forces determine expressed attitudes: expectations, experiences, social pressure, and so on. The analysis of relationships between past experiences, expressed attitudes, and future behaviour seems remarkably undeveloped. Embedding attitude reports in a lifetime of behaviours would permit this area of research to develop in new ways. Furthermore, research on modern racism can inform statistical and experimental research by examining relevant individual characteristics (*e.g.*, personal values) and features of encounters (*e.g.*, interdependence, accountability). Some social science models, such as the theories of reasoned action and planned behaviour, provide a framework for incorporating a variety of factors to predict behaviour and evaluating the respective weights and values of own beliefs, perceived social norms, and perceived behavioural control, as well as own prior behaviour (Ajzen, 2001).

Measures of Explicit Racism

Not all white Americans eschew overt racial bias. By some estimates, about 10 percent of white Americans openly embrace racial discrimination; if accurate, this figure would mean there is at least one prejudiced white person for every black person in the United States (Fischer *et al.*, 1996). Hence, even this apparently low incidence of prejudice can be viewed as high. Moreover, measures of more explicit racially biased attitudes correlate with more explicit and potentially violent forms of discrimination. Not everyone holding these attitudes is violent, of course, but perpetrators of violence do hold these attitudes. Thus, explicit racism is a necessary but not sufficient predictor of the most serious forms of discrimination.

Three contemporary scales predict endorsement of overtly prejudiced attitudes. One such scale measures blatant or explicit prejudice (Pettigrew and Meertens, 1995), defined as resentment of racial and ethnic minority groups (their allegedly stealing ingroup jobs but also using welfare), as well as rejection of ties to minorities (having a mixed grandchild or an outgroup boss). High scores on this scale predict generalized ethnocentrism and overall rejection of outgroups not one's own, as well as approval of racist political movements and hate crimes (Green *et al.*, 1999). Explicit prejudice stems from perceived threat to the economic status of one's own group.

A related scale measures social dominance orientation (Sidanius and Pratto, 1999); it also focuses on economic and status competition between societal groups. High scores on this scale indicate agreement by respondents that some groups are just more worthy than others, that group hierarchy is inevitable and good and that dominance is necessary. These attitudes correlate with believing that the world is competitive and that force is sometimes necessary to keep inferior groups in their place. They also correlate with explicit racial prejudice.

In addition to perceived economic threat, perceived threat to values predicts discriminatory attitudes. A scale on right-wing authoritarianism (Altemeyer, 1988, 1996) measures belief in old-fashioned ways, censorship, leadership based on superior power, and rejection of troublemakers and deviants. High scores on this scale correlate with social conservatism and predict approval of aggression against nonconformers. They also correlate with limited intergroup contact and limited education.

Summary

Following the enactment of civil rights legislation, overt racial discrimination became illegal and socially unacceptable, and measuring discrimination became increasingly difficult as a result. The more subtle forms of discrimination evident today complicate the way we assess the causes and consequences of discrimination. Surveys provide valuable evidence for understanding the extent of discrimination; however, they cannot directly measure its occurrence. Most survey items are intended to measure self-reported attitudes, perceptions, or experiences of discrimination, and these items can be unreliable for at least two reasons. First, if a discriminatory occurrence is ambiguous, a black or other minority respondent may under-or overreport its incidence. Some subtle forms of discrimination, for instance, may not be easily detected. Second, white respondents are often not willing to admit to practicing or supporting discrimination, which may lead to less-accurate reporting of their true attitudes or beliefs.

On the other hand, although survey measures cannot capture discrimination directly, results to date suggest that valid and reliable data on racially discriminatory attitudes and experiences can be gathered on social surveys. Conducting repeated cross-sectional surveys is very useful to provide time series; the GSS is the best example of a large-scale survey that collects data on changes over time in racial attitudes and experiences with discrimination through yearly interviews with samples of the population. Conducting longitudinal surveys to analyze the incidence, causes, and consequences of changes in attitudes about race and experiences of racial discrimination at the individual level is also very valuable, although none of the major longitudinal surveys to date has included attitudinal or perceptual variables. More generally, research is needed to evaluate and improve the reliability and consistency of survey reports of discriminatory attitudes and behaviour. In particular, as expressions of prejudice and discriminatory behaviour change and become more subtle, survey questions on racial attitudes and experiences of discrimination may be necessary. Scale measures can be very useful to capture complex racial attitudes that can lead to more subtle types of discrimination. Open-ended questions on surveys can provide some of the advantages of in-depth interviews in regard to the detail of information obtained combined with the advantages of surveys of large, representative samples.

6

Caste Discrimination in South Asian Diaspora

Discriminatory and cruel, inhuman, and degrading treatment of a vast global population has been justified on the basis of caste. In much of Asia and parts of Africa, caste is the basis for the definition and exclusion of distinct population groups by reason of their descent. Over 250 million people worldwide continue to suffer under what is often a hidden apartheid of segregation, modern-day slavery, and other extreme forms of discrimination, exploitation, and violence. Caste imposes enormous obstacles to their full attainment of civil, political, economic, social, and cultural rights. Caste is descent-based and hereditary in nature. It is a characteristic determined by one's birth into a particular caste, irrespective of the faith practiced by the individual. Caste denotes a system of rigid social stratification into ranked groups defined by descent and occupation. Under various caste systems throughout the world, caste divisions also dominate in housing, marriage, and general social interaction-divisions that are reinforced through the practice and threat of social ostracism, economic boycotts, and even physical violence.

Among the communities discussed in this report are the Dalits or so-called untouchables of South Asia-including Nepal, Bangladesh, India, Sri Lanka, and Pakistan-the Buraku people of Japan, the Osu of Nigeria's Igbo people, and certain groups in Senegal and Mauritania. The prominence of caste as a social and economic indicator for the widespread South Asian diaspora is also discussed. These communities share many features; features that have allowed even the most appalling practices to escape international scrutiny. In many cases, caste systems coexist with otherwise democratic structures. In countries such as India and Nigeria, governments have also enacted progressive legislation to combat abuses against lower-caste communities. Despite formal protections in law, however, discriminatory treatment remains endemic and discriminatory societal norms continue to be reinforced by government and private structures and practices, in some cases through violent means.

Lower-caste communities are almost invariably indistinguishable in physical appearance from higher-caste communities. This is not, as some would say, a black and white issue. For most outsiders then, the visual cues that otherwise accompany race or ethnicity are often completely lacking. Stark economic disparities between low and high-caste communities also get buried under a seemingly homogenous landscape of poverty. Poverty can be quite deceptive. It makes one conclude that all suffer from it equally. A closer look reveals the discrimination inherent in the allocation of jobs, land, basic resources and amenities, and even physical security. A closer look at victims of violence, bonded labour, and other severe abuses also reveals disproportionate membership in the lowest ranking in the caste order. A perpetual state of economic dependency also allows for abuses to go unpunished, while a biased state machinery looks the other way, or worse, becomes complicit in the abuse.

The language used to describe low and high-caste community characteristics in the examples that follow are striking in their similarity, despite the variation in geographic origin, with ideas of pollution and purity, and filth and cleanliness prevalent. In turn, these designations are used to justify the physical and social segregation of low-caste communities from the rest of society, their exclusion from certain occupations, and their involuntary monopoly over 'unclean' occupations and tasks.

The exploitation of low-caste laborers and the rigid assignment of demeaning occupations on the basis of caste keep lower-caste populations in a position of economic and physical vulnerability. The triple burden of caste, class, and gender effectively ensures that lower-caste women are the farthest removed from legal protections. Only with the honest implementation of the International Convention on the Elimination of All Forms of Racial Discrimination (ICERD) and of domestic laws designed to abolish the vestiges of various caste systems and to protect the economic, social, cultural, civil, and political rights of all, can the process of attaining economic and physical security, and human dignity, begin.

In August 2000, the U.N. Subcommission on the Promotion and Protection of Human Rights passed resolution 2000/4 on Discrimination Based on Work and Descent. The resolution, aimed at addressing the issue of caste, reaffirmed that discrimination based on work and descent is prohibited under international human rights law. The Subcommission also decided to further identify affected communities, examine existing constitutional, legislative, and administrative measures for the abolition of such discrimination, and make concrete recommendations for the effective elimination of such practices.

In August 2001, subcommission expert R.K.W. Goonesekere presented his working paper on work and descent-based discrimination to the subcommission's fifty-third session. The paper was submitted pursuant to Subcommission resolution 2000/4. Because of time and other constraints, Mr. Goonesekere limited the paper's focus to the Asian countries of India, Nepal, Pakistan, Sri Lanka, and Japan but stated that further study of African countries in particular was warranted. The presentation of the paper, and the ensuing debate amongst subcommission experts that followed, marked the first time that caste discrimination was discussed as a major source of human rights violations worldwide by a U.N. human rights body. The subcommission also determined by consensus to extend the study to other regions of the world where work and descent-based discrimination continues to be experienced.

This important resolution underscores the notion that caste systems are inherently economic and social in their consequences and that the exclusion of lower-caste communities extends to the economic and social realms of wages, jobs, education, and land. This report discusses the manifestations of caste and descent-based discrimination and abuse in over a dozen countries. It is not meant to be an exhaustive review but an introduction to the prevalence and global dimensions of this underreported problem. It is also an appeal to governments to give close and systematic attention to the problem of caste discrimination at the World Conference Against Racism, Racial Discrimination, Xenophobia and Related Intolerance and beyond. Despite the magnitude of the problem, as of this writing, caste-based discrimination had been systematically cut out of the WCAR's intergovernmental process through the actions of a handful of governments. This has occurred despite the Committee on the Elimination of Racial Discrimination's repeated affirmations that caste, as a form of descent-based discrimination, falls within the definition of racial discrimination under article 1 of the ICERD.

Concerted international attention and the commitment of resources to assist national governments in this important work are also long overdue. In many parts of the world, the success of the World Conference will turn upon its commitment to effectively addressing the issue of caste. For at least a quarter-billion people worldwide, the end of apartheid in South Africa did not signal the end of segregation and servitude in their own lives. This important conference can and should bring us closer to this important global goal.

Untouchability and Segregation

India's caste system is perhaps the world's longest surviving social hierarchy. A defining feature of Hinduism, caste encompasses a complex ordering of social groups on the basis of ritual purity. A person is considered a member of the caste into which he or she is born and remains within that caste until death, although the particular ranking of that caste may vary among regions and over time.

Differences in status are traditionally justified by the religious doctrine of karma, a belief that one's place in life is determined by one's deeds in previous lifetimes.

Traditional scholarship has described this more than 2,000-year-old system within the context of the four principal varnas, or large caste categories. In order of precedence these are the Brahmins (priests and teachers), the Ksyatriyas (rulers and soldiers), the Vaisyas (merchants and traders) and the Shudras (laborers and artisans). A fifth category falls outside the varna system and consists of those known as 'untouchables' or Dalits; they are often assigned tasks too ritually polluting to merit inclusion within the traditional varna system (Embree (ed.), 1988). Almost identical structures are also visible in Nepal. (A caste system amongst Bali's predominantly Hindu population also mimics India's caste system in structure though not in severity. While people still self-identify as belonging to particular castes, and culturally abide by certain caste norms, the extent of discrimination based on caste is unclear).

Despite its constitutional abolition in 1950, the practice of 'untouchability'-the imposition of social disabilities on persons by reason of birth into a particular caste- remains very much a part of rural India. Representing over one-sixth of India's population-or some 160 million people-Dalits endure near complete social ostracization. In what has been called India's 'hidden apartheid', entire villages in many Indian states remain completely segregated by caste (Human Rights Watch, 1999).

'Untouchability' is reinforced by state allocation of resources and facilities; separate facilities are provided for separate caste-based neighborhoods. Dalits often receive the poorer of the two, if they receive any at all. In many villages, the state administration installs electricity, sanitation facilities, and water pumps in the upper-caste section, but neglects to do the same in the neighboring, segregated Dalit area. Basic amenities such as water taps and wells are also segregated, and medical facilities and the better, thatched-roof houses exist exclusively in the upper-caste colony. As revealed by the case study below on the earthquake in Gujarat, these same practices hold true even in times of great natural disaster.

Earthquake in Gujarat: Caste and its Fault-Lines

On January 26, 2001, a devastating earthquake rocked the northwest Indian state of Gujarat. Within days of the country's worst natural disaster in recent history at least 30,000 were declared dead and over one million were left homeless. In the months since the earthquake, residents of the state of Gujarat have been besieged by a man-made disaster: caste and communal discrimination in the distribution of relief and rehabilitation, corruption in the handling of aid, and political squabbling that has done little to help the earthquake's neediest victims. Six weeks after the earthquake, Human Rights Watch visited the towns of Bhuj, Bhijouri, Khawda, Anjar, and Bhachau in Kutch, the state's most devastated district. In all areas visited by Human Rights Watch, Dalits and Muslims lived separately from upper-caste Hindus. Several residents and survivors told us, "we are surviving the way we lived, that's why we are in separate camps."

While the government has allocated equal amounts of monetary compensation and food supplies to members of all communities, Dalit and Muslim populations did not have the same access to adequate shelter, electricity, running water, and other supplies available to others. This was apparent in several cities near Bhuj, including Anjar and Bhachchau, where the government had provided far superior shelter and basic amenities to upper-caste populations. The attention is now shifting to the process of rehabilitation and reconstruction of homes. As of this writing, it remained to be seen whether the government would construct integrated housing and give effect to its 1950 constitutional abolition of 'untouchability.'

India's caste system naturally finds corollaries in other parts of the sub-continent, including Nepal, Pakistan (Streefland, 1979: 13, 15), Lanka, and Bangladesh. Within the Dalit community of Nepal, there are eight major caste groups and twenty-five identified sub-castes (Bishwakarma, 2001). Some NGOs estimate the Dalit population at 4.5 million, or 21 percent of Nepal's population (*Ibid*). Despite their significant numbers, they continue to be victimized by reason of their caste. Nepal's 1990 constitution prohibits discrimination on the basis of caste (along with religion, race, sex, and ideology). However, an exception was created for Hindu religious practices. As a result, Dalits can and most often are legally excluded from Hindu temples and rituals (Bureau of Democracy, Human Rights and Labour, U.S. Department of State, February 25, 2000). They are also often kept from entering hotels, shops, or homes, and are even excluded from cowsheds due to the belief that they will pollute the milking cows. In a high profile case in 2000, dubbed the "Gaidakot Milk Scandal", the upper castes of the Gaidakot Multipurpose Milk Production Co-operative Institution Limited refused to sell milk from an animal raised by a Dalit. Only after protests and the intervention of NGOs and human rights organizations were Dalits allowed to sell their milk to the cooperative.

As in India, the government has committed itself to developing policies aimed at the social and economic advancement of the Dalit population. In 1998, the Independent Downtrodden and Oppressed Community Council was formed with the objective of coordinating policies and supervising programs to benefit Dalits. Nepal's Ninth Five-Year Plan also adopted several specific policies and programs for Dalit socio-economic development in the areas of education, health, sanitation, training and skills enhancement, and employment (Goonesekere, 2001). On August 16, 2001, the prime minister of Nepal announced that the government would outlaw discrimination against lower-caste Hindus and pledged to pass new legislation to criminalize untouchability practices and enforce the pre-existing constitutional ban on caste discrimination. At this writing, specific legislation had yet to be proposed (*The New York Times*, August 17, 2001).

Unlike India, which persistently argues that "the policies of the Indian Government relating to Scheduled Castes and Scheduled Tribes do not come under the purview of Article 1 of the Convention [on the Elimination of All Forms of Racial Discrimination—CERD/C/299/Add.3, para. 7, April 29, 1996]," Nepal has provided detailed accounts of the country's problems with caste discrimination in several of its reports to CERD. In its fourteenth periodic report under ICERD, the government frankly acknowledged that, "for an overwhelming majority of people the caste system continues to be an extremely salient feature of personal identity and social relationships and, to some extent, determines access to social opportunities." (CERD/C/337/Add.4, para. 22, May 12, 1999) It further stated that: "[R]acial discrimination in the society, especially in rural areas, is still in existence. So-called untouchables cannot even enter the houses of the people of so-called higher and middle-class castes. On one hand, they are socially suppressed by the upper classes and, on the other hand, they suffer from poverty; the intensity of poverty seems to be higher in socially backward people." (Ibid., para. 38) At the Asian Regional Preparatory Meeting for the World Conference Against Racism, Racial Discrimination, Xenophobia and Related Intolerance, held in Tehran in February 2001, the Nepali government also declared that the problem of caste discrimination should be addressed at WCAR.

Within Sri Lanka's majority Sinhala community, the Rodiya were historically excluded from villages and communities, forcing them into street begging, scavenging, and roving. Moreover, Rodiya could only wear caste-specific attire; were restricted from schools and public facilities; segregated at gravesites (Weeratunge, 1988: 61); and made to drink out of disposable coconut shells from local teashops so as not to contaminate the glasses of others. A history of exclusion has carried forward into present-day practices-Rodiya continue to reside in segregated communities with little to no interaction with upper-castes (*Ibid.*, p. 77). According to the U.N. Subcommission on the Promotion and Protection of Human Rights' working paper on work and descent-based discrimination:

In Sri Lanka there are two caste systems, one for the Sinhalese and the other for the Tamils. Although they both have their origin in India, the Sinhalese caste system is not linked to the Hindu varna. It was an aspect of a feudal society which divided people "according to Descent and Blood" or according to their hereditary roles and functions. The caste system was a secular hierarchy.... Social distance was practised but the notion of pollution hardly existed. As an American scholar concluded, "The absence of the Hindu concept had rendered the Sinhalese caste system mild and humanitarian when judged by Indian standards." The exception is the caste of

Rodiyas or Rodi (meaning 'filth') from very early times. Many legends surround their origin, all agreeing that they were banished for a heinous crime and condemned to a life of begging or, more accurately, soliciting for alms. They were denied land and work and subjected to many disadvantages and degrading treatment (Goonesekere, 2001).

Caste differentiation occurs in both of Sri Lanka's main Tamil communities (those descended from plantation workers of Indian origin brought to Sri Lanka by the British colonial government, as well as those with ancestors in Sri Lanka). Marriage bars persist, as do other social bans. Caste-based discrimination is sometimes applied to non-Hindus-including Tamil Christian and Muslim converts, and members of other minority groups. These tensions are exacerbated by conflict-driven displacement, which can place groups of varying caste backgrounds in closer proximity to another (Human Rights Watch interviews, April 1999). Caste differences between Indian-origin Tamil plantation workers also remain prominent. Higher-caste workers will often refuse to touch food offered to them by 'untouchables'. 'Untouchables' are also made to perform specific tasks during Hindu rituals that are particular to their low-caste status (Hollup, 1993: 79-81).

Caste-based divisions of labour are central to several ethnic groups in many West African countries, including the Fulani, Mandinka, and Wolof communities. Various U.N. human rights treaty monitoring bodies have made at least passing reference to caste-based distinctions in Burkina Faso, Mali, Cameroon, and Mauritania. Outside of West Africa, caste in Burundi and Mauritius has also been noted. While this report limits its discussion in West Africa to Mauritania, Senegal, and Nigeria, in addition to the countries mentioned above, caste systems can also be found in Guinea, Guinea Bissau, the Ivory Coast, Gambia, Sierra Leone, and Liberia. Though caste systems exist within several ethnic groups in Senegal, this report confines itself to the Wolof community, the country's largest ethnic group. In July 2001, a coalition of Senegalese nongovernmental organizations held a national workshop on problems faced by caste communities in the country. The one-day meeting was in preparation for the World Conference Against Racism. Among the participants was well-known sociologist Abdoulaye Bara Diop, who has written extensively on caste systems among the Wolof of Senegal. He remarked: "When we speak of castes we think of India where the caste system rigidly structures all of society. Sub-Saharan African also knows castes, among which the griot are the most well-known." He went on to add that castes can be defined as hereditary, endogamous groups that are assigned specific occupations and governed by strict hierarchical relationships. All such characteristics can be found among the Wolof who are principally divided between the geer and the neeno.

The Senegalese constitution proclaims the right of all citizens to equal protection of the law regardless of race, religion, sex, or origin, a reference to one's caste background (article 1) and prohibits all acts of racial, ethnic, and religious discrimination (article 5). Despite these constitutional protections, the extent to which neeno castes approach the courts for legal redress on discrimination claims is negligible. Within the Igbo communities of southeastern Nigeria, the marginalization of those that have been categorized as Osu reportedly remains largely unchecked (Constitutional Rights Project, 1986). The term 'Osu' historically applied to individuals who were held to be 'owned' by deities (*Ibid*). Like caste distinctions in other societies, the distinction of Osu is automatically passed on by inheritance and descent and cannot generally be overcome. Osus cannot be distinguished from others on the basis of their physical appearance or their speech. Though Osu share the same legal status as other Nigerians-the Osu system was outlawed with the passage of the Osu System Law and the Laws of Eastern Nigeria in 1956 and 1963-members of the Osu community are still shunned as pariahs and denied social equality. Mostly landless, Osu can traditionally only marry within their caste, and are buried in separate cemeteries (Okafor, 1993: 33).

Discrimination against Buraku, sometimes known as eta (variously defined as 'pollution abundant' or 'unclean') persists in Japan. Scholarly consensus today holds that the estimated three million Buraku who live in Japan today can trace their ancestry to those who became involved in occupations thought to be unclean during Japan's feudal Tokugawa era in the seventeenth century. These occupations included leather-making, a task shunned by Shintoists and Buddhists who felt that anything which involved the taking of life was unclean. The then-government codified such discrimination against Buraku when it explicitly deemed certain groups distinguished by their occupations to be eta and hinin ('nonperson'). These newly formed lower castes were then further forced into specific occupations. The etas were forced to dispose of dead cattle or take work as hide tanners and other leather-related crafts, while the hinin became security guards and executioners. Beginning in the early 1700s, the Japanese government established specific rules limiting the types of clothes and hairstyles that Buraku could wear, rendering them easily identifiable. Buraku were often prohibited from entering towns at night or frequenting certain religious sites (Neary, 1997: 55). Their gravestones were also marked with names connecting them to slavery or cattle.

The Buraku system was officially abolished by the Emancipation Edict of 1871, though discrimination against Buraku persists to this day. Following the edict, peasants rioted in protest at being ranked as equals to Buraku, setting fire to Buraku villages in western Japan and demanding that the edict be revoked. In modern day Japan, many Buraku still live in segregated communities in cities around the country, including major cities such as Kyoto, Osaka, and Kobe. Burakumin continue to be characterized as 'dirty' and 'inappropriate' to associate with. They are even said to be of a different descent than the majority of Japanese people even though they are racially indistinguishable from the rest of the population (Alldritt, 2000). Today, the Buraku people are the targets of verbal abuse and incitement to violence, often in the form of graffiti or messages posted on the Internet with slogans like 'Kill Buraku People' or 'Exterminate Buraku People'. Offensive emails are frequently sent to NGOs active on Buraku issues, such as the Buraku Liberation Movement (Ishikawa, 2001). Segregation also continues to be a way of life for the Buraku people in rural areas in Japan, though in urban centers many have successfully integrated with non-Buraku communities.

Caste and Marriage

Often, rigid social norms of purity and pollution are socially enforced through strict prohibitions on marriage or other social interaction between castes. While economic and social indicators other than caste have gained in significance, allowing intermarriage among upper castes, in many countries strong social barriers remain in place against marriage between lower and higher castes. In India the condemnation can be quite severe, ranging from social ostracism to punitive violence. On August 6, 2001, in the north Indian state of Uttar Pradesh, an upper-caste Brahmin boy and a lower-caste Jat girl were dragged to the roof of a house and publicly hanged by members of their own families as hundreds of spectators looked on. The public lynching was punishment for refusing to end an inter-caste relationship (Nolen, 2001). Inter-caste marriages can also lead to large-scale attacks on lower-caste communities. In May 2000 in Hardoi district in Uttar Pradesh, a police constable enraged by his daughter's marriage to a Dalit was joined by other relatives in shooting and killing four members of his son-in-law's family. Dalits who marry high-caste persons in Nepal in some cases reportedly have been imprisoned by local authorities because of false cases filed against them by members of the upper-caste families. Dalits are often forbidden from performing marriage or funeral rites in public areas or, in some areas, from speaking to members of upper castes. In both the Tamil and Sinhala communities of Sri Lanka, intermarriage between upper-caste and lower-caste persons is still socially discouraged. Matrimonial ads in Sri Lankan newspapers placed by Tamils and Sinhalese both routinely specify the caste background of the match that the family is seeking.

In Japan, marriage remains a primary source of discrimination for Buraku people today. Suspicions that a person is of Buraku descent often lead to private investigations into his or her family background. These background checks are easy to conduct because family registries are easily obtainable, and Buraku names are distinct and recognizable. Upon discovering that the intended bride or groom is of Buraku descent, the marriage plans are often reportedly cancelled or condemned. Marriages are still expected to fall along caste lines for the Wolof societies of Senegal; a geer who marries someone from the lower castes may be ostracized. Even amongst the neeno, marriage within one's own caste is preferred, particularly amongst the griot community. In parts of southeastern Nigeria, marriage to an Osu by a non-Osu is highly discouraged and even condemned by society, while children of such a union are likely to be ostracized and mistreated.

Caste and Labour

Allocation of labour on the basis of caste is one of the fundamental tenets of many caste systems, with lower-castes typically restricted to tasks and occupations that are deemed too 'filthy' or 'polluting' for higher-caste communities. Among the Wolof of Senegal, the concept of caste is founded on occupational groups, and accordingly divides Wolof Senegalese into one of four categories, each of which are either hereditary or assumed upon marriage. The 'superior' category of the geer was traditionally comprised of farmers, fisherman, warriors and animal breeders-they are still deemed society's noblest. They traditionally can only marry within the group, and are not allowed to practice the traditional professions of the lower castes. Although the lower-caste professions are divided among three distinct castes, they are collectively termed neeno and are thus distinguished from the geer.

The neeno are further divided into subcastes: the jeff-lekk are comprised of artisans while griots and jesters constitute the sab-lekk. A third category of the noole, who are relatively few in number, make up the servants and courtesans. The artisans are further divided into four sub-castes, namely blacksmiths or jewelers, shoemakers, woodcutters, and weavers. Beneath the neeno is the category of jaam or slaves-they are deemed to be outside the caste system. Over time, the migration of Wolofs to cities and larger towns has led to greater access to educational and professional opportunities for neeno castes, though serious problems remain. Sanitation jobs-including street cleaning and the handling of human waste and animal carcasses-are functions almost exclusively performed by Dalits in India, Sri Lanka, Bangladesh, and Nepal.

Dalits in Bangladesh-who originally migrated from India under British rule and remained after the partition of the subcontinent in 1947-work principally as municipal cleaners and domestic workers, lowly jobs that are shunned by the country's majority Muslim Bengali population (Indian Express, September 20, 2000). In the country's capital, for example, Dalits make up the majority of the 5,500 cleaners working for Dhaka City Corporation. They live in small, squalid quarters provided by the city corporation with no gas or electricity and are paid a little over U.S. $1 a day. Dalits also breed pigs for Dhaka's minority Hindu and Christian population and work as vendors and rickshaw pullers (*Ibid*).

Tamils of Indian-origin in Sri Lanka continue to face severe social discrimination. For many of the country's minority Tamils, little has changed occupationally since the eighteenth century when members of lower-castes from southern India were brought to Sri Lanka as captive labour to work on plantations and as city cleaners. To this day, the traditional division of labour continues to be perpetuated (Sivapragasam, 2001). At the bottom of the caste hierarchy in the Indian Tamil community are three untouchable castes. While Pallas and Nalavas can work on upper-caste land for wages, Paraiyars are predominantly engaged in 'unclean' sanitation work (Goonesekere, 2001). Plantation laborers also remain marginalized from economic, educational, and social opportunities, and suffer from poor health care and an inability to participate in political life (*Ibid*). According to the subcommission's working paper on work and descent-based discrimination: "A recent allegation of discrimination based on descent is that made by Tamils of Indian origin employed mainly as tea estate workers in the hill country. With regard to wages, housing, sanitation, health and educational facilities, they were an oppressed group. Improvements have slowly been made as a result of government policies and powerful trade union action. Integration with the rest of society is more difficult owing to prejudice, but this is breaking down. There are signs of upward mobility through education and non-discriminatory laws. Caste distinctions exist among themselves and complaints have been made that workers (mostly Dalits) are kept out of trade union office by high caste supervisors" (*Ibid.*, para. 36). The Sri Lankan government's development and social welfare programs have also failed to integrate the Rodiya into mainstream society, leaving many to rely on menial wage labour as sanitation workers and hospital attendants.

Most Dalits in India also continue to live in extreme poverty, without land or opportunities for better employment or education. With the exception of a minority who have benefited from India's policy of quotas in education and government jobs, Dalits are relegated to the most menial of tasks as removers of human waste and dead animals, leather workers, street sweepers, and cobblers. Dalit children make up the majority of children sold into bondage to pay off debts to upper-caste creditors. According to government statistics, an estimated one million Dalits in India are 'manual scavengers' (a majority of them women) who clear feces from public and private latrines and dispose of dead animals; unofficial estimates are much higher. Handling of human waste is a caste-based occupation, deemed too 'polluting and filthy' for anyone but Dalits. Manual scavengers exist under different caste names throughout the country, such as the Bhangis in Gujarat, the Pakhis in Andhra Pradesh, and the Sikkaliars in Tamil Nadu. Members of these communities are invariably placed at the very bottom of the caste hierarchy, and even the hierarchy of Dalit sub-castes. Using little more than a broom, a tin plate, and a basket, they are made to clear feces from public and private latrines and carry waste to dumping grounds and disposal sites. Though long outlawed, the practice of manual scavenging continues in most states.

In November 1999, after a cyclone slammed into India's eastern state of Orissa, killing thousands and rendering millions homeless, the government brought in two hundred Dalit manual scavengers from New Delhi, and planned to bring five hundred more from other parts of Orissa, to load animal carcasses onto hand-drawn carts and take them away to be burned. Government officials had reportedly offered local upper-caste residents more than the daily minimum wage for each animal burned but they refused, citing the decayed conditions of the carcasses and the fact that the task was beneath them: they had "some self-respect left" (Misra, 1999). As witnessed with the earthquake in Gujarat, even in times of natural disaster, the laws of 'purity and pollution' prevail and the government's actions often reinforce the prejudice. Discrimination against Buraku persists in Japan's economy. In a high profile case in 1998, according to Buraku civil rights groups, over seven hundred companies were discovered to have hired private investigators to unearth job applicants' Buraku origins, ethnic background, nationality, ideology, religion, and political affiliation. After factoring in each characteristic, an applicant was ranked from 'excellent' to "advisable not to hire." However, a person discovered to be of Buraku origin was not rated and consequently not hired (Tomonaga, 2000).

Already years before, in 1975, the practice of selling 'Buraku lists' had been exposed. Also compiled by investigative companies, these lists included information on the names and locations of Buraku households and were marketed to private companies for the purposes of screening job applicants and to families seeking to arrange and approve marriages (*Ibid*). Some claim that the lists were used to counter the Buraku rights movement, which successfully campaigned for a standard job application for high school students, and for the prohibition of the discriminatory use of family registers to be legally mandated (*Ibid*). Such lists were reported to be in circulation as recently as 1996.

Debt Bondage and Slavery

The poor remuneration of manual scavenging, agricultural labour, and other forms of low-caste employment often force families of lower castes or caste-like groups into bondage. A lack of enforcement of relevant legislation prohibiting debt bondage in most of the countries concerned allows for the practice to continue unabated. An estimated forty million people in India, among them some fifteen million children, are working in slave-like conditions in order to pay off debts as bonded laborers. Due to the high interest rates charged, the employers' control over records, and the abysmally low wages paid, the debts are seldom settled. Bonded laborers are frequently low-caste, illiterate, and extremely poor, while the creditors/

employers are usually higher-caste, literate, comparatively wealthy, and relatively more powerful members of the community. The Bonded Labour System (Abolition) Act, 1976, abolishes all agreements and obligations arising out of the bonded labour system. It aims to release all laborers from bondage, cancel any outstanding debt, prohibit the creation of new bondage agreements, and order the economic rehabilitation of freed bonded laborers by the state. It also punishes attempts to compel persons into bondage with a maximum of three years in prison and a Rs. 2,000 (U.S.$43) fine. However, relatively few bonded laborers have been identified, released, and rehabilitated in the country.

In Pakistan the debt bondage system is most prevalent in the agricultural provinces of southern Punjab and Sindh. Most laborers in these areas are minority Hindus from lower castes (Los Angeles Times, August 20, 1999). According to a report by the Asian Development Bank, bonded agricultural laborers in Sindh province in Pakistan, known as Haris, hail from lower caste and 'untouchable' groups of Indian origin. In lower Sindh, many live in 'unregistered villages' and so have no political rights. Many are illiterate and often ignorant of the laws that are meant to protect them. Haris work as contract laborers, migrant workers, and sharecroppers. Under current systems, Haris can never receive compensation worth more than one-fourth of the crop that they have farmed (Asian Development Bank, "Sindh Rural Development Project (TA 3132-PAK) Final Report, Volume 1," October 2000). In a pattern similar to that practiced in India, the charging of exorbitantly high interest rates ensure that loans from landowners never get repaid. While the loan agreement is often made between the landowner and the male head of the peasant household, the work to pay off the loan is performed by the entire family, including women and children (Human Rights Watch, 1995: 12-13).

Women have also been held in custody by landowners when bonded male members of the family leave the land or area, and have even been sold into marriage or prostitution should the male family member fail to return (*Ibid.*). As in India, children often inherit their families' debts and remain trapped in a cycle of debt bondage. (To ensure the sustainability of the practice of debt bondage, landowners in Pakistan have also been known to bribe teachers to stay at home, instead of teaching at schools attended by the children of bonded laborers. A 1999 report found that Pakistani newspapers and education groups have documented at least 5,000 `ghost schools-many of them in rural areas-where no students study because landlords often pay the teachers to stay at home.). A disturbing reflection of the slavery of centuries past is the well-documented practice of tying up or chaining bonded laborers to hinder their escape. Of the 7,500 bonded laborers reported to have escaped or been released since 1995 in the southern Sindh province, human rights organizations report that 'several hundred' of them were found "tied up or in chains." Similarly, in 1991 the Pakistani army reportedly conducted a raid that unearthed the illegal detention of 295 laborers, including 132 children, all of whom were shackled each night. Most were only given flour and chili peppers as food and had no access to plumbing facilities or medical care (http://www.dol.gov/dol/ilab/public/media/reports/iclp/sweat2/bonded.htm (accessed May 16, 2001)). National legislation in Pakistan prohibiting these practices reportedly has done little to eradicate them. Provincial governments responsible for their enforcement have yet to establish mechanisms to put them into practice. According to the United Nation Development Programme's "Nepal Human Development Report 1998," despite legal pronouncements to the contrary, bonded labour has not been eradicated in Nepal. The report adds:

In the mid-western and far western hills, the debt-bonded agricultural labourers, haliyas, mainly from 'untouchable' castes, work under this system. The Anti-Slavery International and INSEC73 in 1996 rarely observed haliyas from among members of the high caste groups.... Their report also revealed that in the regions noted above, members of 'untouchable' households were charged very high rates of interest - as high as 10 percent/month - on loans forwarded by their landlords, while members of 'high caste' households were generally charged only 2-3 percent/month. Such discrimination was designed to keep alive and intensify the system of debt bondage. The 'low caste' Tarai groups like Musahar, Dusadh,

Dom, Chamar, etc., face a similar problem: repayment of loans is actively discouraged by the landlords (ibid.). Because the primary interest of the landlord lies in continued cultivation of his land and in regular assurance of labour supply, his lending is not directed towards earning interest in cash (NRB 1988). The kamaiya bonded labour system is also prevalent in western Nepal. According to the UNDP report, kamaiyas are "mostly landless and homeless, and belong to the Tharu ethnic group.... A kamaiya is heavily burdened with debts and often remains as such for a long period. Debts are inter-generationally transferable. Frequently, therefore, a kamaiya household remains in bondage through multiple generations" (*Ibid*). In July 2000, the Nepali government responded to years of sustained advocacy by local NGOs and issued a decree canceling all debts arising from the illegal practice of bonded labour. The decree liberated thousands of kamaiya laborers but it remains unclear whether haliyas were affected. Many kamaiyas were forcibly driven from their homes and dispossessed of all their belongings as a result of landlord retaliation. As of February 2001, a lack of government rehabilitation services had kept many displaced laborers in makeshift camps that lacked adequate shelter, water, food, and sanitation (Limbu, 2001).

The legacy of slavery as a form of caste and descent-based discrimination in Mauritania is an issue the government must do more to address (Human Rights Watch, 1994). While President Maaouiya Ould Sid'Ahmed Ould Taya has brought public attention to modern-day slavery practices throughout the country-and while the government purports to have implemented relevant education and agrarian reforms-its record on enforcing slavery-specific legislation, and legislation promoting the civil rights of former slaves, is weak (Ibid., 79). Both the Arab and Afro-Mauritanian groups have long distinguished community members on the basis of caste, and both included a caste-like designation of 'slave' within these systems. To this day a former 'slave' distinction-particularly for the Haratines, Arabic speakers of Sub-Saharan African origin-still carries significant social implications. At best, members of higher and lower castes are discouraged from intermarrying. In Soninke communities, members of the slave caste are also buried in separate cemeteries (http://www.erieri.com/codes/MAURITANIA.htm (accessed March 22, 2001)). At worst, however, there is a widespread system of unpaid servitude required of communities whose members still self-identify as slaves. Though the government has long outlawed slave-like distinctions and practices, it has taken few steps to enforce these laws. A weak economy also leaves former slaves with few options other than remaining with the families of masters who owned their ancestors (*Ibid*). Caste systems similar to those found among the Wolof of Senegal can also be found among Soninke, Halpular, and Wolof Afro-Mauritanians.

Caste and Socio-Economic Disparities

Significant economic and educational disparities persist between lower and higher-caste communities in the countries highlighted in this report. Lower-caste communities are often plagued by low literacy levels and a lack of access to health care and education. A lack of formal education or training, as well as discrimination that effectively bars them from many forms of employment, and the nonenforcement of protective legislation, perpetuates caste-based employment and keeps its hereditary nature alive. As of 1997, there were reportedly only two Dalit medical doctors and fifteen Dalit engineers in Nepal (Vishwakarma, 1997). The life expectancy rate of Nepal's Dalits is five years short of the national average of 55. Children face a higher incidence of malnutrition and the general population lacks access to clean drinking water or proper health services.

Nepal's 1998 Human Development Report revealed that development indicators closely followed caste lines. Without a single exception, the lower the caste, the lower the life expectancy, the literacy rate, years of schooling, and per capita income (Fourteenth Report of States Parties Due in 1998: Nepal", CERD/C/337/Add.4, Annex, May 12, 1999). In 1999, Nepal's fourteenth periodic report to CERD also frankly and constructively highlighted the economic disparities that continue to persist between low- and high-caste populations: "[A]wareness creation, income generation, education and health facilities programmes were implemented to address the problems of the backward communities. However, the gap between so-called higher and lower castes has not narrowed. There have hardly been any changes in the society or the living standard of the poor. Consequently, the people of backward communities have felt discriminated against and could not believe that the Government was doing anything for their welfare and development. The main reasons for this are: lack of integrated programmes, weak implementation and sustainability, failure to mainstream backward communities and repressed people into the national development process, centre-oriented/based programmes rather than community-based/participatory programmes, little attention to human resource development and lack of encouragement to the development and modernization of traditional occupations and skills, lack of effective institutional mechanisms, etc".

Access to Education

High drop-out and lower literacy rates among lower-caste populations have rather simplistically been characterized as the natural consequences of poverty and underdevelopment. Though these rates are partly attributable to the need for low-caste children to supplement their family wages through labour, more insidious and less well-documented is the discriminatory and abusive treatment faced by low-caste children who attempt to attend school, at the hands of their teachers and fellow students. Over fifty years since India's constitutional promise of free, compulsory, primary education for all children up to the age of fourteen-with special care and consideration to be given to promote the educational progress of scheduled castes-illiteracy still plagues almost two-thirds of the Dalit population as compared to about one-half of the general population. The literacy gap between Dalits and the rest of the population fell a scant 0.39 percent between 1961 and 1991. Most of the government schools in which Dalit students are enrolled are deficient in basic infrastructure, classrooms, teachers, and teaching aids. A majority of Dalit students are also enrolled in vernacular schools whose students suffer serious disadvantages in the job market as compared to those who learn in English-speaking schools (India: National Campaign on Dalit Human Rights, 1999).

Despite state assistance in primary education, Dalits also suffer from an alarming drop-out rate. According to the National Commission for Scheduled Castes and Scheduled Tribes' 1996-1997 and 1997-1998 Report, the national drop-out rate for Dalit children-who often sit in the back of classrooms-was a staggering 49.35 percent at the primary level, 67.77 percent for middle school, and 77.65 percent for secondary school. Rodiya children in Sri Lanka rarely study past elementary levels, if at all. Instead, their parents require them to realize their income-earning potential even as young children, and often prematurely take them out of school. Lower-caste Tamil plantation workers of Indian origin in Sri Lanka also have low literacy levels. According to a Srı Lankan activists only 65 percent of plantation workers can read or write, compared to a high 90 percent national average. Higher drop out rates among children of plantation workers stems partly from the employment of these children as domestic workers, hotel workers, or sanitation cleaners (Sivapragasam, 2001).

The Buraku of Japan also suffer from lower levels of higher education than the national average, and higher dropout rates than the broader society. In particular, Buraku women report lower levels of literacy, high school and university enrollment, and employment. Special scholarship programs that bolstered national averages of Buraku education are expected to be phased out by March 2002, despite the considerable success they had in bridging the education gap between Buraku and non-Buraku. In Nepal, the literacy rate for Dalits is appallingly low at 10 percent for men and 3.2 percent for women, compared to a national literacy rate that exceeds 50 percent. According to the government's own fourteenth periodic report under ICERD, "The lowest literacy is among the occupational castes. Women constitute more than two thirds of the illiterates."

Access to Land

Most Dalit victims of abuse in India are landless agricultural laborers who form the backbone of the nation's agrarian economy. Despite decades of land reform legislation, over 86 percent of Dalit households today are landless or near landless. Those who own land often own very little. Land is the prime asset in rural areas that determines an individual's standard of living and social status. As with many other low-caste populations, lack of access to land makes Dalits economically vulnerable; their dependency is exploited by upper- and middle-caste landlords and allows for many abuses to go unpunished. Landless agricultural laborers throughout the country work for a few kilograms of rice or Rs. 15 to Rs. 35 (US$0.32 to $0.75) a day, well below the minimum wage prescribed in their state. Many laborers owe debts to their employers or other moneylenders.

Indian laws and regulations that prohibit alienation of Dalit lands, set ceilings on a single landowner's holdings, or allocate surplus government lands to scheduled castes and scheduled tribes have been largely ignored, or worse, manipulated by upper castes with the help of district administrations. Although many of Nepal's agricultural laborers are Dalits, Dalits also have a startlingly low rate of land ownership-only 3.1 percent of Dalits own more than twenty-one ropanies of land and collectively Dalits own only about 1 percent of Nepal's total cultivable land. Moreover, 90 percent of Nepal Dalits live below the poverty line, compared to 45 percent of the overall population. Their per capita income amounts to a paltry U.S.$39.60 while the rest of Nepalese average U.S.$210 per year.94 Nepali Dalits are among the world's poorest of the poor.

Political Representation and Political Rights

India's policy of 'reservations' or caste-based quotas is an attempt by the central government to remedy past injustices related to low-caste status. To allow for proportional representation in certain state and federal institutions, the constitution reserves 22.5 percent of federal government jobs, seats in state legislatures, the lower house of parliament, and educational institutions for scheduled castes and scheduled tribes. The reservation policy, however, has not been fully implemented. The National Commission for Scheduled Castes and Scheduled Tribes' (1996-1997 and 1997-1998) report indicates that of the total scheduled caste reservation quota in the Central Government, 54 percent remains unfilled. More than 88 percent of posts reserved in the public sector remain unfilled as do 45 percent in state banks. A closer examination of the caste composition of government services, institutions of education and other services, however, reveals what Dalit activists call an "unacknowledged reservation policy" for upper-castes, particularly Brahmins, built into the system. Though they represented only 5 percent of the population in 1989, Brahmins comprised 70 percent of the Class I officers in governmental services. At universities, upper-castes occupy 90 percent of the teaching posts in the social sciences and percent in the sciences, while Dalit representation is only 1.2 and 0.5 percent, respectively.

Dalits throughout India also suffer in many instances from de facto disenfranchisement. While India remains the world's largest democracy, for many of its Dalit citizens democracy has been a sham. During elections, many are routinely threatened and beaten by political party strongmen in order to compel them to vote for certain candidates. Already under the thumb of local landlords and police officials, Dalit villagers who do not comply have been harassed, beaten, and murdered. Police and upper-caste militias, operating at the behest of powerful political leaders in India's states, have also punished Dalit voters. In February 1998, police raided a Dalit village in Tamil Nadu that had boycotted the national parliamentary elections. Women were kicked and beaten, their clothing was torn, and police forced sticks and iron pipes into their mouths. Kerosene was poured into stored food grains and grocery items and police reportedly urinated in cooking vessels. In Bihar, political candidates ensure their majority vote with the help of senas, civilian militias, whose members intimidate and kill. The Ranvir Sena, a private militia of upper-caste landlords, was responsible for killing more than fifty people during Bihar's 1995 state election campaign. The sena was again used to intimidate voters in Ara district, Bihar, during the February 1998 national parliamentary elections. Dalits who have contested political office in village councils and municipalities through seats that have been constitutionally 'reserved' for them have been threatened with physical abuse and even death in order to get them to withdraw from the campaign. In the village of Melavalavu, in

Tamil Nadu's Madurai district, following the election of a Dalit to the village council presidency, members of a higher-caste group murdered six Dalits in June 1997, including the elected council president, whom they beheaded.

Unlike India, Nepal does not provide for reservations of posts or quotas in political bodies, civil sector jobs, and institutions of higher learning. Though they comprise over 20 percent of the population, lower castes are dramatically underrepresented in government. Since 1958, only fourteen Dalits in Nepal have become members of parliament (upper house) through a system of nomination, all of them men. Only one Dalit has been elected to the House of Representatives. Furthermore, there has been a dearth of Dalits in Nepal's administrative and judicial system; and discrimination continues to persist in the Nepal Royal Army (*Kathmandu Post*, July 27, 1997). Conversely, according to an NGO study on discrimination against Dalits in Nepal, while Brahmins constitute only 16 percent of the population, they represent 57 percent of parliament and a staggering 89 percent of the judiciary.100 The result is that a full one-fifth of Nepal's population is effectively excluded. In Sri Lanka, Indian-origin Tamils-who have resided in the country since the nineteenth century-can only become citizens through registration. They are denied the right to citizenship by descent to which the rest of the Sri Lankan population is entitled.

Physical and Economic Retaliation

A principal weapon in sustaining the low status of Dalits in India is the use of social and economic boycotts and acts of retaliatory violence. Dalits are physically abused and threatened with economic and social ostracism from the community for refusing to carry out various caste-based tasks. Any attempt to alter village customs, defy the social order, or to demand land, increased wages, or political rights leads to violence and economic retaliation on the part of those most threatened by changes in the status quo. Dalit communities as a whole are summarily punished for individual transgressions; Dalits are cut off from community land and employment during social boycotts, Dalit women bear the brunt of physical attacks, and the law is rarely enforced. Large-scale clashes between caste communities in Tamil Nadu's southern districts in recent years, for example, have often been triggered by Dalits' efforts to draw water from a 'forbidden' well or by their refusal to perform a delegated task. Since the early 1990s, violence against Dalits has escalated dramatically in response to growing Dalit rights movements. Between 1995 and 1997, a total of 90,925 cases were registered with the police nationwide as crimes and 'atrocities' against scheduled castes. Of these 1,617 were for murder, 12,591 for hurt, 2,824 for rape, and 31,376 for offenses listed under the Prevention of Atrocities Act. Under the act, atrocities are defined to include forcing members of a scheduled caste or scheduled tribe to drink or eat any inedible or obnoxious substance; dumping excreta, waste matter, carcasses or any other obnoxious substance in their premises or neighborhood; forcibly removing their clothes and parading them naked or with painted face or body; interfering with their rights to land; compelling a member of a scheduled caste or scheduled tribe into forms of forced or bonded labour; corrupting or fouling the water of any spring, reservoir or any other source ordinarily used by scheduled castes or scheduled tribes; denying right of passage to a place of public resort; and using a position of dominance to exploit a scheduled caste or scheduled tribe woman sexually. Given that Dalits are often both reluctant and unable (for lack of police cooperation) to report crimes against themselves, the actual number of abuses is presumably much higher (Human Rights Watch, 1999).

India's National Commission for Scheduled Castes and Scheduled Tribes has reported that these cases typically fall into one of three categories: cases relating to the practice of 'untouchability' and attempts to defy the social order; cases relating to land disputes and demands for minimum wages; and cases of atrocities by police and forest officials. Most of the conflicts take place within very narrow segments of the caste hierarchy, between the poor and the not so poor, the landless laborer and the marginal landowner. The differences lie in the considerable amount of leverage that the higher-caste Hindus or non-Dalits are able to wield over local police, district administrations, and even state governments (Ibid., 4). On the night of December 1, 1997, an upper-caste landlord militia called the Ranvir Sena shot dead sixteen children, twenty-seven women, and eighteen men in the village of Laxmanpur-Bathe, Jehanabad district Bihar. Five teenage girls were raped and mutilated before being shot in the chest. The villagers were alleged to have been sympathetic to a guerilla group known as Naxalites that had been demanding more equitable land redistribution in the area. When asked why the sena killed children and women, one sena member told Human Rights Watch, "We kill children because they will grow up to become Naxalites. We kill women because they will give birth to Naxalites" (*Ibid.*, p. 5).

The senas, which claim many politicians as members, operate with virtual impunity. In some cases, police have accompanied them on raids and have stood by as they killed villagers and burned down their homes. On April 10, 1997, in the village of Ekwari, located in the Bhojpur district of Bihar, police stationed in the area to protect lower-caste villagers instead pried open the doors of their residences as members of the sena entered and killed eight residents. In other cases, police raids have followed attacks by the senas. Sena leaders are rarely prosecuted for such killings, and the villagers are rarely or inadequately compensated for their losses. Even in cases where police are not hostile to Dalits, they are generally not accessible to call upon: most police camps are located in the upper-caste section of the village and Dalits are simply unable to approach them for protection.

Caste and Gender

Lower-caste women are singularly positioned at the bottom of caste, class, and gender hierarchies. Largely uneducated and consistently paid less than their male counterparts worldwide they invariably bear the brunt of exploitation, discrimination, and physical attacks. Sexual abuse and other forms of violence against women are often used by landlords and the police to inflict political 'lessons' and crush dissent within the community. Lower-caste women also suffer disproportionately in terms of access to health care, education, and subsistence wages as compared to women of higher castes. Dalit women in India and Nepal make up the majority of landless laborers and scavengers, as well as a significant percentage of the women forced into prostitution in rural areas or sold into urban brothels. As such, they come into greater contact with landlords and enforcement agencies than their upper-caste counterparts. Their subordinate position is exploited by those in power who carry out their attacks with impunity. Incidents of gang-rape, stripping, and parading women naked through the streets, and making them eat excrement are all crimes specific to Dalit women in India. Sexual violence is also linked to debt bondage in India, Pakistan, and Nepal. According to a Tamil Nadu state government official, the rape of Dalit women exposes the hypocrisy of the caste system as "no one practices untouchability when it comes to sex" (*Ibid.*, p. 3). Like other Indian women whose relatives are sought by the police, Dalit women have also been arrested and tortured in custody as a means of punishing their male relatives who are hiding from the authorities.

Gender-specific violence is a problem of epidemic proportions among low-caste plantation workers in Sri Lanka. In Nepal, Dalit women are economically marginalized and exploited, both within and outside their families. As the largest group of those engaged in manual labour and agricultural production, their jobs often include waste disposal, clearing carcasses, and doing leatherwork. Despite their grueling tasks and long hours, exploitative wages ensure that Dalit women are unable to earn a subsistence living. In some rural areas Dalit women scarcely earn ten to twenty kilograms of food grain a year, barely enough to sustain a family (Dalit NGO Federation (Nepal) "Nepal Alternative Country Report 2001). Many have been driven to prostitution. One caste in particular, known as badis, is viewed as a prostitution caste. Many Dalit women and girls, including those from the badi caste, are trafficked into sex work in Indian brothels (Sob, 995). Under the devadasi system, thousands of Dalit girls in India's southern states are ceremonially 'dedicated' or married to a deity or to a temple. Once dedicated, they are forced to become prostitutes for upper-caste community members, and eventually auctioned into an urban brothel (Consideration of Report by India to the Human Rights Committee, CCPR/C/79/Add.81, August 4, 1997). In Pakistan human rights organizations report that the rape of female bonded laborers is one of the most pressing problems facing the movement to end debt bondage. Not only is it a widespread, violent problem, but there is little legal recourse (Jahangir and Jilani, 1990). In Mauritania, women are particularly burdened by the designation of 'slave'. While men are sometimes able to escape, and by law cannot be forced to return to their 'masters', women are often forced to remain as their 'masters' threaten to keep their children. The tenuous legal status of slave children also keeps women tied to their masters (http://www.erieri.com (accessed March 22, 2001)).

Caste and the South Asian Diaspora

Caste has migrated with the South Asian diaspora to firmly take root in East and South Africa, Mauritius, Fiji, Suriname, the Middle East, Malaysia, the Caribbean, the United Kingdom, North America, and other regions. Prakash Jain of Delhi's Jawaharlal Nehru University has analyzed major clusters of the Indian diaspora. The following summary appeared in an article in the weekly magazine India Today: "There are approximately 15-20 million Indians across the globe. Other than Nepal, this population has emerged in five different ways. The first arose in the mid-19th and early 20th century when the British took Indian labour to raise sugar plantations in countries like South Africa, Mauritius, Trinidad, Jamaica, Guyana and Fiji. This numbers about 3.3 million. The second cluster of about 1.5 million in Sri Lanka, Malaysia and Myanmar has descended from kingani/maistry labour. The third category numbering over two lakh [200,000] is made up of free passage emigrants, largely from Gujarat, who went to Kenya, Tanzania and Zambia. The fourth group comprises workers in Saudi Arabia, UAE, Oman, Kuwait, Bahrain, Qatar and other West Asian countries, now estimated at about three million. The final group comprises around four million emigrants to the US, UK, Canada, Australia and other western countries."

Among migrant communities in North America and Europe, caste ideologies are perpetuated by families returning to India to seek out marriage partners within their own caste. U.S.-based matrimonial services, including regional conventions, are burgeoning alongside a growing population of Indian origin (Seenarine, 2001). Families openly advertise their caste preference in the matrimonial sections of Indian community papers in North America and Europe (a practice quite common within India as well), as well as on Internet matchmaking sites. In the United States, a rising number of caste-based groups-each with chapters throughout many major cities-also points to the importance of caste as an identifier for migrant Indian communities. Such caste-based associations in the United States are providing funds and political support for a resurgence of caste fundamentalism in South Asia as well (*Ibid*). In Britain emigrant Dalits must also worship in segregated temples and have thus formed an umbrella group for low-caste temples-Guru Ravidass UK (Puri, 2001). Twenty-two of these temples withheld (and ultimately redirected) funds raised for earthquake victims in Gujarat due to incidents of caste discrimination in the distribution of earthquake relief (*Ibid*).

Also in Britain caste tensions frequently erupt between high-caste Punjabis (Jats) and low-caste Punjabis (Chamars). Physical violence has also been known to erupt following intermarriage between the two communities (Muman, 2001). Caste consciousness becomes especially problematic given the sizable population of both Jats and Chamars in the United Kingdom. According Sat Pal Muman, a presenter at the September 2000 International Dalit Human Rights Conference in London, inquiries about one's caste background are often made in privately run or Jat-run educational institutions and places of employment. In the city of Wolverhampton incidents of upper-caste Jats refusing to share water taps or make any physical contact with lower-caste persons have also been reported. At a sports competition in Birmingham in 1999 Jats reportedly refused to eat food that came from the Chamar community (*Ibid*).

In Suriname, Indians of Dalit-descent continue to be largely distinguished by their various caste-based occupations. Chamars traditionally worked as drum beaters, beggars, hawkers, and shoemakers; Pallen as landless laborers; Dhobis as washers; Collies as porters; and Dasis as house servants. A higher-caste group includes Kurmis as cultivators, Ahir as cow herders, and Chettyar as weavers, barbers, shopkeepers, and moneylenders. The third and highest caste category consists of priests, scribes, and schoolmasters.

In Mauritius, with its large concentration of people of Indian origin, social organization is based on family, kinship networks, and "to a not negligible extent, caste-based organization" (Eriksen, 1992). Caste-based considerations have also been reported in the political and employment sector (*Ibid*). Caste distinctions play a role in both private life and political organization within Malaysia's minority 'Indian' community although the extent of its influence on Malaysian Indian society is the subject of considerable debate. Most Malaysians of South Asian descent are Tamils whose ancestors came from South India. But the term 'Indian' also includes Sri Lankans, northern Indians and people from elsewhere in South Asia. Caste considerations are most obvious in the private sphere, particularly in the community's attitudes towards intermarriage. Many families seeking to arrange marriages place matrimonial ads that include caste requirements, and marriage brokers may be expected to take caste into account when finding suitable matches (Muthiah, 1997). As one researcher observed, "Caste has, indeed, such a strong hold in marriage matters that intercaste marriages between different categories of higher caste status sometimes do not take place with parents' approval, much less between higher and lower caste members. Abolition of caste discrimination in this area remains a distant dream" (Ramasamy, 1984: 46). Though interactions outside the home seem to take place without much emphasis on caste, within the home contact with castes thought to be polluting may be quite limited. Some families, for example, refuse to dine with or accept food and drinks from people they suspect of being lower caste.

In the political sphere, caste was a driving force in a lengthy dispute between two prominent Malaysian Indian politicians, All Malaysian Indian Progressive Front (IPF) president Datuk M.G.

Pandithan, and Malaysian Indian Congress (MIC) party president Datuk Seri S. Samy Vellu. In 1988, Pandithan, then the MIC's vice president, was expelled from the party for accusing the MIC of practicing caste-based politics that favored higher castes. "Pandithan's dilemma - to be or not to be in MIC," Utusan Express, January 26, 2001. In 1997, Vellu rejected Pandithan's claim that "casteism is a deep-rooted issue in Malaysia which is silently but strongly being practised." Pandithan was particularly critical of the existence of some twenty-two registered caste-based associations in Malaysia dedicated to assisting members of their own caste socially and financially. These associations sometimes impose caste-based restrictions on members, such as banning exogamous marriages (Muthiah, 1997; Ramasamy, 1984: 74-75). Mass migration of higher and lower-caste Indians to Bahrain, Kuwait, the United Arab Emirates, and other Gulf states has brought with it vestiges of the caste system as well.

Failure to Implement Domestic and International Law

The practice of untouchability, other caste-based discrimination, violence against lower-caste men, women, and children, and other abuses outlined in this report violate numerous domestic and international laws. International human rights law imposes on governments a duty to guarantee the rights of all people without discrimination and to punish those who engage in caste-based exploitation, violence, and discrimination. In its August 2000 resolution, the U.N. Subcommission on the Promotion and Protection of Human Rights urged governments to ensure that "appropriate legal penalties and sanctions, including criminal sanctions, are prescribed for and applied to all persons or entities within the jurisdiction of the Governments concerned who may be found to have engaged in practices of discrimination on the basis of work and descent". The subcommission's working paper on work and descent-based discrimination noted a year later, "The laws are there, but there is a clear lack of will on the part of law enforcement officers to take action owing to caste prejudice on their part or deference shown to higher-caste perpetrators." Though constitutional guarantees and other national legislation banning caste discrimination suggest that various governments have successfully tackled caste-related violations, much of the legislation remains unenforced. Official condemnation alone has proven insufficient in many countries in abolishing caste-based abuses.

In India, for example, laws are openly flouted while state complicity in attacks on Dalit communities continues to reflect a well-documented pattern. India's own constitutional and statutory bodies, including the National Human Rights Commission and the National Commission for Scheduled Castes and Scheduled Tribes, have repeatedly confirmed and decried the prevalence of the abuses outlined in this report. Other government authorities, however, have facilitated continued discrimination. Indeed it would be difficult to convince Dalits that, over fifty-four years after independence, the government had done anything to end the violence and discrimination that has ruled their lives. The message sent from the judiciary on caste discrimination is equally disturbing: in July 1998 in the state of Uttar Pradesh, an Allahabad High Court judge reportedly had his chambers "purified with Ganga jal," water from the River Ganges, because it had earlier been occupied by a Dalit judge (*Times of India* (Bombay), July 23, 1998).

The state's failure to prosecute atrocities against Dalits is well illustrated by its manipulation of the Scheduled Castes and Scheduled Tribes (Prevention of Atrocities) Act. Enacted in 1989, the act provides for certain stiffer punishments for abuses against members of scheduled castes and scheduled tribes when committed by non-scheduled caste or tribe members. Its enactment represented an acknowledgment on the part of the government that abuses, in their most degrading and violent forms, were still perpetrated against Dalits despite the constitutional abolition of 'untouchability' four decades earlier. The potential of the Scheduled Castes and Scheduled Tribes (Prevention of Atrocities) Act, 1989, to bring about social change, however, has been hampered by police corruption and caste bias, with the result that many allegations of caste crimes are not entered in police records. Ignorance of procedures and a lack of knowledge of the act have also affected its implementation. Even when cases are registered, the absence of special courts to try them can delay prosecutions for up to three to four years. Some state governments dominated by higher castes have attempted to repeal the legislation altogether.

In 1957, the government of Sri Lanka passed the Prevention of Social Disabilities Act making it an offense to deny access to various public places to persons by reason of their caste. A 1971 amendment imposed stiffer punishments for the commission of offenses under the 1957 act. According to the U.N. Subcommission's working paper: "Initially there were some prosecutions in the North but there was a tendency for the police not to take action against violations. In a celebrated temple-entry case, the Act was challenged as interfering with customs and ancient usages that prohibited defilement of a Hindu temple by the entry of low-caste persons. This argument was rejected by the Supreme Court and Privy Council."

Unlike India's constitution, Sri Lanka's 1978 Constitution does not provide for community-based affirmative action. It does however prohibit discrimination on the grounds of caste, including caste-based restrictions on access to shops, public restaurants, hotels, places of public entertainment, and places of worship of one's own religion. Despite these constitutional prohibitions, serious problems remain. Prohibitions on the denial of fundamental freedoms to Nigeria's Osu community are part and parcel of the country's constitution and domestic laws. Legislation abolishing the Osu system has been in force since the 1950s, and constitutional provisions prohibit discriminatory practices and promote equal implementation of legal protections. Nigeria has also incorporated the African Charter on Human and People's Rights into its national legislation, strengthening its commitment on paper to end discriminatory practices such as the Osu caste system. However, these laws remain largely unenforced. According to the 1984 report of an expert to the then-U.N. Subcommission on Prevention of Discrimination and Protection of Minorities, slavery "as an institution protected by law has been genuinely abolished in Mauritania.... Nevertheless... it cannot be denied that in certain remote corners of the country over which the administration has little control certain situations of de facto slavery may still persist" (Bossuyt, 1984). Still many human rights groups, including Human Rights Watch, have pointed to Mauritanian government inaction in enforcing its own ban on slave-like practices.

In their oral submission before the fiftieth session of the U.N. Subcommission on Prevention of Discrimination and Protection of Minorities in 1998, Anti-Slavery International stated that, "the government does not have a pro-slavery policy, but its silence and inaction on this issue allow centuries-old caste servitude to continue with impunity." In a 1999 letter Human Rights Watch noted the following on the enforcement of laws against slavery: The government has not taken any forceful steps to remove what it considers the 'vestiges' or 'after effects' (sequelles) of slavery. While the courts have upheld individual rights in a few cases, judges have failed to enforce systematically the laws abolishing slavery, in some cases returning 'slaves' to their 'masters' even though this relationship in theory has ceased to exist. Few lawyers are able and willing to appear in court to defend the rights of 'slaves'. There is no law providing for the practice of slavery or forced labour to be an offense; while provisions in the 1980 law for compensation to be provided to slave-owners (but not slaves) have never been implemented, encouraging an attitude among 'masters' that they need take no action to ensure substantive freedom for their 'slaves' (Bales, 1999). The success of legislation to combat caste discrimination in Japan may be coming to an end. To counter various forms of discrimination against the Buraku population, the Japanese government instituted the "Law on Special Measures for Dowa Projects." This series of reform efforts had considerable success in improving housing areas for Buraku communities and increasing education and literacy rates among Buraku children. As a case in point, from 1963 to 1997, the enrolment of Buraku children in high school and public vocational schools rose from 30 percent to 92 percent, while university and junior college rates rose from 14.2 percent to 28.6 percent.139 With the Special Measures set to lapse in March 2002, civil rights activists in Japan worry that that progress will be halted and have urged the government to consider the need for further such legislation. Discrimination based on occupation and descent affects some 250 million people worldwide. The elimination of caste-based discrimination and related human rights abuses, too long neglected, must become a global priority. Despite the existence of significant constitutional protections and progressive legislation, in many countries the reality for many millions remains unchanged. The solution lies in concerted international attention to assist national governments in this important and long overdue work.

Bibliography

Ajzen, I. (1991). The theory of planned behaviour. *Organizational Behaviour and Human Decision Processes,* 50, 179–211.

Alba, R. (1990). *Ethnic Identity,* New Haven, CT: Yale University Press.

Alba, R., A. Lutz and E. Vesselinov (2001). How enduring were the inequalities among European immigrant groups in the United States? *Demography,* 38, 349–356.

Alexander, K.L., D.R. Entwisle and R. Herman (1999). In the eye of the beholder: Parents' and teachers' ratings of children's behavioural style. In *Contemporary Perspectives on Family Research,* 1, C. L. Shehan, ed. Greenwich, CT: JAI Press.

Alldritt, Leslie D. (2000). The Burakumin: The Complicity of Japanese Buddhism in Oppression and an Opportunity for Liberation. *Journal of Buddhist Ethics,* 7.

Allen, J. (1995). A possible remedy for unthinking discrimination. *Brooklyn Law Review,* 61, 1299.

Allen, M. (2003). Bush issues ban on racial profiling. *The Washington Post,* A14.

Allport, G. (1954). *The Nature of Prejudice.* Reading, MA: Addison-Wesley.

Altemeyer, B. (1988). *Enemies of Freedom: Understanding Right-Wing Authoritarianism.* San Francisco, CA: Jossey-Bass.

Altonji, J.G. and C.R. Pierret (2001). Employer learning and statistical discrimination. *Quarterly Journal of Economics,* 1–37.

Altonji, J.G. and U. Doraszelski (2002). The Role of Permanent Income and Demographics in Black/White Differences in Wealth. Yale University Economic Growth Center Discussion Paper No. 850.

Altonji, J.G. and R. Blank (1999). Race and gender in the labour market. *Handbook of Labour Economics,* 3, 3143–3259.

Anderson, B.R. (1983). *Imagined Communities: Reflections on the Origin and Spread of Nationalism.* London: Verso.

Anderson, M. (1988). *The American Census: A Social History.* New Haven, CT: Yale University Press.

Anderson, M. and S. Fienberg (1999). To sample or not to sample? The 2000 census controversy. *Journal of Interdisciplinary History,* 30(1), 1–36.

Anderson, N.B. (1989). Racial differences in stress-induced cardiovascular reactivity and hypertension: Current status and substantive issues. *Psychological Bulletin,* 105, 89–105.

Antecol, H. and P. Kuhn (2000). Gender as an impediment to labour market success: Why do young women report greater harm? *Journal of Labour Economics,* 18(4), 702–728.

Appiah, K.A. (1992). *My Father's House: Africa in the Philosophy of Culture.* Oxford, England: Oxford University Press.

Arrow, K. (1973). The theory of discrimination. In *Discrimination in Labour Markets*, O. Ashenfelter and A. Rees, eds. Princeton, NJ: Princeton University Press.

Augstein, H. F. (ed.) (1996). *Race: the origins of an idea, 1760-1850.* Thoemmes Press, Bristol.

Ayres, I. and P. Siegelman (1995). Race and gender discrimination in bargaining. *American Economic Review,* 85, 304–321.

Bachman, R. (1996). Victim's perceptions of initial police responses to robbery and aggravated assault: Does race matter? *Journal of Quantitative Criminology,* 12(4), 363–390.

Banton, M. (1987). *Racial Theories*, Cambridge University Press.

Banton, M.P. (1983). *Racial and Ethnic Competition.* New York: Cambridge University Press.

Bargh, J.A. and T.L. Chartrand (1999). The unbearable automaticity of being. *American Psychologist,* 54, 462–479.

Bargh, J.A., M. Chen and L. Burrows (1996). Automaticity of social behaviour: Direct effects of trait construct and stereotype priming on action. *Journal of Personality and Social Psychology,* 71, 230–244.

Barker, D.J.P. (1998). *Mothers, Babies, and Health in Later Life*, 2nd ed. Edinburgh, Scotland: Churchill Livingston.

Barsky, R., J. Bound, K.K. Charles and J.P. Lupton (2002). Accounting for the black-white wealth gap: A nonparametric approach. *Journal of the American Statistical Association* 97(459), 663–673.

Barzun, J. (1965). *Race: a study in superstition*, Harper and Row, New York.

Bates, N.A., M. De La Puente, T.J. DeMaio and E.A. Martin (1994). Research on race and ethnicity: Results from questionnaire design tests (disc. P160-6). In *Proceedings of the Bureau of the Census Annual Research Conference*. Washington, DC: U.S. Bureau of the Census.

Beck, E.M. and S.E. Tolnay (1990). The killing fields of the deep South: The market for cotton and the lynching of blacks, 1882–1930. *American Sociological Review,* 55, 526–539.

Becker, G.S. (1957). *The Economics of Discrimination.* Chicago: University of Chicago Press.

Bendick, M., Jr., C.W. Jackson and V.A. Reinoso (1994). Measuring employment discrimination through controlled experiments. *Review of Black Political Economy,* 23, 25–48.

Benson, P.L., S.A. Karabenick and R.M. Lerner (1976). Pretty pleases: The effects of physical attractiveness, race, and sex on receiving help. *Journal of Experimental Social Psychology,* 12, 409–415.

Bertrand, M. and S. Mullainathan (2002). Are Emily and Brendan More Employable than Lakisha and Jamal? A Field Experiment on Labour Market Discrimination. Graduate School of Business Working Paper, University of Chicago.

Bickel, P.J. and J.W. O'Connell (1975). Is there a sex bias in graduate admissions? *Science,* 187, 398–404.

Biernat, M. and D. Kobrynowicz (1997). Gender- and race-based standards of competence: Lower minimum standards but higher ability standards for devalued groups. *Journal of Personality and Social Psychology,* 72(3), 544–557.

Bishwakarma, Padmalal (2001). Caste Discrimination and Untouchability Against Dalits in Nepal, paper prepared by the Society for the Liberation of Oppressed Dalit Castes, Nepal, for the Global Conference on Caste Discrimination, New Delhi.

Black, D. A. Haviland, S. Sanders and L. Taylor (2002). Why Do Minority Men Earn Less? A Study of Wage Differentials Among the Highly Educated. Unpublished paper, Carnegie Mellon University, Pittsburgh, PA.

Black, D.A. (1995). Discrimination in an equilibrium search model. *Journal of Labour Economics,* 13(2), 309–334.

Black, S.E. and P.E. Strahan (2001). The division of spoils: Rent-sharing and discrimination in a regulated industry. *American Economic Review,* 91(4), 814–831.

Blackwell, C. and J. Mehaffey (1983). American Indians, trust and recognition. In *Nonrecognized American Indian Tribes: An Historical and Legal Perspective*, F. Porter III, ed., Occasional Papers Series, No. 7., Chicago: The Newberry Library.

Blair, I.V., C.M. Judd, M.S. Sadler and C. Jenkins (2002). The role of Afrocentric features in person perception: Judging by features and categories. *Journal of Personality and Social Psychology,* 83(1), 5–25.

Blascovich, J., S.J. Spencer, D. Quinn and C. Steele (2001). African Americans and high blood pressure: The role of stereotype threat. *Psychological Science,* 12(3), 225–229.

Blau, F. and A. Beller (1992). Black-white earnings over the 1970s and 1980s: Gender differences in trends. *Review of Economics and Statistics,* 74(2), 276–286.

Blau, F.D. (1977). *Equal Pay in the Office.* Lexington, MA: Lexington Books.

Blau, F.D. and L.M. Kahn (1997). Swimming upstream: Trends in the gender wage differential in the 1980s. *Journal of Labour Economics,* 15(1), 1–42.

Blau, F.D., M.A. Ferber, and A.E. Winkler (1998). *The Economics of Women, Men, and Work.* Upper Saddle River, NJ: Prentice-Hall.

Blaut, J.M. (1993). *The Colonizer's Model of the World: Geographic Diffusionism and Eurocentric History.* New York: Guillford.

Blinder, A. (1973). Wage discrimination: Reduced form and structural variables. *Journal of Human Resources,* 8, 436–455.

Blumstein, A. (1982). On the racial disproportionality of United States' prison populations. *Journal of Criminal Law and Criminology,* 73, 1259–1281.

Bobo, L.D. (1983). Whites' opposition to busing: Symbolic racism or realistic group conflict? *Journal of Personality and Social Psychology,* 45, 1196–1210.

Bobo, L.D. and J.R. Kluegel (1997). Status, ideology, and dimensions of whites' racial beliefs and attitudes: Progress and stagnation. In *Racial Attitudes in the 1990s: Continuity and Change*, S.A. Tuch and J.R. Martin, eds. Westport, CT: Praeger Press.

Bobo, L.D. and M.P. Massagli (2001). Stereotyping and urban inequality. In *Urban Inequality: Evidence from Four Cities*, A. O'Conner, C. Tilly, and L.D. Bobo, eds. New York: Russell Sage Foundation.

Bobo, L.D. and R. Smith (1998). From Jim Crow racism to laissez faire racism: The transformation of racial attitudes. In *Beyond Pluralism: Essays on the Conception of Groups and Group Identities in America*, W. Katkin, N. Landsman, and A. Tyree, eds. Urbana: University of Illinois Press.

Bobo, L.D. and S.A. Suh (2000). Surveying racial discrimination: Analyses from a multiethnic labour market. In *Prismatic Metropolis: Inequality in Los Angeles*, L.D. Bobo, M.L. Oliver, J.H. Johnson, Jr. and A. Valenzuela, eds. New York: Russell Sage Foundation.

Bobo, L.D., J. Kluegel and R. Smith (1997). Laissez-faire racism: The crystallization of a kinder, gentler, anti-black ideology. In *Racial Attitudes in the 1990s: Continuity and Change*, S. Tuch and J. Martin, eds. Westport, CT: Praeger.

Bondeson, U.V. (1989). *Prisoners in Prison Societies.* New Brunswick, NJ: Transaction Publishers.

Bonilla-Silva, E. and T.A. Forman (2000). "I am not a racist but...": Mapping white college students' racial ideology in the USA. *Discourse and Society,* 11(1), 50–85.

Boozer, M., A. Krueger, S. and Wolkon (1992). Race and school quality since Brown v. Board of Education. *Papers on Economic Activity–Microeconomics*, 269–338.

Borjas, G.J. (1994). Long-run convergence of ethnic skill differentials: The children and grandchildren of the great migration. *Industrial and Labour Relations Review,* 47, 553–573.

Borjas, G.J. and S.G. Bronars (1989). Consumer discrimination and self-employment. *Journal of Political Economy,* 97(3), 581–606.

Bossuyt, Marc (1984). *Slavery and Slavery-like Practices*, New York: United Nations.

Bowlus, A.J. and Z. Eckstein (2002). Discrimination and skill differences in an equilibrium search model. *International Economic Review,* 43(4), 1309–1345.

Bowman, P.J. and C. Howard (1985). Race-related socialization, motivation, and academic achievement: A study of black youth in three-generation families. *Journal of the American Academy of Child Psychiatry,* 24, 134–141.

Boykin, A.W. and F. Toms (1985). Black child socialization: A conceptual framework. In *Black Children: Social, Educational, and Parental Environments*, H. McAdoo and J. McAdoo, eds. Thousand Oaks, CA: Sage.

Braddock, J.H. and J.M. McPartland (1987). How minorities continue to be excluded from equal employment opportunities: Research on labour market and institutional barriers. *Journal of Social Issues,* 43, 5–39.

Brewer, M.B. and R. Brown (1998). Intergroup relations. In *The Handbook of Social Psychology*, 4th Edition, D. Gilbert, S.T. Fiske, and G. Lindzy, eds. New York: McGraw-Hill.

Brooks-Gunn, J., G.J. Duncan and J.L. Aber (1997). *Neighborhood Poverty: Context and Consequences for Children.* New York: Russell Sage Foundation.

Brown, T.N. (2001). Measuring self-perceived racial and ethnic discrimination in social survey. *Sociological Spectrum,* 21, 377–392.

Brundage, W.F. (1993). *Lynching in the New South: Georgia and Virginia, 1880–1930.* Urbana: University of Illinois Press.

Camarillo, A.M. and F. Bonilla (2001). Hispanics in a multicultural society: A new American dilemma? In *America Becoming: Racial Trends and Their Consequences*, Vol. I, N.J. Smelser, W.J. Wilson, and F.

Mitchell, eds. Commission on Behavioural and Social Sciences and Education, National Research Council. Washington, DC: National Academy Press.

Campbell, D.T. and J.C. Stanley (1963). *Experimental and Quasi-Experimental Designs for Research.* Chicago: Rand McNally College Publishing Company.

Card, D. and A. Krueger (1992). School quality and black-white relative earnings: A direct assessment. *Quarterly Journal of Economics,* 107, 151–200.

Card, D. and T. Lemieux (1994). *Changing Wage Structure and Black-White Differentials Among Men and Women: A Longitudinal Analysis.* (NBER Working Paper 4755.) Cambridge, MA: National Bureau of Economic Research.

Carr, J.H. and I.F. Megbolugbe (1993). The Federal Reserve Bank of Boston study on mortgage lending revisited. *Journal of Housing Research,* 4, 277–314.

Case, A., D. Lubotsky and C. Paxson (2002). Economic status and health in childhood: The origins of the gradient. *American Economic Review,* 92(5), 1308–1334.

Cavalli-Sforza, L.L. (2000). *Genes, Peoples, and Languages.* New York: North Point Press.

Charles, C.Z. (2001). Processes of residential segregation. In *Urban Inequality: Evidence from Four Cities,* A. O'Connor, C. Tilly, and L. Bobo, eds. New York: Russell Sage Foundation.

Charles, K. and E. Hurst (2002). The transition to home ownership and the black-white wealth gap. *Review of Economics and Statistics,* 84(2), 281–297.

Chay, K.Y. (1998). The impact of federal civil rights policy on black economic progress: Evidence from the Equal Opportunity Act of 1972. *Industrial and Labour Relations Review,* 51(4), 608–632.

Chay, K.Y. and M. Greenstone (2000). The convergence in black-white infant mortality rates during the 1960's. *American Economic Review,* 90(2), 326–332.

Chen, M. and J.A. Bargh (1997). Nonconscious behavioural confirmation processes: The self-fulfilling nature of automatically-activated stereotypes. *Journal of Experimental Social Psychology,* 33, 541–560.

Chin, M.H., J.X. Zhang and K. Merrell (1998). Diabetes in the African-American Medicare population: Morbidity, quality of care, and resource utilization. *Diabetes Care,* 21(7), 1090–1095.

Coate, S. and G.C. Loury (1993). Will affirmative-action policies eliminate negative stereotypes? *American Economic Review,* 83(5), 1220–1240.

Cochran, W.G. (1965). The planning of observational studies of human populations (with discussion). *Journal of the Royal Statistical Society, Series A,* 128, 234–266.

Coleman, M.G., W.A. Darity, Jr. and R.V. Sharpe (2002). Are Reports of Discrimination Valid? Considering the Moral Hazard Effect. Unpublished paper, Pennsylvania State University, State College.

Collins, J.W., Jr., R.J. David, R. Symons, A. Handler, S.N. Wall and L. Dwyer (2000). Low-income, African-American mother's perceptions of exposure to racial discrimination and infant birth weight. *Epidemiology,* 11, 337–339.

Conley, D. (1999). *Being Black, Living in the Red: Race, Wealth and Social Policy in America.* Berkeley: University of California Press.

Cook, P.J. and J.H. Laub (1998). The unprecedented epidemic in youth violence. In *Youth Violence, Crime and Justice,* Vol. 24, M. Tonry and M. H. Moore, eds. Chicago: University of Chicago Press.

Cook, S.W. and M. Pelfrey (1985). Reactions to being helped in cooperating interracial groups: A context effect. *Journal of Personality and Social Psychology,* 49, 1231–1245.

Cordner, G., B. Williams and M. Zuniga (2000). *Vehicle Stop Study: Mid-Year Report.* San Diego, CA: San Diego Police Department.

Correll, J., B. Park, C.M. Judd and B. Wittenbrink (2002). The police officer's dilemma: Using ethnicity to disambiguate potentially threatening individuals. *Journal of Personality and Social Psychology,* 83(6), 1314–1329.

Cox, S.M., S.E. Pease, D.S. Miller and C.B. Tyson (2001). *Interim Report of Traffic Stops Statistics for the State of Connecticut,* Rocky Hill, CT: Division of Criminal Justice.

Crosby, F. (1984). The denial of personal discrimination. *American Behavioural Scientist,* 27, 371–386.

Crosby, F., S. Bromley and L. Saxe (1980). Recent unobtrusive studies of black and white discrimination and prejudice: A literature review. *Psychological Bulletin* 87, 546–563.

Cross, H., G. Kenney, J. Mell and W. Zimmerman (1990) *Employer Hiring Practices: Differential Treatment of Hispanic and Anglo Job Seekers.* Washington, DC: Urban Institute Press.

Crow, J.F. (2002). Unequal by nature: A geneticist's perspective on human differences. *Daedalus,* 81–88.

Cunningham, W.A., K.J. Preacher and M.R. Banaji (2001). Implicit attitude measures: Consistency, stability, and convergent validity. *Psychological Science,* 121(2), 163–170.

Darity, Jr., W.A. (2003). Employment discrimination, segregation, and health. *American Journal of Public Health,* 93(2), 226–231.

Darity, W.A., Jr. and P.L. Mason (1998). Evidence on discrimination in employment: Codes of color, codes of gender. *Journal of Economic Perspectives,* 12, 63–90.

Darity, W.A., Jr., J. Dietrich and D.K. Guilkey (2001). Persistent advantage or disadvantage? Evidence in support of the intergenerational drag hypothesis. *American Journal of Economics and Sociology,* 60(2), 435–470.

Darley, J.M. and P.H. Gross (1983). A hypothesis-confirming bias in labeling effects. *Journal of Personality and Social Psychology,* 44, 20–33.

Darley, J.M. and R.H. Fazio (1980). Expectancy confirmation processes arising in the social interaction sequence. *American Psychologist,* 35(10), 867–881.

Davis, J.A., T.W. Smith and P.V. Marsden (2001). *General Social Survey, 1972–2000: Cumulative Codebook.* Chicago: National Opinion Research Center.

Dawid, A.P. (2000) Causal inference without counterfactuals. *Journal of the American Statistical Association,* 95, 407–448.

de la Garza, R.L., L. DeSipio, F. Garcia, J. Garcia, and A. Falcon (1992). *Latino Voices: Mexican, Puerto Rican and Cuban Perspectives on American Politics.* Boulder, CO: Westview Press.

Deaton, A. (2003). Health, income, and inequality. *NBER Reporter,* 9–12.

Degler, C.N. (1971). *Neither Black nor White, Slavery and Race Relations in Brazil and the United States.* New York: Macmillan.

Del Conte, A. and J. Kling (2001). A synthesis of MTO research on self-sufficiency, safety and health, and behaviour and delinquency.

Quarterly Newsletter of the Northwestern University/University of Chicago Joint Center for Poverty Research, 15(1).

del Pinal, J. (2003). *Race and Ethnicity in Census 2000.* (Census 2000 Testing, Experimentation, and Evaluation Program, Topic Report 9.) Washington, DC: U.S. Census Bureau.

Denton, N.A. and D.S. Massey (1989). Racial identity among Caribbean Hispanics: The effect of double minority status on residential segregation. *American Sociological Review,* 54, 790–808.

Dertke, M.C., L.A. Penner and K. Ulrich (1974). Observer's reporting of shoplifting as a function of thief's race and sex. *Journal of Social Psychology,* 94, 213–221.

Devine, P.G. (1989). Stereotypes and prejudice: Their automatic and controlled components. *Journal of Personality and Social Psychology,* 56, 5–18.

Dike, Victor (2001). The Caste System in Nigeria, Democratization and Culture: Socio-political and Civil Rights Implications. *African Economic Analysis.*

DiNardo, J., N. Fortin and T. Lemieux (1996). Labour market institutions and the distribution of wages, 1973–1992: A semi-parametric approach. *Econometrica,* 64, 1001–1044.

Dion, K.L. (2001). Immigrants' perceptions of housing discrimination in Toronto: The housing new Canadians project. *Journal of Social Issues,* 57, 523–540.

Donnerstein, E., M. Donnerstein and C. Koch (1975). Racial discrimination in apartment rentals: A replication. *Journal of Social Psychology,* 96, 37–38.

Donohue, J.J., J. Heckman and P. Todd (2002). The schooling of southern blacks: The roles of legal activism and private philanthropy. *Quarterly Journal of Economics,* 117(1), 225–268.

Dovidio, J.F. (1993), The subtlety of racism. *Training and Development,* 47, 51–57.

Dovidio, J.F. and S.L. Gaertner (eds.) (1986). *Prejudice, Discrimination, and Racism.* San Diego, CA: Academic Press.

Dovidio, J.F., J.C. Brigham, B.T. Johnson and S.L. Gaertner (1996). Stereotyping, prejudice, and discrimination: Another look. In

Stereotypes and Stereotyping, C.N. Macrae, C. Stangor, and M. Hewstone, eds. New York: Guilford Press.

Dovidio, J.F., K. Kawakami and S.L. Gaertner (2002). Implicit and explicit prejudice and interracial interaction. *Journal of Personality and Social Psychology*, 82, 62–68.

Dovidio, J.F., K. Kawakami, C. Johnson, B. Johnson and A. Howard (1997). On the nature of prejudice: Automatic and controlled processes. *Journal of Experimental Social Psychology*, 33(5), 510–540.

Dovidio, J.F., N. Evans and R.B. Tyler (1986). Racial stereotypes: The contents of their cognitive representations. *Journal of Experimental Social Psychology*, 22, 22–37.

Duckitt, J. (2001). A dual-process cognitive-motivational theory of ideology and prejudice. In *Advances in Experimental Social Psychology*, Vol. 33, M.P. Zanna, ed. San Diego, CA: Academic Press.

Duncan, G. and K. Magnuson (2001). Off with Hollingshead: Socioeconomic resources, parenting, and child development. In *Socioeconomic Status, Parenting, and Child Development*, M. Bornstein and R. Bradley, eds. Mahwah, NJ: Lawrence Erlbaum.

Duncan, O.D. (1968). Inheritance of poverty or inheritance of race? In *On Understanding Poverty*, D. Moynihan, ed. New York: Basic Books.

Eagly, A. and S. Chaiken (1993). *Psychology of Attitudes.* Fort Worth, TX: Harcourt Brace Jovanovich.

Elder, G.H. (1974). *Children of the Great Depression: Social Change in Life Experience.* Chicago: University of Chicago Press.

Embree, Ainslie ed. (1988). *Sources of Indian Tradition: From the Beginnings to 1800,* New York: Columbia University Press.

Emerson, M.O. and C. Smith (2000). *Divided by Faith: Evangelical Religion and the Problem of Race in America.* New York: Oxford University Press.

Emerson, M.O., G. Yancey and K.J. Chai (2001). Does race matter in residential segregation? Exploring the preferences of white Americans. *American Sociological Review*, 66, 922–935.

Engel, R.S, J.M Calnon and T.J. Bernard (2002). Theory and racial profiling: Shortcomings and future directions in research. *Justice Quarterly*, 19(2), 249–273.

Entwisle, D. and K. Alexander (1992). Summer setback: Race, poverty, school composition, and mathematics achievement in the first two years of school. *American Sociological Review*, 57, 72–84.

Entwisle, D., K.L. Alexander and L.S. Olson (1997). *Children, Schools, and Inequality.* Boulder, CO: Westview Press.

Epstein, A.M., J.Z. Ayanian, .H. Keogh, S.J. Noonan, N. Armistead, P.D. Cleary, J.S. Weissman, J.A. David-Kasdan, D. Carlson, J. Fuller, D. March, and R. Conti (2000). Racial disparities in access to renal transplantation. *New England Journal of Medicine*, 343(21), 1537–1544.

Eriksen, Thomas Hylland (1992). Indians in New Worlds: Mauritius and Trinidad. *Social and Economic Studies*, 1.

Esmail, A. and S. Everington (1993). Racial discrimination against doctors from ethnic minorities. *British Medical Journal*, 306, 691–692.

Essed, P. (1991). *Understanding Everyday Racism*, Thousand Oaks, CA: Sage.

Evans, A.S., Jr. (2001). Hate Crime in America: A Sociological Perspective. Paper presented at the Annual Meeting of the Southern Sociological Society, Atlanta, GA, April.

Everett, R.S. and R.A. Wojtkiewicz (2002). Difference, disparity, and race/ethnic bias in federal sentencing. *Journal of Quantitative Criminology*, 18(2), 189–211.

Fagan, J. (2002). Law, social science, and racial profiling. *Justice Research and Policy*, 4(Special Issue).

Farkas, G. (2003). Racial disparities and discrimination in education: What do we know, how do we know it, and what do we need to know? *Teachers College Record*, 105(6), 1119–1146.

Farley, R. (1990). Blacks, Hispanics, and white ethnic groups: Are blacks uniquely disadvantaged? *American Economic Review*, 80(2), 237–241.

Farmer, J.J., Jr. (2001). *Monitors' Quarterly and Training Evaluation Report Track State Police Progress: Attorney General Releases*

Traffic Survey and Semiannual Data on Statewide State Police Traffic Enforcement and Trooper Conduct. Trenton: New Jersey Department of Law and Public Safety.

Fazio, R.H. and M.A. Olson (2003). Implicit measures in social cognition research: Their meaning and uses. *Annual Review of Psychology,* 54, 297–327.

Fazio, R.H., J.R. Jackson, B.C. Dunton and C.J. Williams (1995). Variability in automatic activation as an unobtrusive measure of racial attitudes: A bona fide pipeline? *Journal of Personality and Social Psychology,* 69, 1013–1027.

Feagin, J.R. (1991). The continuing significance of race: Anti-black discrimination in public places. *American Sociological Review,* 56, 101–116.

Feagin, J.R. and C.B. Feagin (1996). *Racial and Ethnic Relations*, 5th ed. Upper Saddle River, NJ: Prentice-Hall.

Feagin, J.R. and M.P. Sikes (1994). *Living with Racism: The Black Middle-Class Experience.* Boston, MA: Beacon Press.

Ferguson, R.F. (1998). Can schools narrow the black–white test score gap? In *The Black–White Test Score Gap*, C. Jencks and M. Phillips, eds. Washington, DC: Brookings Institution Press.

Fernandez, R. and L. Sosa (2003). Gendering the Job: Networks and Recruitment at a Call Center. Unpublished manuscript, MIT Sloan School of Management, Cambridge, MA.

Fernandez, R.M. (1997). Spatial mismatch: Housing, transportation, and employment in regional perspective. In *The Urban Crisis: Linking Research to Action*, B. Weisbrod and J. Worthy, eds. Evanston, IL: Northwestern University Press.

Fernandez, R.M. and N. Weinberg (1997). Sifting and sorting: Personal contacts and hiring in a retail bank. *American Sociological Review,* 62, 883–902.

Fernandez, R.M., E. Castilla and P. Moore (2000). Social capital at work: Networks and employment at a phone center. *American Journal of Sociology,* 105(5), 1288–1356.

Filkins, Dexter (1999). Serfs Cast Off Chains in Pakistan. *Los Angeles Times.*

Fischer C.S., M. Hout, M.S. Jankowski, S.R. Lucas, A. Swidler and K. Voss (1996). *Inequality by Design: Cracking the Myth of the Bell Curve.* Princeton, NJ: Princeton University Press.

Fisher, R.A. (1935). The logic of inductive inference. *Journal of the Royal Statistical Society Series A,* 98, 39–54.

Fiske, S.T. (1998). Stereotyping, prejudice, and discrimination. In *The Handbook of Social Psychology,* 4th ed., D. Gilbert, S.T. Fiske, and G. Lindzey, eds. New York: McGraw-Hill.

Fiske, S.T., A.J. Cuddy, P. Glick and J. Xu (2002). A model of (often mixed) stereotype content: Competence and warmth respectively follow from perceived status and competition. *Journal of Personality and Social Psychology,* 82, 878–902.

Fiske, S.T. and S.E. Taylor (1991). *Social Cognition,* New York: McGraw-Hill.

Fix, M. and M.A. Turner (1998). *A National Report Card on Discrimination in America: The Role of Testing,* Washington, DC: Urban Institute Press.

Fix, M., G. Galster and R. Struyk (1993). An overview of auditing for discrimination. In *Clear and Convincing Evidence: Measurement of Discrimination in America,* M. Fix and R.J. Struyk, eds. Washington, DC: Urban Institute Press.

Fowler, F.J. (1993). *Survey Research Methods,* 2nd edition. Thousand Oaks, CA: Sage.

Fredrickson, G.M. (2002). *Racism: A Short History.* Princeton, NJ: Princeton University Press.

Freedman, D. (2000). From Association to Causation: Some Remarks on the History of Statistics. Technical Report No. 521, Department of Statistics, University of California, Berkeley.

Freeman, R. (1973). Changes in the labour market for black Americans, 1948–72. *Brookings Paper on Economic Activity,* 1, 67–120.

Gaertner, S.L. and J.P. McLaughlin (1983). Racial stereotypes: Associations and ascriptions of positive and negative characteristics. *Social Psychology Quarterly,* 46, 23–30.

Gaertner, S.L. and L. Bickman (1971). Effects of race on the elicitation of helping behaviour: The wrong number technique. *Journal of Personality and Social Psychology,* 20, 218–222.

Gail, M.H. (1996). Statistics in action. *Journal of the American Statistical Association,* 433, 1–13.

Galster, G.C. (1990a). Racial discrimination in housing markets during the 1980s: A review of the audit evidence. *Journal of Planning Education and Research,* 9(3), 165–175.

Gamoran, A. and R.D. Mare (1989). Secondary school tracking and educational inequality: Compensation, reinforcement, or neutrality? *American Journal of Sociology,* 94, 1146–1183.

Garrett, B. (2001). Remedying racial profiling. *Columbia Human Rights Law Review,* 33, 41.

Gary, L.E. (1995). African American men's perceptions of racial discrimination: A sociocultural analysis. *Social Work Research,* 19, 207–217.

Gilens, M. (1996). "Race coding" and white opposition to welfare. *American Political Science Review,* 90, 593–604.

Glaser, J. (2003). The Efficacy and Effect of Racial Profiling. Unpublished manuscript. Goldman School of Public Policy, University of California, Berkeley.

Glaser, J., J. Dixit and D.P. Green (2002). Studying hate crime with the Internet: What makes racists advocate racial violence? *Journal of Social Issues* 58(1), 177–194.

Glick, P. and S.T. Fiske (1996). The ambivalent sexism inventory: Differentiating hostile and benevolent sexism. *Journal of Personality and Social Psychology,* 70, 491–512.

Goldin, C. and C. Rouse (2000). Orchestrating impartiality: The impact of "blind" auditions on female musicians. *American Economic Review,* 90(4), 715 741.

Goldsmith, A.H., J.R. Veum and W. Darity, Jr. (2000). Motivation and labour market outcomes. *Worker Well-Being,* 19, 109–146.

Gomez, J.P. and S.J. Trierweiler (2001). Does discrimination terminology create response bias in questionnaire studies of discrimination? *Personality and Social Psychology Bulletin* 27, 630–638.

Goodman, L.A. (1961). Snowball sampling. *Annals of Mathematical Statistics,* 20, 572–579.

Goonesekere, R.K.W. (2001). *Prevention of Discrimination and Protection of Indigenous Peoples and Minorities*, New York: United Nations,

Gordon, M.M. (1964). *Assimilation in American Life: The Role of Race, Religion, and National Origins.* New York: Oxford University Press.

Graham, R. (1990). *The Idea of Race in Latin America 1870–1940.* Austin: University of Texas Press.

Green, D.P., D.Z. Strolovitch and J.S. Wong (1998). Defended neighborhoods, integration, and racially motivated crime. *American Journal of Sociology,* 104(2), 372–403.

Green, D.P., L.H. McFalls and J.K. Smith (2001). Hate crime: An emergent research agenda. *Annual Review of Sociology* 27, 479–504.

Green, D.P., R.P. Abelson and M. Garnett (1999). The distinctive political views of hate-crime perpetrators and white supremacists. In *Cultural Divides: Understanding and Overcoming Group Conflict*, D.A. Prentice and D.T. Miller, eds. New York: Russell Sage Foundation.

Greenwald, A.G. and M.R. Banaji (1995). Implicit social cognition: Attitudes, self-esteem, and stereotypes. *Psychological Review,* 102(1), 4–27.

Greenwald, A.G., D.E. McGhee and J.L.K. Schwartz (1998). Measuring individual differences in implicit cognition: The implicit association test. *Journal of Personality and Social Psychology,* 74(6), 1464–1480.

Griffin, J.H. (1996). *Black Like Me,* New York: Signet.

Guryan, J. (2001). *Desegregation and Black Dropout Rates.* (NBER Working Paper 8345.) Cambridge, MA: National Bureau of Economic Research.

Hagan, J. (1993). The social embeddedness of crime and unemployment. *Criminology,* 31, 465–491.

Hallinan, M.T. (1998). Diversity effects on student outcomes: Social science evidence. *Ohio State Law Journal,* 59, 733–754.

Hannaford, I. (1996). *Race. The history of an idea in the West*, Johns Hopkins University Press, Baltimore.

Hannaford, I. (1996). *Race: The History of an Idea in the West.* Baltimore, MD: Johns Hopkins University Press.

Harrell, J.P., S. Hall and J. Taliaferro (2003). Physiological responses to racism and discrimination: An assessment of the evidence. *American Journal of Public Health,* 93(2), 243–248.

Harrell, S.P. (2000). A multidimensional conceptualization of racism-related stress: Implications for well-being of people of color. *American Journal of Orthopsychiatry,* 70, 42–57.

Harris, D.A. (1997). "Driving while black" and all other traffic offenses: The Supreme Court and pretextual traffic stops. *Journal of Criminal Law and Criminology,* 87(2), 544–582.

Harris, D.R. (2002). Racial Classification and the 2000 Census. Unpublished paper prepared for the National Research Council Panel to Review the 2000 Census, Washington, DC. Institute for Social Research, University of Michigan.

Harrison, G.W. (1998). Mortgage lending in Boston: A reconsideration of the evidence. *Economic Inquiry,* 36(1), 29–38.

Harrison, R.J. (2002). Inadequacies of multiple race response data in the federal statistical system. In *Mixed Results*, J. Perlman and M. Waters, eds. New York: Russell Sage Foundation.

Hart, A.J., P.J. Whalen, L.M. Shin, S.C. McInerney, H. Fischer, and S.L. Rauch (2000). Differential response in the human amygdala to racial outgroups vs. ingroup face stimuli. *Neuroreport for Rapid Communication of Neuroscience Research,* 11, 2351–2355.

Hauser, R.M., S.J. Simmons and D.I. Pager (2002). High School Dropout, Race-Ethnicity, and Social Background from 1970s to the 1990s. CDE Working Paper No. 2000-12. Center for Demography and Ecology, University of Wisconsin-Madison.

Heckman, J.J. (1979). Sample selection bias as a specification error. *Econometrica,* 47, 153–161.

Heckman, J.J. and B.S. Payner (1989). Determining the impact of federal anti-discrimination policy on the economic status of blacks: A study of South Carolina. *American Economic Review* 79(1), 138–177.

Heckman, J.J. and P. Siegelman (1993). The Urban Institute audit studies: Their methods and findings. In *Clear and Convincing Evidence: Measurement of Discrimination in America*, M. Fix and R.J. Struyk, eds. Washington, DC: Urban Institute Press.

Hellerstein, J.K. and D. Neumark (1998). Wage discrimination, segregation, and sex differences in wages and productivity within and between plants. *Industrial Relations,* 37(2), 232–260.

Henderson-King, E.I. and R.E. Nisbett (1996). Anti-black prejudice as a function of exposure to the negative behaviour of a single black person. *Journal of Personality and Social Psychology,* 654–664.

Hewstone, M., M. Rubin and H. Willis (2002). Intergroup bias. *Annual Review of Psychology,* 53, 575–604.

Heyns, B. (1978). *Summer Learning and the Effects of Schooling.* New York: Academic Press.

Higginbotham, A. (1996). *Shades of Freedom: Racial Politics and Presumptions of the American Legal Process.* New York: Oxford University Press.

Hill, A.B. (1987). The environment and disease: Association or causation? In *Evolution of Epidemiologic Ideas: Annotated Readings on Concepts in Methods*, S. Greenland, ed. Newton Lower Falls, MA: Epidemiology Resources Inc.

Hirschman, C., R. Alba and R. Farley (2000). The meaning and measurement of race in the U.S. census: Glimpses into the future. *Demography,* 37(2), 381–393.

Hobsbawm, E. (1992). Introduction: Inventing traditions. In *The Invention of Tradition*, E. Hobsbawm and T. Ranger, eds. Cambridge, England: Cambridge University Press.

Holland, P.W. (1986). Statistics and causal inference (with comments). *Journal of the American Statistical Association,* 396, 945–970.

Hollinger, D. (2000). *Postethnic America: Beyond Multiculturalism*, 2nd ed. New York: Basic Books. Holzer, H.J.

Hollup, Oddvar (1993). Caste Identity and Cultural Continuity Among Tamil plantation workers in Sri Lanka. *Journal of Asian and African studies*, 28(1-2), 79–81.

Holzer, H.J. and J. Ludwig (2003). Measuring discrimination in education: Are methodologies from labour and housing markets useful? *Teachers College Record,* 105(6), 1147–1178.

Hsiao, C. (1986). *Analysis of Panel Data.* Cambridge, England: Cambridge University Press.

Huddy, L. and S. Virtanen (1995). Subgroup differentiation and subgroup bias among Latinos as a function of familiarity and positive distinctiveness. *Journal of Personality and Social Psychology,* 68, 97–108.

Hughes, D. and L. Chen (1999). Parents' race-related messages to children: A developmental perspective. In *Child Psychology: A Handbook of Contemporary Issues*, C. Tamis-Lemonda and L. Balter, eds. New York: New York University Press.

Hurh, W.M. and K.C. Kim (1989). The "success" image of Asian Americans: Its validity and its practical and theoretical implications. *Ethnic and Racial Studies,* 12(4), 512–537.

Ichioka, Y. (1977). The early Japanese quest for citizenship: The background of the 1922 Ozawa case. *Amerasia Journal,* 4, 1–22.

Ignatiev, N. (1995). *How the Irish Became White,* New York: Routledge.

Ihlanfeldt, K.R. and D.L. Sjoquist (1998). The spatial mismatch hypothesis: A review of recent studies and their implication for welfare reform. *Housing Policy Debate,* 9(4), 849–92.

Imperato, P.J., R.P. Nenner and T.O. Will (1996). Radical prostatectomy: Lower rates among African American men. *Journal of the National Medical Association,* 88(9), 589–594.

Ishikawa, Yuka (2001). Rights Activists and Rights Violations: The Burakumin Case in Japan, paper prepared by the Buraku Liberation League for the Global Conference Against Racism and Caste Based Discrimination, New Delhi, India.

Jackman, M.R. (1994). *The Velvet Glove: Paternalism and Conflict in Gender, Class, and Race Relations.* Berkeley: University of California Press.

Jacobson, J., C. Olsen, J.K. Rice, S. Sweetland and J. Ralph (2001). *Educational Achievement and Black-White Inequality.* (NCES 2001-061.) Washington, DC: National Center for Education Statistics.

Jahangir, Asma and Jilani, Hina (1990). *The Hudood Ordinances: A Divine Sanction*? Lahore: Rhota Books.

Jencks, C. and S. Mayer (1990). The social consequences of growing up in a poor neighborhood. In *Inner-City Poverty in the United States*, L. Lynn and M. McGeary, eds. Committee on National Urban Policy, National Research Council. Washington, DC: National Academy Press.

Johnson, G.E. and F.P. Stafford (1998). Alternative approaches to occupational exclusion. In *Women's Work and Wages*, I. Persson and C. Jonung, eds. London: Routledge.

Johnson, W.R. and D.A. Neal (1998). Black skills and the black-white earnings gap. In *The Black-White Test Score Gap*, C. Jencks and M. Phillips, eds. Washington, DC: Brookings Institution Press.

Jones, F.L. (1983). On decomposing the wage gap: A critical comment on Blinder's method. *Journal of Human Resources,* 18, 126–130.

Jones, J.M. (1997). *Prejudice and Racism*, 2nd ed. New York: McGraw Hill.

Judd, C.M., B. Park, C.S. Ryan, M. Brauer and S. Kraus (1995). Stereotypes and ethnocentrism: Diverging interethnic perceptions of African American and white American youth. *Journal of Personality and Social Psychology,* 69(3), 460–481.

Jussim, L. (1989). Teacher expectations: Self-fulfilling prophecies, perceptual biases, and accuracy. *Journal of Personality and Social Psychology,* 57(3), 469–480.

Jussim, L. and J.S. Eccles (1992). Teacher expectations II: Construction and reflection of student achievement. *Journal of Personality and Social Psychology,* 63(6), 947–961.

Jussim, L., J. Eccles and S.J. Madon (1996). Social perception, social stereotypes, and teacher expectations: Accuracy and the quest for the powerful self-fulfilling prophecy. *Advances in Experimental Social Psychology,* 29, 281–388.

Kahlenberg, R. (2001). An unambitious legacy. *Education Week,* 48.

Kahn, L.M. (1991) Discrimination in professional sports: A survey of the literature. *Industrial and Labour Relations Review,* 44, 395–418.

Kahn, L.M. and P.D. Sherer (1988). Racial differences in professional basketball players' compensation. *Journal of Labour Economics,* 6(1), 40–61.

Kain, J.F. (1968). Housing segregation, Negro employment, and metropolitan decentralization. *Quarterly Journal of Economics* 82(2), 175–197.

Kasarda, J. and K. Ting (1996). Joblessness and poverty in America's central cities: Causes and policy prescriptions. *Housing Policy Debate,* 7(2), 387–419.

Katz, I. and R.G. Hass (1988). Racial ambivalence and American value conflict: Correlational and priming studies of dual cognitive structures. *Journal of Personality and Social Psychology,* 55, 893–905.

Katz, I., J. Wackenhut and R.G. Hass (1986). Racial ambivalence, value duality, and behaviour. In *Prejudice, Discrimination, and Racism*, J.F. Dovidio and S.L. Gaertner, eds. San Diego, CA: Academic Press.

Kawakami, K. and J.F. Dovidio (2001). The reliability of implicit stereotyping. *Personality and Social Psychology Bulletin* 27(2), 212–225.

Kawakami, K., K.L. Dion and J.F. Dovidio (1998). Racial prejudice and stereotype activation. *Personality and Social Psychology Bulletin,* 24(4), 407–416.

Keith, V.M. and C. Herring (1991). Skin tone and stratification in the black community. *American Journal of Sociology,* 97(3), 760–778.

Keppel, K.G., J.N. Pearcy and D.K. Wagener (2002). Trends in racial and ethnic-specific rates for the health status indicators: United States, 1990–1998. *Healthy People 2000 Statistical Notes,* 1–16.

Kerckhoff, A.C. (1986). Effects of ability grouping in British secondary schools. *American Sociological Review,* 51(6), 842–858.

Kinder, D. and D. Kiewiet (1981). Sociotropic politics: The American case. *British Journal of Politics,* 11, 129–161.

Kinder, D.R. (1998). Opinion and action in the realm of politics. In *Handbook of Social Psychology*, 4th ed., D.T. Gilbert, S.T. Fiske, and G. Lindzey, eds. New York: McGraw-Hill.

Kinder, D.R. and D.O. Sears (1981). Prejudice and politics: Symbolic racism versus racial threats to the good life. *Journal of Personality and Social Psychology,* 40, 414–431.

Kinder, D.R. and L.M. Sanders (1996). *Divided by Color: Racial Politics and Democratic Ideals.* Chicago: University of Chicago Press.

Kirschenman, J. and K.M. Neckerman (1991). "We'd love to hire them, but..." The meaning of race for employers. In *The Urban Underclass*, C. Jencks and P.E. Peterson, eds. Washington, DC: Brookings Institution Press.

Kitano, H.H. and S. Sue (1973). The model minorities. *Journal of Social Issues,* 29(2), 1–10.

Klein, H.S. (1999). *The Atlantic Slave Trade.* New York: Cambridge University Press.

Kluegel, J.R. and L.D. Bobo (2001). Perceived group discrimination and policy attitudes: The sources and consequences of the race and gender gaps. In *Urban Inequality: Evidence from Four Cities*, A. O'Conner, C. Tilly, and L.D. Bobo, eds. New York: Russell Sage Foundation.

Kocieniewski, D. (2002). New Jersey troopers avoid jail in case that highlighted profiling. *The New York Times*, January 15.

Kolenda, Pauline (1978). *Caste in Contemporary India: Beyond Organic Solidarity,* Menlo Park: Benjamin/Cumming Publishing Co.

Kornhaber, M. (1997). Seeking Strengths: Equitable Identification for Gifted Education and the Theory of Multiple Intelligences. Doctoral dissertation, Harvard Graduate School of Education, Cambridge, MA.

Krieger, N. (1990). Racial and gender discrimination: Risk factors for high blood pressure? *Social Science and Medicine,* 39, 1273–1281.

Krieger, N. and S. Sidney (1996). Racial discrimination and blood pressure: The CARDIA study of young black and white adults. *American Journal of Public Health,* 86, 1370–1378.

Krueger, A.B. (2002). What's in a name? Perhaps plenty if you're a job seeker. *The New York Times*.

Kuh, D. and Y. Ben-Shlomo (1997). *A Lifecourse Approach to Chronic Disease Epidemiology: Tracing the Origins of Ill Health from Early to Adult Life.* Oxford: Oxford University Press.

Ladd, H.F. (1998). Evidence on discrimination in mortgage lending. *Journal of Economic Perspectives,* 12, 41–62.

Landrine, H. and E.A. Klonoff (1996). The schedule of racist events: A measure of racial discrimination and a study of its negative physical and mental health consequences. *Journal of Black Psychology,* 22, 144–168.

Lange, J.E., K.O. Blackman and M.B. Johnson (2001). *Speed Violation Survey of the New Jersey Turnpike: Final Report.* Trenton, NJ: Office of the Attorney General.

Lansdowne, W.M. (2000). *Vehicle Stop Demographic Study.* San Jose, CA: San Jose Police Department.

Lee, V.E., D.T. Burkam and L.F. LoGerfo (2001). Who Goes Where? How Kindergartners' Social Background Maps Onto the Quality of the Elementary Schools They Attend. Paper presented at the annual meeting of the American Educational Research Association, Seattle, WA.

Leventhal, T. and J. Brooks-Gunn (2000). The neighborhoods they live in: The effects of neighborhood residence on child and adolescent outcomes. *Psychological Bulletin,* 126(2), 309–337.

Levine, J.M. and R.L. Moreland (1998). Small groups. In *The Handbook of Social Psychology*, 4th ed., D. Gilbert, S. Fiske, and G. Lindzey, eds. Boston, MA: McGraw-Hill.

Lieberman, L. (1993). Race and ethnicity: Overlapping meanings. *ANN World Focus,* 1(1), 3–4.

Lieberman, R.C. (1998). *Shifting the Color Line: Race and the American Welfare State.* Cambridge, MA: Harvard University Press.

Lillie-Blanton, M., P.E. Parson, H. Gayle and A. Dievler (1996). Racial differences in health: Not just black and white, but shades of gray. *Annual Review of Public Health,* 17, 411–448.

Limbu, Ramyata (2001). Lacking homes, freed peasants squat on gov't land. *Inter Press Service.*

Linville, P.W. and E.E. Jones (1980). Polarized appraisals of out-group members. *Journal of Personality and Social Psychology,* 38, 689–703.

Lloyd, K.M, M. Tienda and A. Zajacova (2002). Trends in the educational achievement of minority students since Brown v. Board of Education. In *Achieving High Educational Standards for All*, T. Ready, C. Edley, Jr., and C.E. Snow, eds. Division of Behavioural and Social Sciences and Education, National Research Council. Washington, DC: National Academy Press.

Lochner, L.J. (1999). *Education, Work, and Crime: Theory and Evidence.* (RCER Working Paper No. 465.) Rochester, NY: Rochester Center for Economic Research.

Loury, G.C. (1977). A dynamic theory of racial income differences. In *Women, Minorities and Employment Discrimination*, P.A. Wallace and A.M. LaMond, eds. Lexington, MA: D.C. Heath and Co.

Lucas, S.R. (1994). Effects of Race and Gender Discrimination in the United States: 1940–1980. Unpublished Ph.D. dissertation, University of Wisconsin, Madison.

Lucas, S.R. and A. Gamoran (1991). Race and Track Assignment: A Reconsideration with Course-Based Indicators of Track Locations.

Presentation at the American Sociological Association annual meeting, Cincinnati, OH, August.

Lucas, S.R. and M. Berends (2002). Sociodemographic diversity, correlated achievement, and de facto tracking. *Sociology of Education,* 75(4), 328–348.

Ludwig, J., G.J. Duncan and P. Hirschfield (2001). Urban poverty and juvenile crime: Evidence from a randomized housing-mobility experiment. *Quarterly Journal of Economics,* 116(2), 655–680.

Lundberg, S.J. (1991). The enforcement of equal opportunity laws under imperfect information: Affirmative action and alternatives. *Quarterly Journal of Economics,* 106(1), 309–326.

Lundberg, S.J. and R. Startz (1983). Private discrimination and social intervention in competitive labour markets. *American Economic Review,* 73(3), 340–347.

Luttmer, E.F.P. (2001). Group loyalty and the taste for redistribution. *Journal of Political Economy,* 109(3), 500–528.

Maddox, K.B. and S.A. Gray (2002). Cognitive representations of black Americans: Reexploring the role of skin tone. *Personality and Social Psychology Bulletin,* 28(2), 250–259.

Manski, C.F. (1995). *Identification Problems in Social Sciences.* Cambridge, MA: Harvard University Press.

Mare, R.D. (1995). Changes in educational attainment and social enrollment. In *State of the Union: America in the 1990s*, Vol. 1, R. Farley, ed. New York: Russell Sage Foundation.

Margo, R. (1990). *Race and Schooling in the South, 1880–1950: An Economic History.* Chicago: University of Chicago Press.

Marini, M.M. and B. Singer (1988). Causality in the social sciences. In *Sociological Methodology*, C.C. Clogg, ed. Washington, DC: American Sociological Association.

Marlow, D. and D.P. Crowne (1961). Social desirability and response to perceived situational demands. *Journal of Consulting Psychology,* 25, 109–115.

Martell, R.F., D.M. Lane and C. Emrich (1996). Male-female differences: A computer simulation. *American Psychologist* 51, 157–158.

Martin, E., T.J. DeMaio and P.C. Campanelli (1990). Contest effects for census measure of race and Hispanic origin. *Public Opinion Quarterly,* 54, 551–566.

Massey, D.S. (2001). Residential segregation and neighborhood conditions in U.S. metropolitan areas. In *America Becoming: Racial Trends and Their Consequences*, Vol. 1, N.J. Smelser, W.J. Wilson, and F. Mitchell, eds. Commission on Behavioural and Social Sciences and Education. Washington, DC: National Academy Press.

Massey, D.S. and G. Lundy (2001). Use of black English and racial discrimination in urban housing markets: New methods and findings. *Urban Affairs Review,* 36(4), 452–469.

Massey, D.S. and N.A. Denton (1992). Racial identity and the segregation of Mexicans in the United States. *Social Science Research,* 21, 235–260.

Massey, D.S., C.Z. Charles and G. Dinwiddie (2003). The Continuing Consequences of Segregation: Family Stress and College Academic Performance. Unpublished paper, Department of Sociology, University of Pennsylvania.

Mayberry, R.M., F. Mili and E. Ofili (2000) Racial and ethnic differences in access to medical care. *Medical Care Research and Review, 2000 Supplement, 1,* 57, 108–146.

Mayr, E. (2002). The biology of race and the concept of equality. *Daedalus,* 89–94.

Mays, V.M., L.M. Coleman and J.S. Jackson (1996). Perceived race-based discrimination, employment status, and job stress in a national sample of black women: Implications for health outcomes. *Journal of Occupational Health Psychology,* 1(3), 319–329.

McConahay, J.B. (1986). Modern racism, ambivalence, and the modern racism scale. In *Prejudice, Discrimination, and Racism*, J.F. Dovidio and S.L. Gaertner, eds. San Diego, CA: Academic Press.

McMahon, L.F., R.A. Wolfe, S. Huang, P. Tedeschi, W. Manning, and M.J. Edlund (1999). Racial and gender variation in use of diagnostic colonic procedures in the Michigan Medicare population. *Medical Care,* 37(7), 712–717.

Mead, M., T. Dobzhansky, E. Tobach, and R. Light, eds. (1968). *Science and the Concept of Race.* New York: Columbia University Press.

Meyer, B.D. (1995). Natural and quasi-experiments in economics. *Journal of Business and Economic Statistics,* 13, 151–162.

Mickelson, R.A. (2001). Subverting Swann: First- and second-generation segregation in the Charlotte–Mecklenburg schools. *American Educational Research Journal,* 38, 215–252.

Misra, Neelesh (1999). *Even for Money, Cyclone Survivors Won't Clear Bodies*, Associated Press.

Montagu, A. (1972). *Statement on Race,* New York: Oxford University Press.

Morgan, S.L. (2001). Counterfactuals, causal effect heterogeneity, and the Catholic school effect on learning. *Sociology of Education,* 74, 341–374.

Morin, A. (2001). Misperceptions cloud whites' view of blacks. *The Washington Post.*

Mouw, T. (2000). Job relocation and the racial gap in unemployment in Detroit and Chicago, 1980–1990. *American Sociological Review,* 65, 730–753.

Munnell, A.H., G.M.B. Tootell, L.E. Browne and J. McEneaney (1996). Mortgage lending in Boston: Interpreting HMDA data. *American Economic Review,* 86(1), 25–53.

Munnell, A.H., L.E. Browne, J. McEneaney, and G.M.B. Tootell (1992). *Mortgage Lending in Boston: Interpreting HMDA Data.* (Working Paper No. 92-7.) Boston, MA: Federal Reserve Bank of Boston.

Murnane, R.J., J.B. Willett and F. Levy (1995). *The Growing Importance of Cognitive Skills in Wage Determination.* (NBER Working Paper 5076.) Cambridge, MA: National Bureau of Economic Research.

Murphy, S. (2002). Audit studies and the assessment of discrimination. In *Measuring Housing Discrimination in a National Study: Report of a Workshop*, A.W. Foster, F. Mitchell, and S.E. Fienberg, eds. Division of Behavioural and Social Sciences and Education, National Research Council. Washington, DC: National Academy Press.

Murray, C.B. and J.S. Jackson (1982-83). The conditioned failure model of black educational underachievement. *Humboldt Journal of Social Relations,* 10(1), 276–300.

Muthiah, Wani (1997). Pride and Prejudice. *The Star,* Kuala Lumpur.

Nagel, J. (1994). Constructing ethnicity: Creating and recreating ethnic identity and culture. *Social Problems,* 41,153.

Natriello, G., E.L. McDill and A.M. Pallas (1990). *Schooling Disadvantaged Children: Racing Against Catastrophe.* New York: Teachers College Press.

Neal, D.A. and W.R. Johnson (1996). The role of pre-market factors in black-white wage differences. *Journal of Political Economy,* 104(5), 869–895.

Neary, Ian (1997). Burakumin in Contemporary Japan. In Michael Weiner (ed.), *Japan's Minorities: The Illusion of Homogeneity,* London: Routledge, 55.

Neckerman, K.M. and J. Kirschenman (1991). Hiring strategies, racial bias, and inner-city workers. *Social Problems,* 38, 433–437.

Nelson, R.L. and E. Bennett (2003). Judicial Treatment of Statistical Evidence in Cases Alleging Racial Discrimination in Employment: Now (2000–2002) and Then (1980–82). Unpublished paper, Department of Sociology, Northwestern University, Evanston, IL.

Neumark, D. (1996). Sex discrimination in restaurant hiring: An audit study. *Quarterly Journal of Economics,* 3(3), 915–942.

Neumark, D. and M. McLennan (1995). Sex discrimination and women's labour market outcomes. *Journal of Human Resources,* 30(4), 713–740.

Neumark, D. and W.A. Stock (2001). *The Effects of Race and Sex Discrimination Laws.* (NBER Working Paper 8111.) Cambridge, MA: National Bureau of Economic Research.

Newman, L.S. and R. Erber, eds. (2002). *Understanding Genocide: The Social Psychology of the Holocaust,* New York: Oxford University Press.

Newport, F. (1999). Racial Profiling Is Seen as Widespread, Particularly Among Young Black Men. Gallup Poll Analyses.

Newport, F., J. Ludwig and S. Kearney (2001). Black-White Relations in the United States, 2001 Update. Gallup Poll Social Audit.

Neyman, J. (1923). Sur les applications de la theorie des probabilities aux experiences agricoles: Essai des principes. *Roczniki Nauk Rolniczki* 10:1–51, in Polish. English translation by D. Dabrowska and T. Speed, 1990. *Statistical Science,* 5, 463–480.

Nobles, M. (2000). *Shades of Citizenship: Race and the Census in Modern Politics.* Palo Alto, CA: Stanford University Press.

Nolen, Stephanie (2001). Cross-caste teen lovers brutally slain Families charged in torture, killing of Indian couple who defied ingrained tradition. *Globe and Mail,* Toronto, .

Nopo, H. (2002). Matching as a Tool to Decompose Wage Gaps. Unpublished paper, Department of Economics, Northwestern University, Evanston, IL.

Northrup, D. (1994). *The Atlantic Slave Trade.* Lexington, MA: D.C. Heath and Co.

O'Callaghan, M. (1980). *Sociological Theories: Race and Colonialism.* Paris: United Nations Educational, Social, and Cultural Organization.

O'Conner, A., C. Tilly and L.D. Bobo, eds. (2001). *Urban Inequality: Evidence from Four Cities.* New York: Russell Sage Foundation.

Oakes, J. (1985). *Keeping Track: How Schools Structure Inequality.* New Haven, CT: Yale University Press.

Oakes, J., K. Muir and R. Joseph (2000). Course Taking and Achievement in Math and Science: Inequalities that Endure. Paper presented at the National Institute for Science Education Conference, May, Detroit, MI.

Oaxaca, R.L. (1973). Sex discrimination in wages. In *Discrimination in Labour Markets*, O. Ashenfelter and A. Rees, eds. Princeton, NJ: Princeton University Press.

Oaxaca, R.L. and M.R. Ransom (1999). Identification in detailed wage decompositions. *Review of Economics and Statistics,* 81(1), 154–157.

Okafor, Jerome Njikwulimchukwu (1993). *The Challenge of Osu Caste System to the Igbo Christians*, Onitsha: Veritas Printing and Publishing, 33.

Oliver, M.T. and T.M. Shapiro (1995). *Black Wealth, White Wealth: A New Perspective on Racial Inequality.* New York: Routledge.

Omi, M.A. (2001). The changing meaning of race. In *America Becoming: Racial Trends and Their Consequences*, Vol. 1, N.J. Smelser, W.J. Wilson, and F. Mitchell, eds. Commission on

Omi, M.A. and H. Winant (1986). *Racial Formation in the United States: From the 1960s to the 1990s*, 2nd ed. New York: Routledge.

Ondrich, J., S.L. Ross and J. Yinger (2000). How common is housing discrimination? Improving on traditional measures. *Journal of Urban Economics,* 47, 470–500.

Oppenheimer, D.B. (1993). Negligent discrimination. *University of Pennsylvania Law Review,* 141, 899.

Orfield, G. and S.E. Eaton (1996). *Dismantling Desegregation: The Quiet Reversal of Brown v. Board of Education.* Cambridge, MA: Harvard University Press.

Orne, M.T. (1962). On the social psychology of the psychological experiment: With particular reference to demand characteristics and their implications. *American Psychologist,* 17, 776–783.

Park, R. (1950). *Race and Culture.* Glencoe, IL: The Free Press.

Pearl, J. (2000). *Causality: Models, Reasoning, and Inference.* Cambridge, England: Cambridge University Press.

Petersen, T. and L.A. Morgan (1995). Separate and unequal: Occupation-establishment sex segregation and the gender wage gap. *American Journal of Sociology,* 101, 329–365.

Petersen, T., I. Saporta and M. Seidel (2000). Offering a job: Meritocracy and social networks. *American Journal of Sociology,* 106(3), 763–816.

Pettigrew, T.F. (1998a). Intergroup contact theory. *Annual Review of Psychology,* 49, 65–85.

Pettigrew, T.F. and L.R. Tropp (2000). Does intergroup contact reduce prejudice: Recent meta-analytic findings. In *Reducing Prejudice and Discrimination*, S. Oskamp, ed. Mahwah, NJ: Lawrence Erlbaum.

Pettigrew, T.F. and R.W. Meertens (1995). Subtle and blatant prejudice in Western Europe. *European Journal of Social Psychology,* 25, 57–75.

Petty, R.E. and J.A. Krosnick (1995). *Attitude Strength: Antecedents and Consequences.* Mahwah, NJ: Lawrence Erlbaum.

Pfeffer, J. (1998). Understanding organizations: Concepts and controversies. In *Handbook of Social*

Phelps, E.A., K.J. O'Connor, W.A. Cunningham, E.S. Funayama, J.C. Gatenby, J.C. Gore and M.R. Banaji (2000). Performance on indirect measures of race evaluation predicts amygdala activity. *Journal of Cognitive Neuroscience,* 12, 1–10.

Phelps, E.S. (1972). The statistical theory of racism and sexism. *American Economic Review,* 62, 659–661.

Phillips, M., J. Crouse and J. Ralph (1998). Does the black-white test score gap widen after children enter school? In *The Black-White Test Score Gap*, C. Jenks and M. Phillips, eds. Washington, DC: Brookings Institution Press.

Plous, S. and T. Williams (1995). Racial stereotypes from the days of American slavery: A continuing legacy. *Journal of Applied Social Psychology*, 25, 795–817.

Poliakov, L. (1974). *The Aryan Myth: a history of racist and nationalist ideas in Europe*, Chatto and Heinemann, London

Police Foundation (2001). *Racial Profiling: The State of the Law.* Washington, DC: Police Foundation.

Pratt, J.W. and R. Schlaifer (1984). On the nature and discovery of structure (with discussion). *Journal of the American Statistical Association,* 79, 9–33.

Preston, C. (1998). Perceptions of discriminatory practices and attitudes: A survey of African American librarians. *College and Research Libraries,* 434–445.

Puri, Naresh (2001). Caste Splits Earthquake Appeal. *BBC News*.

Quindlen, A. (2002). Armed with only a neutral lipstick. *Newsweek*, March 18.

Ramasamy, Rajakrishnan (1984). *Caste Consciousness Among Indian Tamils in Malaysia,* Selangor, Malaysia: Pelanduk Publications.

Ramesh, Jairam (2001). Ubiquitous Indians: The Indian Diaspora Living in Two Worlds is an Essential Feature of Globalisation. *India Today.*

Ramirez, D., J. McDevitt and A. Farrell (2000). *A Resource Guide on Racial Profiling Data Collection Systems: Promising Practices and Lessons Learned.* (NCJ 184768.) Washington, DC: U.S. Department of Justice.

Rao, Sandy (2001). *India's Hidden Apartheid: The Caste System and Its Continuation to the Caribbean and America.*

Rees, A. and G.P. Shultz (1970). *Workers and Wages in an Urban Labour Market.* Chicago: University of Chicago Press.

Riach, P.A. and J. Rich (2002). Field experiments of discrimination in the market place. *The Economic Journal* 112, F480–F518.

Ridley, S.E., J.A. Bayton and J.H. Outtz (1989). Taxi Service in the District of Columbia: Is it Influenced by Patron's Race and Destination? Paper prepared for the Washington, D.C., Lawyer's Committee for Civil Rights Under the Law.

Roediger, D.R. (1991). *The Wages of Whiteness: Race and the Making of the American Working Class.* London, England: Verso.

Romero, F.S. (2000). The Supreme Court and the protection of minority rights: An empirical examination of racial discrimination cases. *Law and Society,* 24, 291–313.

Rosenbaum, P. (2001). Replicating effects and biases. *American Statistician,* 55, 223–227.

Rosenberg, N., J.K. Pritchard, J.L. Weber, H.M. Cann, K.K. Kidd, L.A. Zhivotovsky and M. Feldman (2002). Genetic structure of human populations. *Science,* 298, 2381–2385.

Rosenthal, R. (1976). *Experimenter Effects in Behavioural Research.* New York: John Wiley & Sons.

Ross, S.L. (2002). Paired testing and the 2000 Housing Discrimination Survey. In National Research Council, *Measuring Housing Discrimination in a National Study: Report of a Workshop*, A.W. Foster, F. Mitchell, and S.E. Fienberg, eds., Committee on National Statistics, Division of Behavioural and Social Sciences and Education. Washington, DC: National Academy Press.

Ross, S.L. and J. Yinger (2002). Detecting Discrimination: A Comparison of the Methods Used by Scholars and Civil Rights Enforcement Officials. Unpublished paper, Department of Economics, University of Connecticut, Storrs.

Rubin, D. (1974). Estimating causal effects of treatments in randomized and nonrandomized studies. *Journal of Educational Psychology,* 66, 688–701.

Rudman, L.A., A.G. Greenwald, D.S. Mellott, and J.L.K. Schwartz (1999). Measuring the automatic components of prejudice: Flexibility and generality of the Implicit Association Test. *Social Cognition,* 17(4), 437–465.

Ryan, J.E. (2003). Race discrimination in education: A legal perspective. *Teachers College Record,* 105(6), 1087–1118.

Sagar, H. and J.W. Schofield (1980). Racial and behavioural cues in black and white children's perceptions of ambiguously aggressive acts. *Journal of Personality and Social Psychology,* 39, 590–598.

Sampson, R.J. and J.H. Laub (1993). *Crime in the Making: Pathways and Turning Points Through Life.* Cambridge, MA: Harvard University Press.

Sampson, R.J. and J.L. Lauritsen (1997). Racial and ethnic disparities in crime and criminal justice in the United States. *Crime and Justice,* 21, 311–374.

Sarndal, C., B. Swensson and J. Wretman (1992). *1997 Model Assisted Survey Sampling.* New York: Springer-Verlag.

Schafer, R. (1979). Racial discrimination in the Boston housing market. *Journal of Urban Economics,* 6, 176–196.

Schneider, K.T., R.T. Hitlan and P. Radhakrishnan (2000). An examination of the nature and correlates of ethnic harassment experiences in multiple contexts. *Journal of Applied Psychology,* 85(1), 3–12.

Schuman, H., C. Steeh, L. Bobo and M. Krysan (1997). *Racial Attitudes in America: Trends and Interpretations* (completely revised and updated edition). Cambridge, MA: Harvard University Press.

Schuman, H., E. Singer, R. Donovan and C. Selltiz (1983). Discriminatory behaviour in New York restaurants: 1950 and 1981. *Social Indicators Research,* 13, 69–83.

Sears, D.O. and C.L. Funk (1991). The role of self-interest in social and political attitudes. *Advances in Experimental Social Psychology,* 24, 1–91.

Sears, D.O. and T. Jessor (1996). Whites' racial policy attitudes: The role of white racism. *Social Science Quarterly,* 77, 751–759.

Sears, D.O., C. Van Laar, M. Carrillo and R. Kosterman (1997). Is it really racism? The origins of white Americans' opposition to race-targeted policies. *Public Opinion Quarterly,* 61, 16–53.

Seenarine, Moses (2001). *The Persistence of Caste and Anti-Caste Resistance in India and the Diaspora.*

Shadish, W.R., T.D. Cook and D.T. Campbell (2002). *Experimental and Quasi-Experimental Designs for Generalized Causal Inference.* Boston: Houghton Mifflin.

Shivley, S. (2001). Resurgence of the class action lawsuit in employment discrimination cases: New obstacles presented by the 1991 amendments to the Civil Rights Act. *University of Arkansas, Little Rock, Law Review,* 23, 925ff.

Sidanius, J. and F. Pratto (1999). *Social Dominance: An Intergroup Theory of Social Hierarchy and Oppression,* New York: Cambridge University Press.

Sigelman, L. and S. Welch (1991). *Black American's Views of Racial Inequality: The Dream Deferred.* New York: Cambridge University Press.

Sivapragasam, P.P. (2001). Indian Origin Tamils in Sri Lanka: An Oppressed People, paper prepared by the National Campaign on Dalit Human Rights for the Global Conference Against Racism and Caste Based Discrimination/Occupation and Descent Based Discrimination Against Dalits, New Delhi.

Skrentny, J.D. (1996). *The Ironies of Affirmative Action: Politics, Culture, and Justice in America.* Chicago: University of Chicago Press.

Smelser, N.J. and P.B. Baltes, eds. (2001). *International Encyclopedia of the Social and Behavioural Sciences*, Vol. 7. Oxford, England: Elsevier Science.

Smelser, N.J., W.J. Wilson and F. Mitchell (2001). Introduction. In National Research Council, *America Becoming: Racial Trends and Their Consequences*, Vol. 1, N.J. Smelser, W.J. Wilson, and F. Mitchell, eds. Commission on Behavioural and Social Sciences and Education. Washington, DC: National Academy Press.

Smith, M.R. and M. Petrocelli (2001). Racial profiling? A multivariate analysis of police traffic stop data. *Police Quarterly,* 4, 4–27.

Smith, R. and M. Delair (1999). New evidence from lender testing: Discrimination at the pre-application stage. In *Mortgage Lending Discrimination: A Review of Existing Evidence*, M. Turner and F. Skidmore, eds. Urban Institute Monograph Series on Race and Discrimination. Washington, DC: Urban Institute Press.

Smith, T.W. (1993). *Race Relations in New Orleans: An Analysis of a Survey Conducted for the Times Picayune.* Chicago: National Opinion Research Center.

Smith, W.R., D. Tomaskovic-Devey, M. Mason, M.T. Zingraff, C. Chambers, P. Warren and C. Wright (2000). Driving While Black: Establishing a Baseline of Driver Behaviour by Measuring Driving Speed and Demographic Characteristics. Unpublished manuscript, North Carolina State University, Raleigh.

Sniderman, P.M. (1985). *Race and Inequality: A Study in American Values.* Chatham, NJ: Chatham House.

Sniderman, P.M. and E.G. Carmines (1997). Reaching beyond race. *Political Science and Politics,* 30, 466–471.

Sniderman, P.M. and T. Piazza (1993). *The Scar of Race.* Cambridge, MA: Harvard University Press.

Snipp, M. (2000). American Indians and Alaska Natives. In *Encyclopedia of the U.S. Census*, M.J. Anderson, ed. Washington, DC: Congressional Quarterly.

Snyder, M. and W.B. Swann, Jr. (1976). When actions reflect attitudes. The politics of impression management. *Journal of Personality and Social Psychology,* 34, 1034–1042.

Sob, Durga (1995). Caste and Gender Discrimination Against Dalit Women in Nepal. *Feminist Dalit Organization.* See also *Human Rights Watch, Rape for Profit: Trafficking of Nepali Girls and Women to India's Brothels*, New York: Human Rights Watch.

Sobel, M.E. (1995). Causal inference in the social and behavioural sciences. In *Handbook of Statistical Modeling for the Social and Behavioural Sciences*, G. Arminger, C.C. Clogg, and M.E. Sobel, eds. New York: Plenum Press.

Sondik, E.J., J.W. Lucas, J.H. Madans and S.S. Smith (2000). Race/ethnicity and the 2000 census: Implications for public health. *American Journal of Public Health,* 90(11), 1709–1713.

Spirtes, P., C. Glymour and R. Scheines (1993). *Causation, Prediction, and Search.* (Spring Lecture Notes in Statistics, No. 81.) New York: Springer-Verlag.

Spitzer, E. (1999). The New York City Police Department's Stop & Frisk Practices: A Report to the People of the State of New York from the Office of the Attorney General.

Squires, G. and W. Velez (1988). Insurance redlining and the process of discrimination. *Review of Black Political Economy,* 16, 63–75.

Squires, G.D. (1994). *Capital and Communities in Black and White.* Albany: SUNY Press.

Squires, G.D. and S. O'Connor (2001). *Color and Money.* Albany: SUNY Press.

Srinivas, M. N. ed. (1996). *Caste: Its Twentieth Century Avatar,* New Delhi: Viking.

St. Jean, Y. and J.R. Feagin (1998). The family cost of white racism: The case of African American families. *Journal of Comparative Family Studies,* 29, 297–312.

Stackhouse, H.F. and S. Brady (2003). *Census 2000 Mail Response Rates.* (Census 2000 Evaluation A.7.a.) Washington, DC: U.S. Census Bureau.

Staub, E. (1989). *The Roots of Evil: The Origins of Genocide and Other Group Violence.* Cambridge: Cambridge University Press.

Steeh, C. and M. Krysan (1996). Affirmative action and the public, 1970–1985. *Public Opinion Quarterly,* 60, 128–158.

Stephan, W.G. (1985). Intergroup relations. In *The Handbook of Social Psychology*, 3rd ed., Vol. II, G. Lindzey and E. Aronson, eds. New York: Random House.

Stephan, W.G. and C.W. Stephan (1989). Emotional reactions to interracial achievement outcomes. *Journal of Applied Social Psychology,* 19, 608–621.

Stephan, W.G. and D. Rosenfield (1982). Racial and ethnic stereotypes. In *In the Eye of the Beholder*, A.G. Miller, ed. New York: Praeger.

Streefland, Pieter H. (1979). *The Sweepers of the Slaughterhouse: Conflict and Survival in a Karachi Neighborhood,* Assen, the Netherlands: Van Gorcum.

Strom, K.J. (2001). *Hate Crime Reported in NIBRS, 1997–1999.* Washington, DC: U.S. Bureau of Justice Statistics.

Sudman; S. and N.M. Bradburn (1982). *Asking Questions.* San Francisco, CA: Jossey-Bass.

Sue, S. and S. Okazaki (1990). Asian American educational achievements: A phenomenon in search of an explanation. *American Psychologist,* 45(8), 913–920.

Sue, S., D.W. Sue and D. Sue (1975). Asian Americans as a minority group. *American Psychologist,* 30, 906–910.

Suh, S.A. (2000). Women's perceptions of workplace discrimination: Impacts of racial group, gender, and class. In *Prismatic Metropolis: Inequality in Los Angeles*, L.D. Bobo, M.L. Oliver, J.H. Johnson, Jr., and A. Valenzuela, Jr., eds. New York: Russell Sage Foundation.

Supphellen, M., O.A. Kvitastein and S.T. Johansen (1997). Projective questioning and ethnic discrimination: A procedure for measuring employer bias. *Public Opinion Quarterly*, 61, 208–224.

Talaska, C.A., S.T. Fiske and S. Chaiken (2003). Stereotypes, Emotional Prejudices, and the Prediction of Discriminatory Behaviour. Unpublished meta-analysis, Princeton University, Princeton, NJ.

Taylor, D.M., S.C. Wright and K. Ruggiero (1991). The personal/group discrimination discrepancy: Responses to experimentally induced personal and group discrimination. *Journal of Social Psychology*, 131, 847–858.

Thompson, M.S. and V.M. Keith (2001). The blacker the berry: Gender, skin tone, self-esteem, and self-efficacy. *Gender and Society*, 15(3), 336–357.

Thornton, R. (1987). *American Indian Holocaust and Survival: A Population History Since 1492.* Norman: University of Oklahoma Press.

Tomonaga, Kenzo (2000). NGO Report in Response to the First and Second Report Prepared by the Government of Japan Concerning the International Convention on the Elimination of All Forms of Racial Discrimination, Japan: Buraku Liberation and Human Rights Research Institute.

Tonry, M. (1995). *Malign Neglect: Race, Crime, and Punishment in America.* New York: Oxford University Press.

Toplin, R.B. (1974). *Slavery and Race Relations in Latin America.* Westport, CT: Greenwood Press.

Tucker, C. and B. Kojetin (1996). Testing racial and ethnic origin questions in the CPS supplement. *Monthly Labour Review*, 3–7.

Tucker, C. and R. Harrison (1995). The research agenda on issues surrounding the definition of racial and ethnic categories. In *Proceedings of the Section on Government Statistics*. Washington, DC: American Statistical Association.

Tucker, C., S. Miller and J. Parker (2000). Comparing census race data under the old and the new standards. Unpublished paper, Bureau of Labour Statistics, Washington, DC.

Turner, M.A. and F. Skidmore (1999). *Mortgage Lending Discrimination: A Review of Existing Evidence.* (Urban Institute Monograph Series on Race and Discrimination.) Washington, DC: Urban Institute Press.

Turner, M.A., B.A. Bednarz, C. Herbig and S.J. Lee (2003). *Discrimination in Metropolitan Housing Markets: Phase 2, Asians and Pacific Islanders.* Washington, DC: Urban Institute Press.

Turner, M.A., F. Freiberg, E. Godfrey, C. Herbig, D.K. Levy and R.R. Smith (2002a). *All Other Things Being Equal: A Paired Testing Study of Mortgage Lending Institution.* Washington, DC: U.S. Department of Housing and Urban Development.

Turner, M.A., M. Fix and R.J. Struyk (1991b). *Opportunities Denied, Opportunities Diminished: Racial Discrimination in Hiring.* Washington, DC: Urban Institute Press.

Turner, M.A., R. Struyk and J. Yinger (1991a). *Housing Discrimination in America: Summary of Findings from the Housing Discrimination Study.* Washington, DC: Urban Institute Press.

Turner, M.A., S.L. Ross, G.C. Galster and J. Yinger (2002b). *Discrimination in Metropolitan Housing Markets: National Results from Phase I of HDS2000.* Washington, DC: U.S. Department of Housing and Urban Development.

van den Berghe, P. (1967). *Race and Racism: A Comparative Perspective,* New York: John Wiley & Sons.

Van Hook, J. (2002). Immigration and African American educational opportunity: Are limited English proficient students disproportionately transforming minority schools? *Sociology of Education,* 75, 169–189.

Verniero, P. and P.H. Zoubek (1999). *Interim Report of the State Police Review Team Regarding Allegations of Racial Profiling.* Trenton, NJ: Attorney General, State of New Jersey.

Vishwakarma, Hira (1997). Reservations for Nepal's Dalits. *Kathmandu Post.*

Waldinger, R. and M.I. Lichter (2003). *How the Other Half Works: Immigration and the Social Organization of Labour.* Berkeley: University of California Press.

Walker, S. (2001). Searching for the denominator: Problems with police traffic stop data and an early warning system solution. *Justice Research and Policy,* 3, 63–95.

Walker, S., C. Spohn and M. DeLone (1996). *The Color of Justice: Race, Ethnicity, and Crime in America.* Belmont, CA: Wadsworth.

Webb, G. (1999). Driving while black. *Esquire,* 118–127.

Weeratunge, Nireka (1988). Aspects of Ethnicity and Gender Among the Rodi of Sri Lanka. *Sri Lanka: International Centre for Ethnic Studies,* 61.

Weich, R. and C. Angulo (2002). Racial disparities in the American criminal justice system. In *Rights at Risk: Equality in an Age of Terrorism,* D.M. Piche, W.L. Taylor, and R.A. Reed, eds. Washington, DC: Citizen's Civil Rights Commission.

Weinberger, C. and L. Joy (2003). Wage gaps among black college graduates, 1980–2001. Unpublished paper, University of California, Santa Barbara.

Weisberg, S. (1985). *Applied Linear Regression* 2nd ed. New York: John Wiley & Sons.

Weiss, Y. and R. Gronau (1981). Expected interruptions in labour force participation and sex-related differences in earnings growth. *Review of Economic Studies,* 48(4), 607–619.

Weitzer, R. and S.A. Tuch (1999). Race, class, and perceptions of discrimination by the police. *Crime and Delinquency,* 45, 494–507.

Welner, K.G. (2001). *Legal Rights, Local Wrongs. When Community Control Collides with Educational Equity.* Albany: SUNY Press.

Western, B. (2002). The impact of incarceration on wage mobility and inequality. *American Sociological Review,* 67, 477–498.

Western, B. and B. Pettit (2002). Beyond crime and punishment: Prisons and inequality. *Contexts,* 1(3), 37–43.

White, B. (2000). ACLU suit accuses U.S. Customs of "profiling." *Washington Post.*

Wienk, R., C.E. Reid, J.C. Simonson and F.J. Eggers (1979). *Measuring Racial Discrimination in American Housing Markets: The Housing Practices Survey.* Washington, DC: U.S. Department of Housing and Urban Development.

Williams, D.R. and C.A. Collins (1995). U.S. socioeconomic and racial differences in health. *Annual Review of Sociology,* 21, 349–386.

Williams, D.R. and H.W. Neighbors (2001). Racism, discrimination, and hypertension: Evidence and needed research. *Ethnicity and Disease,* 11, 800–816.

Williams, D.R. and R. Williams-Morris (2000). Racism and mental health: The African American experience. *Ethnicity and Health,* 5(3/4), 243–268.

Williams, D.R., H.W. Neighbors and J.S. Jackson (2003). Racial/ethnic discrimination and health: Findings from community studies. *American Journal of Public Health,* 93(2), 200–208.

Wilson, J.Q. and H. Higgins (2002). It isn't easy being screened. *The Wall Street Journal.*

Wilson, W.J. (1987). *The Truly Disadvantaged.* Chicago: University of Chicago Press.

Winant, H. (2001). *The World Is a Ghetto: Race and Democracy Since World War II.* New York: Basic Books.

Winship, C. and M. Sobel (2004). Causal analysis in sociological studies. In *Handbook of Data Analysis*, M. Hardy and A. Bryman eds. Thousand Oaks, CA: Sage.

Winship, C. and S.L. Morgan (1999). The estimation of causal effects from observational data. *Annual Review of Sociology,* 25, 659–707.

Wissoker, D.A., W. Zimmerman and G. Galster (1997). *Testing for Discrimination in Home Insurance.* Washington, DC: Urban Institute Press.

Wittenbrink, B., C.M. Judd and B. Park (1997). Evidence for racial prejudice at the implicit level and its relationship with questionnaire measures. *Journal of Personality and Social Psychology,* 72, 262–274.

Wood, J. (1994). Is "symbolic racism" racism? A review informed by intergroup behaviour. *Journal of Personality and Social Psychology,* 72, 262–274.

Word, C.O., M.P. Zanna and J. Cooper (1974). The nonverbal mediation of self-fulfilling prophecies in interracial interaction. *Journal of Experimental Social Psychology,* 10, 109–120.

Wyly, E.K. and S.R. Holloway (1999). The new color of money: Neighborhood lending patterns in Atlanta revisited. *Housing Facts and Findings,* 1(2), 1–11.

Yen, I.H., D.R. Ragland, B.A. Greiner and J.M. Fisher (1999). Workplace discrimination and alcohol consumption: Findings from the San Francisco Muni Health and Safety Study. *Ethnicity and Disease,* 9, 70–80.

Yinger, J. (1986). Measuring racial discrimination with fair housing audits: Caught in the act. *American Economic Review,* 76, 881–893.

Zax, J. (1989). Race and commutes. *Journal of Urban Economics,* 28, 336–348.

Zuberi, T. (2001). *Thicker Than Blood: How Racial Statistics Lie.* Minneapolis: University of Minnesota Press.

Zuckerman, M. (1990). Some dubious premises in research and theory on racial differences. *American Psychologist,* 45, 1297–1303.

Zweigenhaft, R.L. and G.W. Domhoff (1991). *Blacks in the White Establishment: A Study of Race and Class in America.* New Haven, CT: Yale University Press.

Websites

http://www.erieri.com/codes/MAURITANIA.htm

http://www.wordiq.com/definition/Race

http://www.nap.edu/openbook.php?record_id=10887&page=23

http://www.reference.com/browse/discrimination

http://www.nap.edu/openbook.php?record_id=10887&page=223

http://vig.pearsoned.co.uk/samplechapter/0205790615.pdf

Index